# Varieties of State Regulation

HARVARD EAST ASIAN MONOGRAPHS 436

# Varieties of State Regulation

*How China Regulates Its Socialist Market Economy*

## Yukyung Yeo

Published by the Harvard University Asia Center
Distributed by Harvard University Press
Cambridge (Massachusetts) and London 2020

© 2020 by The President and Fellows of Harvard College
Printed in the United States of America

The Harvard University Asia Center publishes a monograph series and, in coordination with the Fairbank Center for Chinese Studies, the Korea Institute, the Reischauer Institute of Japanese Studies, and other facilities and institutes, administers research projects designed to further scholarly understanding of China, Japan, Korea, Vietnam, and other Asian countries. The Center also sponsors projects addressing multidisciplinary, transnational, and regional issues in Asia.

Library of Congress Cataloging-in-Publication Data

Names: Yeo, Yukyung, author.
Title: Varieties of state regulation : how China regulates its socialist market economy / Yukyung Yeo.
Description: Cambridge : Harvard University Asia Center, [2020] | Series: Harvard East Asian monographs ; 436 | Includes bibliographical references and index. | Summary: "Presents the evolution and current practice of state regulation in China and demonstrates that the form of central state control varies considerably across leading industrial sectors, depending on the dominant mode of state ownership, conception of control, and governing structure. By analyzing and comparing institutional dynamics across various sectors, Yukyung Yeo explains variations in the pattern of China's regulation of its economy"—Provided by publisher.
Identifiers: LCCN 2020025837 | ISBN 9780674247857 (hardcover ; alk. paper) | ISBN 9780674247864 (paperback ; alk. paper)
Subjects: LCSH: Industrial policy—China. | Trade regulation—China. | Economic development—China. | China—Economic policy—1949- | China—Politics and government—1949-
Classification: LCC HD3616.C63 Y46 2020 | DDC 338.951—dc23
LC record available at https://lccn.loc.gov/2020025837

Index by Becky Hornyak

♾ Printed on acid-free paper

Last figure below indicates year of this printing
29  28  27  26  25  24  23  22  21  20

I dedicate this book to my lovely mother.

# Contents

# Tables and Figures

## Tables

*Figures*

# Acknowledgments

This book is the product of countless revisions and updates over the course of more than a decade. Although there were many remarkable changes within and around China during that time, particularly after the 2008 global financial crisis and with Xi Jinping's rise to leadership, what has hardly changed is my scholarly curiosity regarding China's political economy. Beyond providing a normative assessment of the country's pathways and future, I hope this book will introduce readers to how the Chinese Communist Party, governments, and firms (public and private) interact with each other and conduct business in the market.

We often study Anglo-American, continental Europe, or statist East Asian types of state–business relations. The case of China, however, clearly points out the inadequacy of existing analytical frameworks in capturing the complexities and varieties of the Chinese market economy. By unpacking markets as institutions, this book explains how China's pursuit of a socialist market economy cannot help but produce more conflicts and tensions with the United States and other liberal market economies. To be sure, there may be disagreement with portions of my analyses and arguments, but hopefully this study will ultimately lead to further advancements in the analysis of the Chinese political economy.

Perhaps some readers may perceive the influence of Margaret M. Pearson, my dissertation chair and mentor, on my research and perspectives on China. From start to finish, she has been available to discuss this project with great support and encouragement. Without such an amazing adviser, I would never have gained an interest in and jumped into China studies, let alone completed this book.

From my field research, I am indebted to numerous interviewees and institutions. Although I cannot name individuals, many interviewees (scholars, officials, entrepreneurs, and journalists) in Beijing, Shanghai, Changchun, Hangzhou, and Guangzhou generously shared their time and knowledge, always critical for advancing our understanding and explanations for China. This work was supported by a grant from Kyung Hee University in 2015 (KHU-20150518). I am grateful for a generous research grant from City University of Hong Kong in 2010, allowing me to update my field data and revise the manuscript. Some portions of Chapter 2 were published in Yukyung Yeo, "The origins of China's distinctive tiered economy," *China Information* (Vol 34, No. 1), pp. 88–108. Copyright © 2020 SAGE. DOI: 10.1177/0920203X19895747.

Friendship and mentorship matter a great deal for maintaining one's energy during the process of writing a book. Special thanks to Jae Ho Chung, who always reminded me of the importance of writing a scholarly monograph, and Young-Kwan Yoon, who is a role model as a scholar and teacher with a warm heart. In the United States, Hong Kong, China, and Korea, my wonderful colleagues and friends Bidisha Biswas, Ray Yep, Tianbiao Zhu, Fengshi Wu, Buhm-Suk Baek, and Jungwon Lim helped me refine this project at various times and encouraged me whenever essential. Seul-ki Ahn contributed invaluable research assistance from Beijing. Ji Young Lee deserves many thanks for her timely support. She shared her experiences with me and helped me focus on revision by hosting me as a visiting scholar at the American University School of International Service. I also thank three anonymous readers who read the manuscript, and my editor, Bob Graham, at Harvard University Asia Center. Thanks to his attention and keen interest in this project, I was able to make it through the painstaking process of turning a raw manuscript into a book.

This book is the result of much effort over many years, and I am deeply grateful to my family for their love and support, always.

# Abbreviations

| | |
|---|---|
| BAIC | Beijing Automotive Industry Corporation |
| CAAC | Civil Aviation Administration of China |
| CASS | Chinese Academy of Social Sciences |
| CBRC | China Banking Regulatory Commission |
| CCP | Chinese Communist Party |
| CFELSG | Central Finance and Economics Leading Small Group |
| CNAIC | Chinese National Auto Industry Corporation |
| CSRC | China Securities and Regulatory Commission |
| FAW | First Auto Works |
| FYP | Five-Year Plan |
| GLF | Great Leap Forward |
| JV | joint venture |
| LSGs | Leading Small Groups |
| MII | Ministry of Information Industry |
| MIIT | Ministry of Industry and Information Technology |
| MMI | Ministry of Machinery Industry |
| MPI | Ministry of Planning and Investment |
| MPT | Ministry of Posts and Telecommunications |
| NDRC | National Development and Reform Commission |

| | |
|---|---|
| OD | Organization Department |
| PRC | People's Republic of China |
| PTAs | Post and Telecommunications Administrations |
| R&D | research and development |
| SAIC | Shanghai Automotive Industry Corporation |
| SASAC | State-Owned Assets Supervision and Administration Commission |
| SDPC | State Development Planning Commission |
| SETC | State Economic and Trade Commission |
| SM-DRC | Shanghai Municipal Development and Reform Commission |
| SM-SASAC | Shanghai Municipal State-Owned Assets Supervision and Administration Commission |
| SOEs | state-owned enterprises |
| SPC | State Planning Commission |
| VCP | Vietnamese Communist Party |
| WTO | World Trade Organization |

# CHAPTER I

## How Does China Regulate a
## Socialist Market Economy?

Without diversity, nothing interesting happens. With diversity, we
get relatively stable market prices, but when we look at the agents
and how they behave, we see a complex system.

—Scott E. Page, *Diversity and Complexity*

In 2018, when Jack Ma announced he was stepping down as chair of the Alibaba Group—one of China's largest privately owned corporations—many commentators suspected he was bowing to pressure from the Chinese Communist Party (CCP). The fact that he was a member of the party seems to have shocked the international media but came as no surprise to China experts, who are well aware of what a business-person needs to do to succeed in the context of China's political and economic realities.[1] Ma's resignation implies that no enterprise, state or private, is free from regulation by the party-state,[2] even after decades of economic reform and the country's deep integration into the global economy.[3] Indeed, party-state regulation has increased under Xi Jinping's leadership, driven by an increased desire to control capital flows, key technologies, and sensitive information.

International apprehension about party-state control over private firms has increased in recent years. The United States, Australia, and New Zealand have expressed concern over and even banned 5G network technology from China's leading telecommunications equipment firms, Huawei and ZTE. Some countries, including Germany and Japan, are considering asking these companies not to provide information on host markets and countries to the Chinese state.[4] But firms like Huawei and ZTE are unlikely to agree to such requests because China's leading private firms are not autonomous.[5]

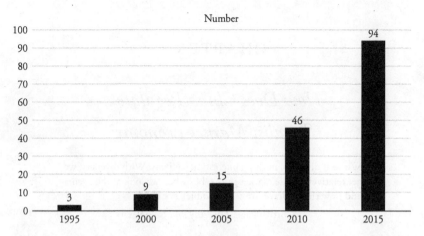

FIGURE I.I: Globalization of Chinese SOEs. This figure includes Chinese state-owned enterprises, excluding private ones, among the Fortune Global 500 list. *Source:* Mansoo Jee, "US-China Trade War and Korea's Action," presentation, Korea Institute of Finance, Seoul, February 23, 2019, 11.

China's party-state rules the markets and regulates business regardless of whether an enterprise is privately owned or state owned. But as explained in this book, the degree of regulation varies, primarily according to the level of ownership. Most enterprises in China are state-owned enterprises (SOEs): some are owned by the central government, and others (the majority) are owned by provincial (or in some cases municipal) governments.[6] Central state-owned enterprises are more tightly regulated than locally or provincially owned enterprises.

The ultimate goal of Chinese leadership is to build a socialist market economy where SOEs central to the economy are under the tight political oversight of the CCP. Since Xi Jinping took office in 2013, efforts to institutionalize the Chinese market economy and socialism have accelerated—the number of SOEs increased from 1.7 million in 2011 to 1.9 million in 2017 (see fig. 1.1).[7]

Any nation's transition to a market-oriented economy requires creating appropriate institutions to smooth the process and uphold the new system. In China under the planned economy, state intervention was ubiquitous.[8] Since the 1990s, as major state firms have spun off from the government ministries that managed them under the central planning system, the nature of the Chinese state in terms of governing the economy has been transformed.[9] The state is now a regulator that does not engage in as much direct and microlevel interference as it did in the past. The Chinese state has retooled its intervention through more indirect and institutionalized channels.[10]

Exactly what system of economic governance has emerged in China? More specifically, how does the Chinese party-state regulate the business of its most strategic industries, which are closely tied to the vested interests of the central party-state?

In this book, I argue that the central party-state exerts tight regulatory control over enterprises when industrial sectors hold strategic value to the national economy. The specific forms of regulation vary across sectors, as well as within sectors when the type of ownership in a sector is diverse (e.g., central party-state, provincial government, and private, as in the automobile industry). When the central party-state holds formal rights to oversee the business of SOEs, it exercises regulation directly. When it does not have formal rights to supervise and intervene in the business of firms—because they are owned privately or by local governments—the central party-state exercises regulation informally and indirectly.

The variations are due to differences in the underlying "market institutions," a phrase that refers to "formal and informal rules of the game that provide economic agents with incentives and constraints."[11] The most influential of market institutions are property rights (the key distinction being not private versus state ownership but level of ownership: central versus local ownership), governance structure, and conceptions of control. I emphasize the significance of *the level of ownership* in fostering party-state regulation in China's political economies. This variation evolved from the party-state's initial approach to modernizing the economy by trying to adapt the heavy industry-centered Soviet model to Chinese realities and needs. The party's desire to maintain absolute control over key infrastructure industries, the recognition of benefits from introducing market forces in certain sectors, and the sheer size of the country all encouraged China's early communist leadership to envision a unique economic system, eventually generating multiple "tiers" in the industrial economy.[12]

I propose the concept of *soft* (informal and indirect) and *hard* (formal and direct) regulation to describe the variations in how China's central party-state regulates the most strategic segments of the economy. Conventional theories of regulation do not adequately explain the nature of regulation in contemporary China. All too often, analysts take a dichotomous approach and focus, for instance, on state control versus market forces. But within a given market, various market institutions can generate different forms of regulation. To understand China's political economies, one needs to disaggregate markets as institutions, and the forms of regulation can be better identified and examined by a "market-institutional framework."

Before explaining what that framework consists of, this chapter defines regulation in the context of the Chinese political economy and briefly addresses the deficiencies of both neoliberal and statist approaches to studying China's market regulation. After outlining the rationale for focusing on automobile manufacturing and telecommunications service and then outlining my main findings, the chapter concludes with a road map of the book.

## Understanding Regulation in China: Concepts and Evolution

What does regulation mean in China? Are the notions and practices of regulation different than those in other advanced market economies, and if so, in what ways?

Although definitions vary and may depend on research disciplines or national traditions, "regulation" broadly denotes the use of public authority to set and enforce rules and standards.[13] Specific administrative agencies are often established to monitor compliance with authoritative rules; market-oriented competition is encouraged and protected by the legal mechanism of regulation (procompetitive regulation).

Until the 1980s, transatlantic differences in the meaning and goal of regulation existed. Governments in continental Europe (particularly France and Germany) understood the concept of regulation to mean a tool with which government could control the economy and society. Regulation referred to all modes of state intervention in economic and social life, and the notions of regulation and state intervention were interchangeable.[14] The United States and the United Kingdom defined regulation more narrowly as a set of authoritative rules and standards that accompany the establishment of sector-specific regulatory institutions.[15] Independence of regulatory institutions and a minimal government role were highly emphasized in these countries.

In the past few decades, different notions and practices of regulation among advanced industrial economies have converged, and the more narrow meaning favored by the United States has come to predominate, as evidenced by the spread of independent regulatory institutions after a global wave of regulatory reform in the 1990s.[16] Indeed, with the dominance of a neoliberal paradigm that stresses deregulation and privatization, decreased state intervention and fewer restrictions on market forces have come to be highly valued and encouraged.

Nevertheless, the emergence of new issues and concerns (e.g., the roles of state capitalism and state-led innovation) and the need to consider national contexts demand modification to the current consensual definition of regulation. According to Jacint Jordana and David Levi-Faur, regulation can be redefined in the following ways:

(1) in the narrowest and simplest sense that stresses the leading role of independent regulatory institutions, as favored in the United States and the United Kingdom; (2) to mean the entire array of efforts by state agencies to steer the economy, as popularized in continental Europe and embraced in Japan (which has a bureaucratic approach to regulating the economy); and (3) in the broadest sense, encompassing all mechanisms of social control, including unintentional and nonstate processes.[17]

Although early studies of regulation and the regulatory state tended to adopt one ideal type of regulation,[18] multiple notions of regulation in and across countries eventually emerged, depending on specific institutional and ideational contexts that stem from historical pathways of development. These different notions reflect the importance of enduring national institutions and visions as well as historical legacies that have come to shape diverse conceptions and forms of regulation.[19]

The global tide of regulatory reform has not left China untouched. Indeed, China's understanding and use of regulation has changed considerably in the past thirty years—but it has changed in a way that is distinctive and probably unique to China. Since the early 1990s, administrative agencies have replaced ministry-led economic governance over a planned economy. The bureaucratic transformation was most pronounced after government restructuring in 1998; the abolition of most industrial ministries, which were the heart of the planned economy, signaled that a new type of state intervention in the economy would have to evolve.[20] The party-state has become a critical player in designing the market, creating competition in it, and protecting the public good, as well as in making the rules.[21] The nature and manner of state intervention in China have shifted from an arbitrary and discretionary control model (planner) to a rule-based one (regulator).

When regulation refers to rule-based state intervention in the economy, the importance of informal rules and norms should not be dismissed.[22] Today, the Chinese party-state's hand, visible or invisible, over the economy is not diminished; instead, state intervention has been transformed into a more rule-based style than what existed during the planned economy. The concept of regulation in the Chinese context is now close to that of continental Europe: a tool used to control the economy and society, implying all modes of state intervention. The ultimate goal of regulation for the Chinese party-state is to exercise control over and steer strategic industries, rather than passively oversee the market in terms of pricing or competition. State planning and state ownership exist despite the market forces. China's modern method of regulation calls for a new analytic framework to better understand and explain the complexities and variations of an economy in transition.[23]

## From Planner to Regulator

Under the planned economy, because all was for the public good, there was no explicit distinction between public and private forms of ownership. The Chinese party-state was the sole planner, producer, and provider of societal and collective goods. Authorities relied on administrative planning (*xingzheng jihua*) and maintained a monopoly over the economy, partly because legal rules or institutions barely existed.[24] Because the party-state dominated the operation of the planned economy, there was no formal mechanism of competition or supervision. As a result, state intervention in the economy was very arbitrary.

After the reforms of the 1990s, a market-oriented mechanism for the provision of public goods was gradually introduced to encourage competition and the participation of private firms.[25] Competition was expected to break up the monopoly of the state and to enhance the distribution and quality of public goods, with a greater emphasis on social services such as education and health.[26]

The modern Chinese notion of how regulation is practiced is grounded on a socialist market economy, which envisions an economic system where the means of production and capital for the heart of the economy (e.g., the infrastructure sectors) are publicly or collectively owned but other resources are ruled by market forces.[27] Thus, the Chinese pursuit of a socialist market economy involves more than simply passively monitoring compliance with rules and fair competition; political principals, such as the CCP, actively plan for the market and manage competition. This is particularly relevant in the case of strategic industrial sectors, where central leadership often exercises control over the most lucrative segments of the economy. Encouraging the creation of national champions and a national industrial policy is part of this strategic regulation, and public ownership serves as an institutional backdrop to effectively keep an eye on the business of strategic sectors.[28]

In other words, the Chinese party-state as a regulator plans for (not just creates) the markets, manages (not just oversees) competition, and closely monitors the business and personnel of key state firms as well as their compliance with rules by employing formal and informal institutions when necessary to ensure compliance with the central party-state's guidelines (see table 1.1).

This web of formal and informal regulations does not catch only domestic companies. Foreign companies trying to penetrate the Chinese market are also entangled in the party-state's regulatory web. In regulating foreign investment, the party-state employs foreign ownership restrictions, such as joint venture requirements and foreign equity limitations, imposes prohibitions or limitations on the scope of business investments, and requires firms to submit themselves to the administrative licensing and approvals process and regulatory approval procedures.[29] The ownership

Table 1.1
The Chinese State as Planner and Regulator

| Government Intervention | Role of Government | |
| --- | --- | --- |
| | Planner | Regulator |
| Scope | • Micro and macro | • Macro |
| Depth | • Predominant role for the party-state | • Central role for the party-state, but market forces are allowed to have more influence |
| | • Plan, produce, distribute | • Plan, but markets produce and distribute most resources and products |
| Tools | • Arbitrary and discretionary control | • More rule-based control: formal and informal rules/norms |
| | • Few rules and legal institutions | • Facilitating competition: precompetitive regulation (*jianguan*, infrastructure) or strategic regulation (*xietiao*, manufacturing) |
| Goals | • Socialist planned economy | • Socialist market economy |

restrictions mandate that foreign investors do business in China only in partnership with a Chinese company; foreign equity cannot exceed 50 percent of a joint venture with a Chinese partner.[30] As my case study of the automobile sector shows, the business of foreign companies in China has been strictly regulated by these requirements, which the Chinese party-state uses as part of its strategy to offer access to its enormous market in return for foreign investors offering access to advanced technology. The issue of the forced transfer of technology between China and the United States has arisen largely because of China's formal requirement and informal pressure for foreign investors to transfer their key technology to access the market.[31] Since 1983, China's regulations on joint ventures have explicitly stated that "joint venture equity should raise China's level of science and technology."[32] Most foreign business groups confront a tough choice between "allowing Chinese partner access to their technology and losing market access."[33]

Another influential measure currently used to regulate the business of foreign investors is the internal party committee. For many years,

Chinese law has required "companies, including foreign ones, to establish a party organization," but that rule "had long been regarded by many executives as more symbolic than anything to worry about."[34] However, as the role of the party has been increasingly active since Xi assumed leadership, the internal party committee has come to exert *real* regulatory control over business operations and investment and personnel decisions. Some foreign companies complain of increasing political pressure "to revise the terms of their joint ventures with state-owned partners to allow the party final say over business management."[35]

## Markets as Institutions: An Alternative

The legacies of a socialist economy limit the application of conventional theories of regulation to China. Until the 1990s, China's efforts to reform its economic system and governance could be characterized as limited marketization or state capitalism.[36] This is largely because of its continued emphasis on the centrality of SOEs and the CCP's invisible but powerful influence on market actors, an influence that has increased under Xi.[37]

The role the CCP plays in both government and business and its informal role in leading SOEs undermine the utility of conventional approaches in analyzing regulation and economic governance in China. Several contending perspectives have been proposed, but consensus has yet to be reached.[38] On one hand, scholars who highlight the effect of government restructuring on economic governance since the late 1990s argue that China has turned into a "minimalist state," departing from its former role of totalitarian planner and making meaningful progress toward a market economy.[39] On the other hand, skeptical views call for more attention to the dark side of reform and growth, suggesting that China has degenerated into a highly decentralized "predatory state" because of a governance deficit in the political sense, such as the accumulated problems of corruption, mounting local governments' debts, and an imbalance in distribution.[40] A more balanced approach takes into account what China has achieved and the deep-seated political and economic constraints on a true market-oriented economy, such as the continued centrality of state ownership and the CCP.[41]

The key issue is perhaps not whether the role of the state (or state intervention) in the economy has increased or decreased. Rather, it is how the institutional legacies of a transitional economy and the persistent idea of a socialist market economy have generated various forms of regulation in China. Considering such resilient socialist political-economic institutions as state planning, public ownership, and the CCP, I propose that a *market-institutional approach* to elucidating how distinctive sets of institutions grow out of the planned economy to create, foster, and oversee the markets demands different logic and rules than does a liberal and statist market economy.[42] Thus, dichotomous ownership (public or private) is a poor guide for examining state–business relations in China.

China's practices of regulation are based not on property rights per se but on the level of ownership (central versus provincial) of an enterprise. The country has forged a new path by selectively adopting lessons from advanced market economies and gradually adapting them to suit Chinese realities and goals.[43]

The notion that there are only two possible forms of political economies—capitalism and communism—has long been contested. According to Karl Polanyi, writing in 1944, "a range of alternatives in political economy are possible, because markets can be embedded in a range of different ways. Many varieties of political economy have been developed as a result of different social and political choices implemented through state intervention."[44] Polanyi considers the neoliberal belief in the benefits of minimalist governments and self-regulating markets an unachievable utopian dream.[45] One can expect various patterns of regulation to emerge because of various political-economic realities in and across countries.

Influenced by Polanyi's contention, sociologist Neil Fligstein has proposed a view of markets as institutions, emphasizing the central role of the state in creating, fostering, and monitoring markets.[46] According to Fligstein, when a country is in transition to a more market-oriented system or capitalist society, the state must develop rules because market actors themselves are not able to create them. Thus, transitional economies inevitably require the state to play a more active role in markets than do capitalist ones. The main change from the planned economy, therefore, is the goals and manner of state intervention; that is, the state remains central, with different responsibilities and tools to control economic and social life. As Steven Vogel claims, "freer markets require more rules," and transitional economies are no exception.[47]

Hence, some kind of state regulation must occur even as market-oriented reforms are pushed for. In this book, "market institutions" refer to both "formal and informal rules of the game that provide economic agents with incentives and constraints, inducing stable patterns of behavior."[48]

Fligstein points to four kinds of rules that produce social structures in markets: property rights, governance structure, rules of exchange, and conceptions of control.[49] Because the actual practices and significance of those rules differ across sectors and institutions, formal and informal rules and patterns of market governance can vary within a single country. By disaggregating markets as a set of institutions, the market-institutional approach opens up the possibility that the system of regulation may exhibit variations because the rules of the game are structured in different ways across sectors and societies, even within a country. In studying the system of Chinese regulation, a market-institutional approach is particularly useful in two respects.

First, a market-institutional approach admits the need of the state to create rules and oversee compliance with them. Because China's regulatory reform has deepened since the 1990s, proactive state planning for markets and the enhanced function of ownership to supervise major state firms should not be considered in opposition to the efforts of market-oriented reform. Even Adam Smith noted that "a strong state would create and reproduce the conditions for the existence of the market and regulate its operation by using the market as an effective instrument of government."[50] In other words, active state intervention is necessary to create the conditions for the market, such as rules, as well as to correct or counter market failure that results in socially and politically undesirable outcomes.[51]

Second, because a market-institutional approach assumes diversity in terms of property rights, governance structure, and conceptions of control, complexity will emerge across industrial sectors within a country. There may be variations in the form of regulation because of underlying cultural and historical elements specific to a certain industry or society.

China's vision of a socialist market economy has generated a tiered industrial structure by selectively opening industries to market coordination while maintaining bureaucratic coordination through strict state ownership in others. This has led to multiple varieties of state regulation in China.

China's tiered industrial structure has been examined by scholars. For example, in a study of China's information technology industry, Dieter Ernst and Barry Naughton argue that China's emerging industrial economy consists of a three-tier structure.[52] The size of a firm and the dominant sector it operates in determine which tier a firm is in. The first tier is composed of large, central state-owned firms that operate primarily in natural monopoly sectors, whereas medium-sized firms operating in competitive markets are categorized as second-tier firms.[53] Second-tier firms have somewhat diverse origins (such as the state sector or foreign investment) and are often characterized as hybrid firms, with substantial stakes of public and private ownership.[54] The third tier consists of the small-scale sector that has relatively low technology and labor-intensive production.[55]

Margaret Pearson shares Ernst and Naughton's notion of a three-tiered industrial system in China but contends that what determines a tier is not the size or nature of the firms but the strategic importance of the sectors in the eyes of top leadership.[56] Her focus is on what the "industries" represent to the Chinese national economy. According to Pearson, the top tier is composed of the most important "economy lifeline" (*jingji mingmai*) or "commanding heights" industries, which are under the state's direct control. The middle tier consists of sectors that are strategically important but with less state control in terms of enterprise ownership and foreign investment. The bottom tier comprises the private and collective firms that have the least strategic importance.[57]

Although studies on the tiered economy tend to focus on the structure of tiers and their respective features, less attention has been paid to how the state rules markets across tiers. In other words, the forms of state regulation and its actual practices have not received attention. Because markets across tiers tend to operate according to different rules, a market-institutional framework is beneficial for explaining how different sets of institutions across tiers (or sectors) create the varieties of state regulation in China.

## A Political-Economic Framework

In this book, I focus on the sources of variation in Chinese regulation. In doing so, three kinds of market institutions—property rights (level of ownership), governance structure, and conceptions of control—are useful for examining the system of Chinese regulation—a system in which state ownership, state planning, and the organizations of the CCP are crucial.

### PROPERTY RIGHTS

Property rights define the power relationship between constituencies in and around firms.[58] Fligstein views property rights as the "rules that define who has claims on the profits of firms"—in other words, who controls an enterprise and who has rights to claim the surplus.[59] In this regard, property rights affect control over a firm's profits and political influence over the firm in China.

In the case of China's strategic industries, whose property rights are largely central state-owned, the central state (specifically, the State-Owned Assets Supervision and Administration Commission, or SASAC) retains the right to control a firm's business management and personnel. Yet a number of state firms under the jurisdiction of provincial or municipal governments are in strategic sectors, such as the automobile and steel industries. Depending on the dominant mode of state ownership in the sector (central or provincial), the power relations between central and local authorities exhibit a different dynamic. More important, as with the automobile industry, major private firms in strategic sectors are *not* free from central state oversight in China. Private firms share important similarities with state firms in terms of state access, influence, and privileges.[60] Some scholars point to an ownership bias that refers to public or private ownership, but that is poor guidance for understanding state–business relations in the Chinese political economy.[61] What makes China different from other countries is the level of ownership (central versus provincial) rather than whether ownership is state or private.

## GOVERNANCE STRUCTURE

This book defines governance structure as the rules that underpin power relations among authorities, vertically (*tiaotiao*, 条条) and horizontally (*kuaikuai*, 块块), as well as between the state and firms within sectors. Vertically structured and centralized governance can be horizontally fragmented with overlapped authorities, as China's telecom service industry indicates; horizontally structured and decentralized governance can create different power relations with central authorities (bounded or unbounded decentralized governing structures), depending on who has substantial decision-making power. To some extent, this concept helps one understand why the level of ownership is not the only determinant of the varieties of regulation in China; level of ownership, governance structure, and conceptions of control all play roles.

Much attention has been paid to Leninist institutions, such as planning and ownership commissions and party organizations, and their formal and informal exercise of political power over the business of leading sectors. One aspect of China's transition toward a market economy is the resilience and even empowerment of comprehensive state commissions, such as the National Development and Reform Commission and the SASAC, along with the growth of market forces. In other words, market reforms in China paradoxically have led to strengthening the state planning commission and the nominal owner of major state enterprises. In particular, the way the party's organizations exercise political clout, formally and informally, inside government and state firms cannot be dismissed. Viewing the comprehensive state commissions and party organizations as proxies of governance structures helps us examine how resilient socialist institutions, which are critical but largely missing in conventional approaches, generate the system of regulation Chinese-style.

## CONCEPTIONS OF CONTROL

"Conceptions of control" refer to shared ideas on the appropriate manner of state intervention, which can be specific to certain industries and societies. According to Fligstein, conceptions of control are cultural in that "they form a set of understandings and practices about how things work in a particular market setting."[62] Conceptions of control can mirror "market-specific arrangements between actors in firms on principles of internal organization, tactics for competition or cooperation, and hierarchy or status ordering of firms in a given market."[63] Each industry has developed from its historical background (such as mode of ownership or rules for investment), understanding, and practices, so that ideas on how to develop a specific industry are varied. Such variation is particularly remarkable in the Chinese economy because of its *selective approach* to introducing market mechanisms across sectors, which occurred even before reform.

For example, in developing the auto industry, central leadership adopted an inclusive approach, allowing foreign investors to cooperate with domestic auto producers from the outset, relying on a decentralized state ownership that brought about fierce competition in the market. In contrast, Chinese leaders' perception of the desirable manner of control for the telecom service sector resulted in the adoption of an exclusive approach. For infrastructure industries such as telecommunications, absolute control has been pursued and emphasized. Central state ownership is preferred, and the entry of foreign companies and foreign capital has been denied historically and is still restricted.

Such historically different paths and development strategies indicate the Chinese leadership's selective approaches to steering sectors based on the respective conception of what is a desirable way of regulating the market.[64] Historically and culturally formed notions of control contribute to generating a tiered structure of industries, reinforcing the varieties of state regulation in China. In this respect, the market-institutional approach is useful for exploring how the patterns of Chinese regulation may vary depending on the underlying characteristics of level of ownership, governance structure, and conceptions of control.[65]

## Research Focus: Two Strategic Industries

In studying a country the size of China, a sectoral focus allows one to examine contending and identifiable collective interests. The observation of sectoral governance can offer "an intimate view of the profound role power and politics play in shaping institutions of the sector."[66] Major changes in a sectoral regime significantly affect economic performance and policies in that sector.[67]

For example, the global wave of regulatory reform has brought about different effects on institutional design across sectors. The diffusion of independent regulatory agencies and the promotion of competition have occurred rapidly in the infrastructure and financial services sectors, but not in others. Some studies have taken a sector-specific or sectoral comparison approach to identifying and explaining institutional changes and development across various issue areas.[68] Li Rongrong, the first SASAC director, published a list of seven strategically important sectors (*zhanlue zhongyao bufen*, 战略重要部分) that are critical to the national economy.[69] Such primacy remains intact despite Xi Jinping's emphasis on deepening reform (*shenhua gaige*, 深化改革) at the Eighteenth Party Congress of 2013. Along with the commanding heights (*jingji mingmai*, 经济命脉), the pillar sectors (*zhizhu chanye*, 支柱产业) are considered strategic industries given China's consistent emphasis on their contribution toward rapid industrialization and modernization of the economy.[70]

Two strategic sectors were chosen for this study: automobile manufacturing and telecommunications services. The automobile industry is one of the most decentralized industries in terms of ownership and governance structure, but it is crucial to the national economy. Although it is often assumed that regulation from the center is fragmented and relatively loose, central regulation does happen. The automobile sector thus serves as a critical case in Chinese regulation. According to critical case logic, if the mechanism of central regulation exists in the most decentralized industry, then other decentralized but strategic sectors will probably fall under central regulatory control.

To enhance the possibility of generalizing my findings, and to highlight the varieties of regulation within China, I selected another strategic but highly centralized sector: telecommunications. Most previous studies have been limited to the areas of infrastructure and financial services or the rationalization of administrative organization.[71]

The comparative case studies of the automobile manufacturing and telecom service sectors provide examples of how two strategic sectors engender varieties of regulation from the central party-state. The system of regulation and its actual practice in these crucial segments of the national economy show how the party-state maintains regulatory control over the heart of the economy while embracing market forces.

The research for this book involved collecting empirical observations about political behavior and the economic interests of the Chinese central leadership from various sources.[72] In doing so, I conducted 102 interviews with midlevel officials and cadres, senior managers of state enterprises, and Chinese scholars in state research institutions. Midlevel officials often have an accurate idea about the political incentives facing top-level leaders, and the consistency of their answers about elite motivation reflects this knowledge.

## The Argument in Brief

Regardless of inherent sectoral characteristics and decentralized political-economic institutions, central regulation exists in strategic industries in China.[73] Yet the patterns of regulation vary across sectors (or tiers); this book explains the variations through a market-institutional framework. Automobile manufacturing, one of the most decentralized but strategic sectors, offers an excellent comparative case, whereas the highly centralized telecommunications industry demonstrates how the Chinese central leadership exerts regulatory control over major state-owned firms. My findings indicate that strong local components do not necessarily lead to a deficiency of central regulation.[74]

What actually gives rise to the varieties of regulation across China's strategic sectors is the level of ownership (central or provincial) rather than state versus private ownership, while the underlying governance structure and conceptions of control across sectors reinforce (not cause) patterns. The central party-state exercises tight regulation for the central state-owned auto companies (e.g., First Auto Works) and telecommunications service carriers, whereas its oversight of local state auto firms (e.g., Shanghai Automotive Industry Corporation) is relatively loose and indirect through informal channels. The concept of soft and hard regulation is used to highlight the different forms and sources of central regulation for China's strategic industries. This finding leads to three insights into the field of Chinese political economy and the study of regulation in general.

First, the varieties of state regulation reflect China's tactical approach to introducing the mechanism of market coordination to certain parts of the economy while keeping bureaucratic coordination, as the central position of state planning and public ownership evidences. In this sense, it is less fruitful to conclude that the Chinese system of regulation and economic governance is either market-oriented or state-led because more market forces do not necessarily lead to less state in the economy, as Steven Vogel finds in his study of regulation in the advanced industrial economies.[75] Rather, in China, more markets have renewed state plans and adapted regulation to growing market forces. The limits of a binary view of markets versus states help justify the benefits of disaggregating markets as institutions. By analyzing markets as institutions based on property rights, governance structure, and conceptions of control, one can better understand China's multifaceted market realities and varieties of state regulation.

Second, my analysis of the CCP's leading small groups (*lingdao xiaozu*, 领导小组) and central inspection groups (*zhongyang xunshizu*, 中央巡视组) presents how the CCP continues to maintain, formally and informally, its political influence and supervision over policy making and the compliance of leading sectors.

Last, my findings on resilient socialist institutions that continue to adapt to new challenges from reform help political economy scholars expand the scope of the existing analysis and theory on the subject of regulation into the socialist market economy that China strives for. These insights also apply to the study of regulation in general (see fig 1.2).

## *The Organization of This Book*

Chapter 2 examines some early efforts to develop and manage industrial sectors during and after Mao Zedong's rule, focusing on how and why Mao devised such a selective approach in nurturing industrial sectors. The chapter explains how Deng Xiaoping's vision of a socialist market economy promoted the construction of regulatory governance, Chinese-style: a state ownership–centered economy (*guoyou zhongxin jingji*, 国有中心经济), a tiered industrial structure, and the resilience of state planning and the

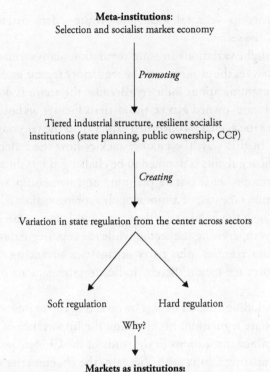

**Meta-institutions:**
Selection and socialist market economy

*Promoting*

Tiered industrial structure, resilient socialist
institutions (state planning, public ownership, CCP)

*Creating*

Variation in state regulation from the center across sectors

Soft regulation        Hard regulation

Why?

**Markets as institutions:**
Property rights/level of ownership, governance structure, and conceptions of control

FIGURE I.2: Varieties of State Regulation, Chinese-Style.

party organization as a governing structure. The chapter then discusses how the planning model has been modified from mandatory and direct planning to guidance and indicative planning, making way for the rise of a regulatory state in the post-Mao era.

Chapters 3 and 4 present the variation in the forms of central regulation by analyzing the conceptions of control and political-economic institutions in two strategic sectors. Chapter 3 examines how the central party-state exerts regulatory control over one of the most decentralized but strategic industries—automobile manufacturing. After reviewing the reform process that remade planning for market regulation in the auto industry, the chapter analyzes how local state ownership, along with governance structure and conceptions of control, play key roles in making central regulation soft. Case studies of three auto firms with different types of ownership—central, local, and private—demonstrate the variations within the sector.

To highlight variations in state regulation across strategic sectors, chapter 4 analyzes the evolution of the regulatory regime and institutions of the telecommunications industry. Because the sector is dominated by three central state–owned giants, the analysis focuses on bureaucratic realities among the agencies concerned rather than the telecom companies themselves. In this way, the chapter tackles how the independence of sector-specific regulators is doomed to be challenged by China's hard regulation by comprehensive state planning and ownership agencies. The chapter examines the case of antimonopoly probing against telecom giants to evidence how the Ministry of Industry and Information Technology is deficient in supervising the sector, while the supraregulators (planning and ownership agencies, plus party organs) are advancing their regulatory power over the sector, thereby indicating the paradox of regulatory reform.

The concluding chapter begins by revisiting the sources of variations in Chinese state regulation, highlighting the importance of formal and informal Leninist institutions in the study of the Chinese political economy. By comparing China with Vietnam, the chapter tests whether the findings from Chinese industrial regulation are applicable to other countries with similar political-economic institutions. The chapter discusses why Chinese practices are relevant to the broader study of regulation, which has previously been dominated by theories and practices from advanced industrial economies. The book concludes with some thoughts about China's path forward, which—given Xi Jinping's recent emphasis on the leading roles of SOEs and CCP organizations in both business and government—seems likely to involve continuing strict regulation of foreign firms regardless of the outcome of US–China trade war negotiations. More broadly, it makes clear that China's efforts to establish a socialist market economy and its distinctive approach to regulating the market will continue to cause friction with the paradigm of the liberal market economy. Therefore, we need to better understand how the system of Chinese political economy actually operates, rather than trying to interpret it through the distorting lens of the orthodox approach to studying regulation.

# CHAPTER 2

## *The Evolution of China's Multifaceted Industrial Regulation*

> We cannot understand where we are going without an understanding of where we have been.
>
> —Douglas North, *Understanding the Process of Economic Change*

The evolution of China's socialist market economy suggests that a consistent theme has been present from the implementation of Mao's command economy to the present state-planned economy: a desire for the party-state to administer market forces while maintaining close oversight of lifeline industries, the heart of the top leadership's power base. In this sense, as Xi Jinping's vision of a socialist market economy indicates, the point of regulatory reform in China has never been to establish a liberal market economy.[1] Instead, the key concern has been how to better administer the enforcement of state regulation in the markets. The enduring emphasis on the centrality of a state-owned economy (*guoyou zhongxin jingji*, 国有中心经济) and the Chinese Communist Party (CCP)'s political oversight of both government and business reflect this ambition.

In this chapter, I demonstrate how China's tiered structure of industries has evolved from Mao Zedong's concept of a planned economy. First, I examine the historical background and evolution of the regulatory state in China and the ideological transformation that has been a driving force in the effort to remake state regulation in the Chinese industrial economy. I highlight industrial management and development under Mao and discuss ideological notions behind the socialist market economy, which is based on the concept that meta-institutions are central to regulatory governance.[2] I review Mao's efforts to manage industrial sectors to implement an efficient and productive command economy and the legacies of these efforts.

How and why did Mao devise a selective approach to nurturing and supervising industrial sectors, even under a command economy? The answer, I argue, is that his emphasis on control over economic lifeline industries (e.g., finance, energy, and communications) and development of heavy industries was affected not only by the Soviet model but also by experiences during the Sino-Japanese War of the 1930s.[3] This selective approach was a departure from the Soviet model of the late 1950s.

Under Deng Xiaoping's leadership, China continued to regulate a dual-track and particularistic contracting system, but Deng's vision of a socialist market economy was an important ideological transformation departing from Mao's vision of collective production and a command economy. This chapter argues that Deng's pursuit of a socialist market economy with Leninist political-economic institutions at the core incrementally and consistently shaped China's tiered industrial structure. The Chinese state's role as a regulator relying on various tactics contrasts with postsocialist Soviet Union and Eastern European experiences, where state regulation was exercised mostly unilaterally. As Douglas North notes, "successful development entails a complex structure of institutions."[4] Deng's vision of a socialist market economy, a vision that still guides China's leaders, fueled a complex structure by steering state planning, state ownership, and the CCP toward a market-oriented economy (fig. 2.1).

To show how China successfully adapted socialist political-economic institutions to market forces, I examine the changing nature and roles of planning agencies in the rise of the regulatory state in the post-Mao era. I explore the evolution of the Central Finance and Economy Leading Small Group (ZCLX, Zhongyang Caijing Lingdao Xiaozu, 中央财经领导小组) to highlight how the CCP has formally engaged in policy making in the economic sector, exerting political leverage over state planning to this day. This chapter focuses on the period from the late 1940s to the early 2000s; the case studies in chapters 3 and 4, which show how the Chinese state uses various tactics in its role as regulator, focus on developments in the past two decades.

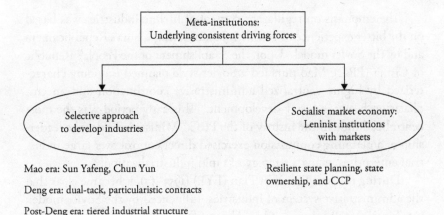

FIGURE 2.1: Historical Origin of Variation in China's Regulation. *Sources:* China Association of Automobile Manufacturers and China Automotive Technology & Research Center, *China Automobile Industry Yearbook 1989–2015* (Beijing: Jixie gongye chubanshe, 1989–2015).

## Economic Regulation under Mao

As many pundits note, China's approach to opening and modernizing industrial sectors has not been unilateral across sectors. The selective approach has resulted in a tiered industrial structure based on different kinds of ownership, governance structures, and conceptions of control among sectors, leading to varieties of state regulation across industries. In this section, I discuss Mao's role in the selective approach to developing and overseeing industries that had been dominated by state-owned enterprises.

As early as the 1940s, Mao addressed the need for the party-state's ownership over big banks, big industries, and large commercial establishments.[5] In 1949, he stressed that "the Communist state would control the economic lifelines of the nation and make the state-owned sector the leading sector of the entire national economy, while allowing the development of private capitalism within the framework of the economic policy and economic planning of the People's Republic."[6] This moment was the birth of China's selective approach to engineering industrial development, thereby shaping a tiered industrial structure.

The emphasis on regulatory control of lifeline industries was based on the bitter experience of war with Japan during China's Republican era and by the Soviet model.[7] Upon the establishment of the People's Republic of China (PRC), Mao pursued a Soviet-style planned economy characterized by highly centralized administrative coordination and an emphasis on heavy industry development.[8] This early period was the most centralized time in the history of the PRC.[9] Ministries under the leadership of a planning commission exercised direct control over large industrial enterprises, using a strategy of rapid industrialization.

During the first Five-Year Plan (FYP) (1953–57), it became clear that the administrative system of industries, influenced by the Soviet model, was hierarchically structured.[10] "About fifty percent of industrial investment during the first Five-Year Plan was either for equipment imported from the USSR and Eastern Europe or for domestic projects that were directly supported by the Soviet plants."[11]

Well before the eruption of Sino-Soviet conflict, Chinese economists and leaders began to question the cost of adopting the Soviet model, which seemed overly repressive and hierarchical. Particularly after the "Khrushchev thaw" in the 1950s, the shortcomings of the Stalinist system were discussed among Chinese elites. Economists proposed various options, and some (e.g., Gu Zhun, 顾准) suggested a move toward a more market-oriented system.[12]

Mao's main concern was how to use state planning to improve the productivity and efficiency of a command economy, particularly the performance of state-owned enterprises (SOEs). Defects of the Soviet-style economy, such as excessive centralization of power in central authorities and emphasis on heavy industries, were recognized by Mao and other leaders by 1956.[13] In modifying a rigid and hierarchically bureaucratized system, China sought to delegate power to authorities and enterprises at lower levels, attempting to rebalance the industrial structure to encompass agriculture and light and heavy industries.

The initial effort was specified in Provisions on Improving the Planning Administration System (1958), which allowed planning to be designed and balanced by local authorities.[14] Another early effort, Provisions on Transferring the Control of Industrial Enterprises, transferred control over state firms to local governments.[15] The delegation of some industrial, commercial, and financial administrative functions to local agencies aimed to give local governments and enterprises more decision-making authority.[16] Decentralizing economic management also allowed local party and government officials to better engage in designing industrialization schemes, an incentive for local officials to mobilize resources under their control into industry.[17]

The delegation of decision making and production to local contexts contributed to the smooth process of the Great Leap Forward (GLF) campaign, which started in 1958. But the GLF ended in economic deterioration and social disorder. Mao later claimed that this failure was the major shortcoming of the GLF, believing that "over-delegation of power in the administration, financial resources, commerce, and industry should be taken back by central and provincial governments."[18]

In 1962, the Central Financial and Economic Leading Group, headed by Chen Yun, took several measures to "recentralize the administration of government finance, credit, and enterprises and to establish a system even more centralized than that of the 1950s."[19] The rupture with the Soviet Union in the 1960s and the ensuing hostility and tension caused the Chinese leadership to reformulate an economic strategy that was independent from the Soviet Union.

Despite painful memories from the GLF, regulatory control over most state enterprises was decentralized to provinces and below. Provinces were given "contractual responsibility" for most of their budgetary revenues and investment, creating financial resources for SOEs and local governments and decreasing the need for central party-state oversight.[20] Consequently, the command economy, which had been focused on the largest SOEs, was restructured into a regionally based arrangement as the central government's control over the economy ebbed.[21]

The decentralization of economic administration shaped the hierarchical structure of the Chinese SOE system by subordinating many state enterprises to the provincial level.[22] By the late 1970s, China's state-owned industrial enterprises were under three systems of control: central, dual, and local.[23] Large and strategic SOEs were controlled by central authorities; small and medium-sized state firms with relatively less strategic value were supervised by local authorities.[24] SOEs under dual control, such as the automobile industry, were subject to control by both central and local authorities, although they were considered centrally controlled or locally controlled depending on the predominant ownership.[25] As a result, "the predominantly centrally controlled enterprises were confined mainly to the electricity generating industry, whereas the predominantly locally controlled enterprises were mostly in light industry and textiles."[26]

To some extent, this selective categorization exhibits how China's emphasis on heavy industries created layers of SOEs across industrial sectors by distinguishing which enterprises were subject to central state ownership. The central government's authority to control the allocation of materials and investment capital enabled it to retain control over all SOEs, even though the degree of control was different across sectors.

## Market-Oriented Reform

Reform-minded economist Sun Yefang (孙冶方) proposed a model of a socialist economy that separated major (national priority) issues and non-major issues according to the degree of market forces. Sun's key proposition was to centralize power over major issues while decentralizing authority over minor ones.[27] Decision-making power regarding extended production with new funds (major issues) was the government's responsibility, and minor issues that required simple production with existing funds were granted to enterprises, giving them some autonomy.[28]

Sun's proposal was a pioneering effort to exercise state control *selectively* over industries and economic affairs. His theory implied that a planned economy does not necessarily mean unilateral absolute control over the entire industrial economy, but that there is room for non-state actors to operate beyond lifeline industries, such as in heavy industries.

Some observers consider Sun's proposal similar to Wlodzimierz Brus's decentralized model of reform.[29] Sun's proposal did not gain much attention under Mao, although Deng widely promoted it. In fact, market-oriented reform was not acceptable because of ideological obstacles until the downfall of the Gang of Four in 1976, by which time a tiered industrial system had emerged, making the command economy based on state planning and SOEs productive and efficient.

## Deng's Evolving Approaches

Although Deng officially declared the goal of "reform and opening" (*gaige kaifang*, 改革开放) upon assuming leadership in 1978, efforts to modify the command economy were moderate and unorganized during the initial stage of reform (1978–93). There were fierce discussions among Chinese scholars and officials (e.g., He Jianzhang, Liu Guoguang, Zhao Renwei) regarding how to adjust markets to state planning in a socialist economy.[30] During Deng's early years, the major departure from Mao was the introduction of market forces while maintaining the primacy of state planning. In this period, the primary task was regulating the scope and depth of introducing market forces into a state-planned (not command) economy.

Chinese leadership attempted to regulate the process of reform to achieve economic stability and development by introducing the idea of guidance planning (*zhidao xing jihua*, 指导性计划), which combined planning with a market mechanism to increase micro-flexibility while maintaining macro-control.[31] This approach was distinct from the rigid, mandatory planning style of the Soviets, in that targets for micro-units (i.e., state enterprises or agriculture producers) were not binding but were adjustable based on a unit's conditions or market demand. For example, with respect to price setting, traditional planning hardly considered possible changes in supply by assuming little in the long run; as a result, unreasonable pricing led to a lack of products in certain markets and missed opportunities for appropriate supply.[32]

Guidance planning grew out of reformist efforts to complement, not replace, a rigid mandatory planning model that failed to consider changing demands from enterprises and society in general.[33] Under Deng, the Chinese state tried to raise incentives for enterprises or producers while maintaining indirect control over overall production volume and the economy's macro-balance.[34] Chinese state planning underwent a transformation from wholesale/unitary mandatory planning (*zhiling xing jihua*, 指令性计划) to a flexible type of planning by incorporating market adjustment (*tiaojie*, 调节).

By the mid-1980s, the implementation of guidance planning was no longer the subject of debate; discussion had shifted to its scope. The 1984

Tentative Regulation on Reforming the Planning System from the State
Planning Commission (SPC) allowed enterprises to make their own decisions regarding production plans and management based on market
conditions and social needs, even though the enhanced autonomy of enterprises was still bounded by state planning.[35]

To ensure stability and address the party-state's primary concerns,
investments in energy and infrastructure continued to be planned by
the state, which gradually introduced market-oriented mechanisms to
less strategic sectors. To regulate the scope and depth of market forces in
state planning, dual-track and particularistic contracting systems were
adopted.

## DUAL TRACKS

The dual-track system in China was devised as the temporary coexistence
of planning and market channels for allocating a given good.[36] For
example, peasants agreed to turn over a certain amount of grain to the government and release the remainder to the market.[37] The dual-track system
thus harbored two coordination mechanisms—plan and market—
rather than replacing plan with market.[38]

Deng's incremental decentralization reform policies reinforced the
administrative hierarchy through the dual-track system.[39] According to
Barry Naughton, "the advantages of the dual-track system were dependent upon the survival of the administrative hierarchy as an organization
capable of delivering effective commands, in that the allocation of goods
by an authoritative plan indeed requires a hierarchy to aggregate and
disaggregate allocation decisions."[40] Economic administration in the
Deng era was indeed decentralized. With a dual-track economy, China
was better positioned to maintain a hierarchy while market forces gradually marched around it.[41]

In the late 1980s, increasing signs of economic instability and market
failures, such as severe inflation and the ensuing shortage of goods and
daily necessities, demanded more mandatory and tight state control in
distributing resources.[42] As a result, while the combination of a planned
economy and market adjustments was largely maintained, state planning
was reemphasized as the leading tool for distributing resources.[43] Likewise, the rise of guidance planning that incorporated a market mecha-

nism into the rigid command economy led to neither the end of state planning nor the collapse of the traditional planned economy, even though the authoritative power of the central government, including the SPC, dwindled.[44]

Despite the remarkable decentralization that generated diverse actors and rules,[45] local authorities still had to get endorsement from Beijing when national priorities were at stake.[46] To some extent, this partial delegation was intended to maintain central leadership control over issues of national priority (or major issues) while increasing efficiency and productivity in nonmajor issues. Although the administrative hierarchy was in turmoil during the political crisis around the Tiananmen Square protests in June 1989, it survived until the central government realized that the dual-track system was not credible in maximizing the profits in the long run and abolished it in 1993 with a declaration of moving toward a socialist market economy.[47]

In summary, regulatory governance under Deng had two notable characteristics. First, state planning remained primary, while the market-adjusting mechanism played a supplementary role, although the benefits and importance of a market-complementary role were stressed.[48] In other words, even though the scope of mandatory planning decreased, the production and distribution of important products continued to be under the direct control of state targets.[49] The strategy of mandatory planning combined with a supplementary guidance plan was solidified.[50] Second, as early as the Twelfth Party Congress in 1982, efforts were made to implement state planning via particularistic contracting.[51]

## PARTICULARISTIC CONTRACTING

Long before economic reform was initiated, Chinese leadership was well aware of the need to develop different means to promote state planning. During the first FYP, Chen Yun, dissatisfied with the Soviet type of rigid economic planning, proposed dividing the Chinese economy into three sectors: "A dominant planned sector under state control, a guided market sector under various degrees of plan guidance, and a free market sector for minor local products."[52]

With insight from the successful practices of the dual-track system in rural reform, policy makers eventually implemented mandatory state planning (*zhiling*, 指令), guidance planning (*zhidao*, 指导), and market regulation.[53] The size and significance of enterprises and the type of industry were the criteria by which the modes of state planning were allocated. Large state-run enterprises (*guoying qiye*, 国营企业) of key industries (e.g., heavy industry) remained in the domain of mandatory state planning, whereas medium and small enterprises in less important sectors were in the domain of guidance planning. As residuals, various small products or special agricultural products were permitted to rely on market regulation rather than state planning.[54]

The idea of contracts was expanded into urban industrial reform. The expectation was that this would enable central leadership to maintain control over some crucial parts of the economy while letting other parts freely transact in the market. Certain enterprises signed profit contracts, promising to turn over to the government a specified amount of annual revenue based on particularistic contracting when dealing with materials of strategic importance or specialized materials.[55]

## THE MIDDLE ROAD

As reform expanded into the industrial and commercial sectors, decision-making power and resources were transferred to lower units. But the demands for approval from Beijing on major issues, such as pricing, investment, and market entry, remained in place, discouraging local actors from acting independently from the center. In this way, the core interests of the central authorities could be secured through particularistic contracts and the dual-track strategy.[56] Such incremental but selective reform approaches led to various forms of state control across sectors and localities, because decentralization and dual-track strategies were not carried out in a unified manner.[57]

Thus, various forms of state control emerged. For example, as in the Mao era, first-category materials, comprising industries of strategic importance and heavy industries, were planned and allocated by the central government, such as the SPC or the State Material Bureau. Specialized materials (second-category material, such as copper and textile machinery) were planned and allocated by individual branch ministries; all other materials, known as third-category goods, were planned by local governments or left to enterprises.[58] As a result, a few large and strategic industrial enterprises were administered directly by the Central Economic Commission, and most industrial enterprises were under the administration of economic commissions at various localities.[59]

The state monopoly over state sectors and firms in the Mao era was not completely transferred to local authorities and firms in the 1980s. Depending on the significance of an industry to the national economy, state control was hierarchically structured, developing into a tiered industrial system. The seventh FYP (1986–90) formalized the distinction between strategic and nonstrategic industries.[60] The central government designated "major pillar industries" (*zhongyao zhizhu chanye*, 重要支柱产业), attempting to make them competitive by maintaining economies of scale or assisting the lagging enterprises in key sectors. As an intermediate road to a more market-oriented economy, the dual-track and particularistic contracting systems contributed to variation in the state's market regulation amid industrial development in China.

## TOWARD A SOCIALIST MARKET ECONOMY

Efforts to reform the economy did not fizzle out in the late 1980s, despite political and economic turmoil; rather, they were invigorated. Perhaps a major departure was a shift in underlying norms toward a market-oriented economy by putting markets first.

The pursuit of a socialist market economy had a profound effect on other institutional reforms. Major steps include dropping the dual-track strategy and the gradual removal of the number of mandatory plans from the SPC (table 2.1). Such a shift in direction and depth of reform was first declared in the Third Plenary Session of the Fourteenth Party Congress in 1978, reinforced by decisions on issues regarding the establishment of a socialist market economic system in 1993.

China's ultimate goal of economic reform was to establish a market economy with socialist characteristics, reflecting continuity with the past rather than any clear features of a liberal market economy.[61] At the Nineteenth Party Congress in 2017, Xi Jinping reaffirmed the consistent move toward a socialist market economy.

Table 2.1
Changes in the Mandatory Planning of Industrial Products under the SPC

| Year | Number of Products | Proportion of Total Industrial Output Value of the Whole Country (%) |
|---|---|---|
| 1980 | 120 | 40 |
| 1985 | 60 | 20 |
| 1992 | 59 | 11.7 |
| 1993 | 36 | 6.8 |
| 1994 | 33 | 4.5 |
| 1998 | 12 | 4 |
| 2002 | 5 | n.a. |

*Sources:* Wei et al., *Shehuizhuyi shichang jingji*, 292; Ma and Cao, *Jihua jingji tizhi xiang*, 239; Beijing shifan daxue jingji yu ziyuan guanli yanjiusuo, *2003 nian zhongguo shichang*.

## A Move toward Indicative Planning

The meaning of "socialist market economy" began to encompass bureaucratic coordination; enhanced market coordination, such as corporatization or legalization; state planning; state ownership; and the CCP. While the markets remained complementary under guidance planning, the rise of indicative planning reflected the fact that the Chinese planned for markets. Primacy shifted to market forces.

Some observers believe that indicative planning refers to "the action of the state in coordinating information from private agents about their intentions, thereby improving forecasts of the future and improving intertemporal resource allocation."[62] However, a more active conceptualization defines indicative planning as "an attempt to influence outcomes with information, not simply affording information."[63] In using governmental forecasting (e.g., statements that estimate growth potential in certain industries), signaling (e.g., preferential policies for small and medium enterprises), and indirect incentives (e.g., improved access to bank credit and domestic/overseas markets), indicative planning aims to stimulate market incentives and mobilize resources in sectors the government identifies as having development potential. The key lies in greater reliance on market forces than on state plans.

For example, local actors will respond strategically to the notices of state policy, because local actors (including local authorities and local state firms) know that the central government will arrange specific instruments to achieve its policy goals. Indeed, the eighth FYP (1991–95) elaborated this new concept of "plan," for the first time suggesting the significance of developing pillar industries, including machine-electronic, petroleum-chemical, auto machinery, and construction.[64] State planning transformed from directly commanding and controlling micro-affairs into a vehicle, along with market-oriented industrial policies, for macro-control and development.[65] The ultimate goal of planning was an attempt to alter the economic structure by motivating the incentives of the actors.[66]

Accordingly, significant modification of the roles and tools of the SPC took place.[67] The role of the SPC shifted from direct *jihua* (计划) over microeconomic affairs to macroeconomic coordination by making long- and medium-term *guihua* (规划), or industrial and regional development policies.[68] The SPC took more responsibility for coordinating macro-development and issuing economic information, as well as setting up the indicative annual planning index.

Based on macro-level assessments, the SPC published policy suggestions on some important issues.[69] For example, because the commission was keen to establish and support infrastructure and pillar industries, related policies were promoted accordingly.[70] The outline of the national industrial policy for the 1990s and the auto industrial policy in 1994, as well as regulations on guiding the direction of foreign commercial investment and guidance on foreign commercial investment industry in 1995, offer examples of how China modified its means of control (i.e., regulation) and refined itself as an indicative planner.[71]

With the creation of a socialist market economy system, the SPC's regulatory function was further modified from guidance planning that used micro- and macro-control to indicative planning that featured indirect macro-control.[72] The renaming of the SPC to the State Development and Planning Commission (SDPC) in 1998 confirmed the changing nature and tools of state regulation.[73] China's pursuit of a socialist market economy also opened up the possibility of diverse actors, institutions, and property rights, ultimately resulting in a variety of regulatory styles to govern the economy. For example, the leadership proposed a system that allowed central authorities to gain a hold over strategically important industries (such as infrastructure and finance) while allowing more market forces in the other sectors.

Thus, the selective approach to regulating sectors was cemented under Deng's vision of a socialist market economy. Efforts to selectively embrace market forces generated a tiered industrial structure. Although scholars do not agree on what criteria to use to group the sectors as tiers, they concur that the Chinese industrial economy is organized into three tiers: top, middle, and bottom.[74]

The tiered industrial structure was enhanced under Deng because the idea of a socialist market economy encourages a selective approach to regulating sectors depending on their importance to the national economy and security. Therefore, different depths of state regulation across tiers (or sectors) contributed to creating the varieties of China's regulatory tactics.

The emphasis on building a socialist market economy suggests that organizational components, such as planning agency and state ownership, were resilient. Xi Jinping has reinforced this concept. The existence of market forces and institutions does not necessarily imply languishing socialist political-economic institutions. Instead, their roles and forms have been adapted to new realities and challenges, ultimately aiming to better administer the state-planned (as opposed to command) economy.

This shift in ideology brought about changes in the tools of control (regulation) from micro-level planning and allocation to macro-direction and indirect intervention in the economy. The changing manners of control also involved a policy move from decentralization and particularistic contracting to recentralization, combined with a greater arm's-length regulatory approach to economic units competing in the marketplace.[75] This view of the regulatory function of the state was initially proposed by leading economists and officials in the late 1970s and early 1980s.[76] According to one such pioneering vision:

> First, the form of *central planning* should change from mandatory to indicative planning, so that the state provided guidance and long-term forecasting, but did not intervene directly. Second, *state ownership* system should be confined to the infrastructure of the economy, such as transportation, harbors, and energy. In principle, government departments should not own and manage industrial enterprise directly. Third, *the means of pro-*

*duction* should be reclassified as "commodities," to be allocated through the market. Finally, *the state's role in the economic sphere* should be limited to the use of economic leverage through economic and financial measures (such as the control of credit, revenues and taxation, tariffs, the pricing mechanism, foreign exchange and so on) rather than direct administrative means.[77]

The transition from guidance planning in the 1980s to indicative planning in the 1990s was a notable step in reforming Chinese regulation. Rather than supplementing mandatory planning, the emerging form of indicative planning led to abolishing mandatory planning and its replacement with a market-oriented mechanism. Furthermore, the state planning agency shifted its role from direct intervention in the micro-affairs of enterprises (such as production, investment, distribution, and pricing) to macroeconomic coordination. In doing so, long- and medium-term industrial policies were used as indirect tools of indicative planning that informed local governments or state enterprises of development direction and strategies as well as preferential policies. When compared with the guidance planning of the 1980s, indicative planning was a substantial transformation in the nature of Chinese regulation; the 1998 decision to rename the SPC the SDPC reflects this remarkable shift.

Although the modernization of traditional SOEs and the introduction of corporate governance came to be the primary concerns of regulation, the centrality of state ownership in the Chinese economy did not change fundamentally.[78] In other words, even though the Chinese party-state embraced market forces, state ownership remained central in some selected strategic sectors. This selective approach is clear in the case of SOEs.

According to the policy of "grasping large enterprises, letting small ones go" (*zhuada fangxiao*, 抓大放小) SOE reform efforts adopted in 1997 at the Fifteenth Communist Party Congress were to be directed at large and medium SOEs that were crucial to the national economy, whereas other SOEs would be released and invigorated by means of mergers, leases, contracts, offers for sale, or bankruptcy.[79] *Zhuada fangxiao* emerged from the concept of making strategically important industries state enterprises by merging existing, less competitive, and inefficiently run state firms or letting them go bankrupt. The state's continued control over industries strategic to the national economy was reaffirmed by the Fourth Plenary Session in 1999, which specifically addressed four

Table 2.2
Evolution of the Chinese State from Planner to Regulator

|  | Planner | Regulator | |
|---|---|---|---|
| Nature of state planning | Mandatory planning (1949–78) | Guidance planning (1978–93) | Indicative planning (1993–present) |
| Goals | Productive/efficient command economy | Enhancing planning by markets | Market-oriented state planning (socialist market economy) |
| Coordination mechanism | Bureaucratic and central command | Bureaucratic > market | Market > bureaucratic |
| Tools | Direct/micro | Mixed: micro/macro; direct/indirect | Macro and indirect; legalizing state regulation |

fields: industries related to national security, industries of natural monopolies, industries providing important public goods and services, and key enterprises in backbone and high-tech industries.[80]

The tools of regulation became institutionalized as China's state planning became more indicative.[81] The Company Law of 1993, for example, provided a legal measure to enhance the modernization of traditional state enterprises and develop their corporate governance.[82] Under the law, most traditional state enterprises were transformed into joint-stock corporations or limited liability companies (*youxian gongsi*, 有限公司).

The norm of "separating government from enterprise" (*zhengqi fenkai*, 政企分开) was taken seriously in promoting the Chinese socialist market economy. It ultimately required streamlining the bureaucracy to set up arm's-length regulatory institutions independent of both government and business to ensure effective market oversight. Starting in the mid-1990s, so-called regulatory institutions for specific industries surged, confirming the rise of the regulatory state in China (table 2.2).

## The CCP as the Regulator of State Planning

Often invisible, the CCP frames state planning, coordinates policies, and supervises some crisis management as well as compliance with state plans.

Specifically, the CFELSG engages in the state planning that is the main channel of bureaucratic coordination. Although there have been some efforts to explore the relationship between state planning and the CCP, the subject is relatively understudied despite its importance to understanding the Chinese political economy.[83] Analysis has tended to focus on cadre evaluation or the plan–cadre nexus in the hierarchical structure of the CCP.[84] How the CFELSG interacts with the state planning agency to create a form of Chinese regulation with deep socialist elements has yet to be studied.[85] A sound understanding of the CFELSG is needed to understand how the CCP is formally embedded in regulation in China.

In Chinese politics, leading small groups (LSGs) are effectively a joint venture between the CCP (*dang*, 党) and the government (*zheng*, 政).[86] LSGs (*lingdao xiaozu*, 领导小组) ensure the CCP's continued leadership over economic management and political administration.[87] They form a bridge between the party's top leadership and major government agencies and a conduit for information processing and policy deliberation.[88]

The CFELSG exerts substantial influence on China's economic plans and reform direction.[89] Established in 1958, the group managed the severe failures and chaos in the wake of the GLF.[90] But the government suspended the CFELSG during the Cultural Revolution, strengthening direct engagement of the party under the leadership of the Cultural Revolution LSG.[91] The CFELSG was reinstated in 1980 with the decision of the Central Political Standing Commission to replace the Finance and Economy Commission under the State Council.[92]

Under the leadership of Zhao Zhiyang, the CFELSG became one of the party's key economic decision-making bodies, responsible for national economic development and system reform until the political crisis following the Tiananmen crackdown.[93] The CFELSG was central in coordinating and guiding overall state planning "by requesting research reports, organizing consultations, formulating policy papers and drafting a comprehensive development plan."[94] Since the late 1980s, it has played a leading role in formulating major reform policies and accomplished substantial achievements, including the 1994 tax reform, the 1997–99 SOE reform, the 1998 housing and social security policy, and World Trade Organization membership in 2001.[95] Such remarkable achievements prove the party's supervisory role in designing the state's plans for the markets.[96]

Zhongcaiban (中财办), the CFELSG office (Zhongyang Caijing Lingdao Xiaozu Bangongshi), is responsible for drafting documents and reports for top leadership.[97] Because it enhances coordination between the party and the government, Zhongcaiban is a powerful tool of political control. It prepares official documents for the Central Economy Work Conference (Zhongyang Jingji Gongzuo Huiyi), established in 1994. Participants in the annual conference include the Central Committee of the CCP and the central bureaucracies, as well as local bureaucrats and entrepreneurs. Each year, Zhongcaiban conducts national research, searching for issues and developing solutions.[98] Over the years, Zhongcaiban has had discussions with local cadres and entrepreneurs, and it regularly holds a symposium to collect comprehensive data and ideas. A final report is delivered to the general secretary of the CCP at the annual work conference, where the findings are endorsed for the upcoming year.[99] These reports influence central and local leadership on how to run the market. For example, Decision of Reforming the Economic System in 1984 and the Idea of Building the Socialist Market Economy in 1993 were drafted and developed by Zhongcaiban.[100] Zhongcaiban worked on a report for the Third Plenum of the Eighteenth Party Congress in 2012 in coordination with the Central Policy Research Center (Zhongyang Zhengce Yanjiushi), setting the direction of new economic reform. Zhong-

Table 2.3
Dual Position of the CFELSG Office (*Zhongcaiban*) Head, 1994–2013

| Head of CFELSG Office | Government Rank |
| --- | --- |
| Zeng Peiyan (曾培炎) 1994–98 | 1992–98: Deputy director, SPC (国家计划委员会副主任) |
| Hua Jianmin (华建敏) 1998–2003 | 1996–98: Deputy director, Office of the Central Leading Group for Financial and Economic Affairs (中央财经领导小组办公室副主任) |
| | 2003–8: State councilor and secretary general, State Council (国务委员、国务院秘书长) |
| Wang Chunzheng (王春正) 2003–7 | 2003–7: Deputy director, National Development and Reform Commission (国家发展和改革委员会副主任) |
| Zhu Zhixin (朱之鑫) 2007–13 | 2007–14: Deputy director, National Development and Reform Commission |

caiban also coordinates potential disagreements between the party and the government.[101]

Since 1994, the head of the National Development and Reform Commission has often held the concurrent post of head of Zhongcaiban (table 2.3).[102] Title holders include Zheng Beiyan (1994–98), Wang Chunzheng (2003–7), and Zhu Zixin (2007–13). With a wealth of knowledge about state planning, the head of Zhongcaiban can promote its capacity for information access and professional expertise in drafting documents and proposals, while serving as the head of the National Development and Reform Commission and taking advantage of powerful political capital.[103] Zhongcaiban's deep involvement with the planning agency indicates how the CCP steers China's economy, determining the overall direction of the state plans through bureaucratic coordination.

## A Tiered Structure

Mao's selective approach to industrial management and Deng's pursuit of a socialist market economy eventually generated diversity in coordination mechanisms and property rights across industrial sectors, resulting in tiers of industries in China. Although China's emphasis on retaining central party control over lifeline and heavy industries has endured since Mao, central oversight has not been linear or uniform since Deng's declaration of a socialist market economy. As a result, what emerged is central oversight over leading industries in tandem with the embrace of market forces, resulting in a tiered industrial structure. Even with the inevitable variability of state regulation, China has shown a remarkable consistency in the pursuit of its policies to create a socialist market economy.

# CHAPTER 3

## *The Auto Industry: Soft Regulation*

A mixture of formal institutions, informal institutions, and their
enforcement characteristics define institutional performance.

—Douglas North, *Understanding the Process of
Economic Change*

Is there a discernible pattern of regulation in which ownership is
highly decentralized yet the industry is considered strategic by the central leadership? As a rapidly growing sector, China's auto industry has a
remarkable record. Since 2009, China has emerged as the largest auto
market in the world, with more than 19.3 million vehicle sales in 2012.[1]
Compared with its global market share of the auto market in 2001,
which was only 4 percent at the time, this seems to signal that China,
now tying with the United States, could become the next global auto
power. Since its Seventh Five-Year Plan (FYP; 1985–90), the Chinese
leadership has targeted auto manufacturing as a pillar industry that
could invigorate its lagging command economy. Moreover, its multiplier
effects on modernizing other industries, including the chemical, machinery, electronic, and steel sectors, have resulted in leadership prioritizing development of the auto industry. In China, the modernization
logic that recognized the auto industry as strategic was reaffirmed with
the introduction of the 2009 Auto Industry Restructuring and Rejuvenating Program (Qiche Chanye Tiaozheng he Jinxing Guihua, 汽车产
业调整和进行规划) following the global financial crisis of 2008.[2] In
particular, the Made in China 2025 policy, announced in 2015, evidences the country's ambition to become a global leader in energy-
saving and electronic vehicles.[3] Rather than relying on technology
transfer or importing key components from foreign joint venture (JV)
partners, the ultimate goal of the Made in China 2025 policy seems to

be upgrading manufacturing production to make it more efficient and competitive in the global production chain.

In China today, increased global integration means increased state regulation in terms of market access and technology innovation, as the Made in China 2025 policy shows. However, this is hardly news, although the scale and impact of China's market power are very different from before. As examined in chapter 2, China has been persistently regulating markets, including production, investment, pricing, and agencies, through state plans amid the policy of reforms. Strategic regulation from the central party-state remains significant, regardless of sectoral characteristics or decentralized authorities. This chapter explains how the predominance of local state ownership plays a key role in making Chinese regulation of the auto industry *soft* from the central party-state through indirect and informal measures, while the concepts of control and the governing structure in the auto sector reinforce the pattern of soft regulation.

The main arguments of this chapter are as follows. First, and most important, although auto manufacturing in China is dominated by strong local components in terms of property rights and governing structure, there are still substantial central levers of regulation over the business of local and private auto firms. Yet because of the lack of formal rights enjoyed by local and private business, the means and scope of central regulation remain indirect and informal compared with centrally state-owned auto firms. Second, variation in the form of central regulation in the sector is also notable. This demonstrates the significance of level of ownership in making the forms of state regulation even within the sector. Whereas the central state-owned enterprise (SOE) First Auto Works (FAW) operates under Beijing's direct and tight oversight—like the sectors of infrastructure and finance—the central regulation of local and private auto producers Shanghai Automotive Industry Corporation (SAIC) and Geely Corporation is indirect and informal. Third, considering that the role of the Chinese Communist Party (CCP) in industrial regulation remains understudied, this chapter attempts to add to the literature by examining how party organizations attempt to maintain levers of political supervision through informal measures.

After discussing how the central leadership has refashioned state planning to regulate the auto industry, this chapter elaborates on the sources that make China's central regulation soft, including the concepts of control, property rights (dominance of local state ownership), and governing structure. The chapter then compares three auto companies with different ownership types (central, local state-owned, and private), mapping out each pattern of state regulation from the central party-state. To compare the central regulation of highly decentralized strategic industries to a centrally monopolized industry (e.g., telecommunications), the concept of *soft* regulation is proposed for China's auto industry.

## The Auto Industry's Market Reform Process

Successful development of the auto industry has been a crucial concern for Chinese leadership because it relates closely to economic modernization and the growth of other sectors, such as the chemical, steel, machinery, and service industries. Due to such modernization logic, the auto sector is often perceived as a comprehensive industry (*zonghe hangye*, 综合行业) among Chinese officials and scholars. Hence, central state regulation, despite the decentralized structure of administration and ownership, has remained steadfast through the market-oriented reforms. This section elaborates how China's opening and reform has remade state planning for regulation of the auto industry. In a nutshell, although there is fierce market competition among foreign partners and Chinese producers, such market mechanism is largely coordinated by the bureaucracy, as illustrated by auto industrial policies and FYPs.

### 1949–79 (PREREFORM): COMMAND CONTROL BY MANDATORY PLANNING

China's path of development in the auto industry goes back to the early socialist regime. In 1953, four years after Mao Zedong's visit to the Soviet Union, China's first auto company, FAW, was established in Changchun. Auto production started with the memorable Liberation (*jiefang*, 解放) truck in 1956.[4] Because of a lack of capital and technology, the sector relied heavily on technical assistance and capital investment from the Soviet Union. Following the rise of FAW, the Shanghai Automobile Assembly Plant (later SAIC) and the Second Automotive Work (later

Dongfeng) were established in 1958 and 1969, respectively. During the initial stages of development, China's auto manufacturing production was limited to heavy and light trucks, buses, and jeeps, mainly for transportation or military use. Back then, the manufacture of passenger vehicles was allowed only for government officials, so vehicles were not available for private purchase; in fact, the private purchase of automobiles was not permitted until the mid-1980s. Likewise, the initial development of China's auto industry was entirely mobilized and managed by the centralized bureaucratic coordination through mandatory planning.

For example, the production and development of the auto sector was managed directly by the State Planning Commission (SPC) to achieve target growth and defense construction. Through this process, production items, the production base of factories, technology development, and product distribution were set by the state mandatory plan.[5] Although there were some changes in China's bureaucratic structure, the auto sector was in the hands of the Ministry of Heavy Industry in 1949 and subsequently under the newly restructured Ministry of the First Machinery Industry, specifically the Auto Industry Managing Bureau (Qiche Gongye Guanliju, 汽车工业管理局).[6] During the first FYP (1953–58), the central authorities exercised intensive direct control over state-run enterprises, including economic lifelines and auto state firms.[7]

## 1979–93: REGULATING BY GUIDANCE PLANNING

With economic reform, China's auto sector entered a new stage of development. Although the direct bureaucratic control through state planning remained overriding, the market mechanism was newly introduced to complement—not replace—the centrally managed economy.[8] Efforts to separate the rights of ownership and management of auto firms were one example of integrating a market-oriented system into state-run enterprises. But the subordination of auto firms and factories to the Chinese National Auto Industry Corporation (CNAIC, Zhongguo Qiche Gongye Gongsi, 中国汽车工业公司) delimited the market-based operation of the firms, in that the CNAIC held the rights to manage the auto firms' personnel, as well as to supervise their business management and policy implementation.[9] Established in 1982 under the direct leadership of the Ministry of Machinery Industry (MMI), the CNAIC acted as a quasi-governmental

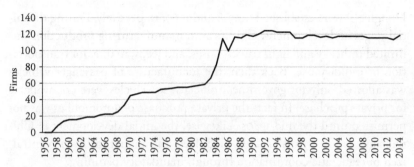

FIGURE 3.1: Number of Automobile Manufacturers in China, 1956–2014. *Sources:* China Association of Automobile Manufacturers and China Automotive Technology & Research Center, *China Automobile Industry Yearbook 1989–2015* (Beijing: Jixie gongye chubanshe, 1989–2015).

agency responsible for coordinating state policies and business between ministries and auto firms. Despite such centralized early bureaucratic architecture, both its longtime regionalized production bases and prior emphasis on self-reliance over the 1950s and 1960s challenged the CNA-IC's regulatory power over the decentralized auto producers. Moreover, its moderated policy for market entry in the early 1980s encouraged local governments to set up their own auto manufacturing plants. Consequently, the number of auto firms surged from 53 in 1976 to 122 in 1995 (fig. 3.1).[10] This fragmented market structure eventually compelled central authorities to push for market consolidation to raise productivity and economies of scale.

As one such endeavor, in 1987 the SPC proposed the creation of "three large firms and three small ones" (*sanda sanxiao*, 三大三小) as the main assemblers of passenger cars, in an attempt to tightly control market entry.[11] Approval of foreign partners and investments became another key lever of direct bureaucratic control for the SPC. Indeed, China was proactive in attracting foreign investment in the form of JVs from the very beginning of the reform. Moreover, given the auto sector's global nature and China's thirst for capital and advanced technology, a JV with foreign producers was favored by Chinese leadership.[12] Such needs and desires have led to a policy of "exchange technology with market" (*huan jishu he shichang*, 换技术和市场). In pursuit of *huan jishu he shichang*, the first JV auto firm, Beijing-Jeep Corporation, was established by Beijing Automobile Corporation and American Motors Corporation in 1983. After that, the SAIC and FAW each set up JV firms with Volkswagen in 1985 and 1991, respectively.

What is notable during this early period of reform is that rather than relying on direct control by the previous mandates, the central leadership attempted to guide the development plans of the auto sector through industrial policies and FYPs. The "Report on Auto Industry Development and Reform" (*Guanyu qiche gongye da fazhan he gaige de baogao*) in the early 1980s was proposed out of such efforts. Moreover, the auto industry, for the first time, was named as a pillar sector in China from the seventh FYP in 1986, and its strategic importance for the national economy was reaffirmed in the eighth FYP.[13] Likewise, centralized bureaucratic regulation was exercised in the form of guidance planning (*yindao jihua*, 引导计划). In the meantime, with the deepening reform, the CNAIC, which had exerted direct control over auto producers, was transformed into the Chinese Auto Industry Association (Zhongguo Qiche Gongye Lianhehui, 中国汽车工业联合会) in 1987, with less authority than before.[14] But the CNAIC was soon reestablished with a new title—the Chinese National Auto Industry General Corporation (Zhongguo Qiche Gongye Zonggongsi, 中国汽车工业总公司)—in the early 1990s, and it was responsible for supervising economic performance of directly subordinated firms.[15]

## 1994–2002: REGULATING BY INDICATIVE PLANNING

Both FYP and auto industry policy send significant signals for the overall direction and strategies to pursue, rather than explicit instructions. As other scholars note,[16] the nature of state planning, such as FYP, appeared to shift toward indicative planning (or program) (*guihua*, 规划), which is designed to influence how the market was structured by providing government and firms with signals. Indeed, the SPC issued a series of industrial policies for selected pillar industries in the early 1990s.[17] For example, the 1994 auto industrial policy was issued to guide (*yindao*, 引导), not command (*zhiling*, 指令), the direction of mid- and long-term strategies for the sector.[18]

Above all, market consolidation and the advancement of technological capacity were stressed as measures to overcome the highly fragmented, inefficient, and sluggish development of the auto sector.[19] Different from the *sanda sanxiao* (big three, small three) strategy of the early 1980s, the 1994 policy did not name particular companies to be made into national champions but indicated its specific plans to promote the creation of two or three large enterprises (*daxing qiye*, 大型企业) and six to seven key enterprises (*gugan qiye*, 骨干企业), not small ones.[20] Ultimately, the central authorities wanted big state firms to form three or four internationally competitive national champions by 2010.[21] Therefore, although the tenth FYP (2001–5) formally addressed China's desire to create large auto business groups,[22] this idea had been harbored and promoted since the mid-1990s through indicative planning. Although some note that the impact of the policy has remained limited due to difficulties in effective local enforcement, it still has significant implications for local and foreign entrepreneurs in designing their business plans.[23] For instance, the SAIC-VW, the largest auto state firms based in Shanghai, established the Department of Auto Industrial Policy Analysis within the group to study national auto industrial policy;[24] the central bureaucracy maintains regulatory oversight by issuing strict rules for technology transfer, product lines, and stock share rate of the enterprises.

## 2003–2012: BACK TO MICRO-CONTROL?

With the rapid growth of the auto market, Chinese leadership began to raise some concerns about the failure of technology transfer through JV with foreign partners since the early 2000s, searching for new strategies to boost the country's own technology and brands in the auto sector. The central authorities believed that the previous policy of "exchanging markets with technology" largely benefited foreign JV partners with great market access to China's enormous potential markets, whereas Chinese producers remained as mere assemblers without learning core technology. In fact, much criticism came from domestic pundits asking for new approaches to upgrading auto development. Emphasis on "indigenous innovation" (*zizhu chuangxin*, 自主创新) resulted from such internal demands, and stricter rules for foreign partners were required for the meaningful transfer of technology to Chinese producers. Hence, such shifts of strategy and approach caused the state planning, which is the main tool of central regulation, to revert to more or less micro-types of control, as exemplified by the 2004 policy for auto industry development and the 2009 rejuvenating auto industry policy.

For example, the 2004 policy delineates at length how to manage investment (articles 40–51, chapter 10), whereas it is addressed in the 1994 policy only briefly.[25] According to the 2004 policy, investment items from provincial governments or enterprise groups should be reported to the National Development and Reform Commission (NDRC) for approval (*pizhun*, 批准);[26] new investments of foreign JVs for passenger cars required the approval of the State Council via the NDRC.[27] Moreover, specific conditions for overall investments and foreign JV were documented in the 2004 policy. This was a considerable change given that China's first auto industry policy in 1994 did not include the particular section for investment control; instead, there were rules on the policy for using foreign capital to boost the development of the domestic auto industry.[28] In this regard, compared with the 1994 policy, the central government retooled its regulatory grip on market entry and investment in the 2004 policy. To this end, the NDRC is more empowered than the SPC by integrating the formerly fragmented authorities across other ministries. Moreover, indigenous innovation was stressed in the 2004 policy in line with the eleventh FYP (2006–10).[29] In nurturing domestic brands and independent capabilities, the NDRC encouraged these firms to collaborate with foreign partners. Such micro-means of regulatory control over the auto industry were further accelerated with the rise of the rejuvenating policy for ten selected sectors in 2009.

To deal with plummeting sales and increasing overcapacity concerns after the 2008 global financial crisis, the 2009 policy put great emphasis on adjusting the market structure and enhancing independent capacity through domestic innovation.[30] While the combined roles of market forces and government guidance were stressed, state-led corporate mergers were set as an objective and were promoted to facilitate market consolidation with two or three large auto business groups that have produced more than two million cars.[31] In effect, when state auto firms intended to merge with private producers, government (local or central) played a leading role in pushing the merger. Consequently, such a move is popularly called *guojin mintui* (国进民退; state advance, private retreat), with some criticism.

In the case of the merger of the Baoling-Beijing auto firms, for example, the Guangdong provincial government, which was in charge of the Baoling firm, pushed the merger with the Beijing Auto Industry Corporation Group through a free asset transfer.[32] Furthermore, in dealing with the overcapacity issue, the central authorities were determined to provide tax incentives and subsidies to residents in rural areas for car purchases.[33]

In short, while China's desire to develop the auto sector as a strategic industrial pillar has remained consistent since the early 1980s, the tools and focus of regulation have shifted from heavy reliance on foreign capital and technology through JVs to nurturing innovative capacity by developing domestic brands. In this procedure, bureaucracy still takes the place of the market mechanism by setting specific plans or targets to achieve, as the past several FYPs and auto industrial policies prove. Moreover, new internal and external challenges, such as industrial overcapacity or the global financial crisis, recall past micro-means of state regulation. As a result, China's highly globalized auto industry paradoxically relies on the centralized regulation through auto industrial policies and FYPs. Yet its pattern of regulation is *soft* compared with that in telecommunications, another strategic sector, because of the underlying conceptions of control, the governing structure, and above all the dominant mode of state ownership, as elaborated in the next section.

## Conceptual Origin of Soft Regulation

According to the Chinese Association for the Automobile, "automobile manufacturing is not a standard manufacturing sector. It is a strategic asset that supports the transformation and upgrading of the national economy."[34] As noted earlier, the auto industry has been considered a pillar sector for China's economic modernization and development since the mid-1980s. Up to now, such perception has generated a range of auto-specific industrial policies—in 1994, 2004, 2009, and 2013 (Made in China 2025 policy)—and its significance has been emphasized consistently in FYPs since the seventh FYP (1986–90). Indeed, FYPs that pointed to the auto sector as the pillar of the national economy have sent government and market actors a signal for the overall direction of development and focus, including the creation of foreign JVs (ninth FYP, 1996–2000), the establishment of large auto business groups (tenth FYP, 2001–5), and the development of indigenous auto brands (eleventh FYP, 2006–10).[35]

Moreover, specific rules of regulation have been elaborated in auto industrial policies. As direct tools of bureaucratic coordination, industrial policies have served as key instruments for allocating resources to specific target sectors, including auto manufacturing.[36] In implementing industrial policies, the Chinese government has granted a considerable number of fiscal subsidies (e.g., bank loans or tax exemptions), export credits, and import restrictions to favored sectors and firms. For those reasons, industrial policy can be seen as a window into the kind of coordination mechanisms that prevail in the sector, indicating the overall set of understandings and practices that shape concepts of control in the sector.

For example, China's first auto industry policy in 1994 focused on two tasks: advancement of its technological capacity and consolidation of the highly fragmented market with the big three and small three firms.[37] Its efforts to create large business groups by merging inefficient small enterprises (later evolved into "grasping large, letting go small") show how the Chinese leadership attempted to benchmark "big business" in Japan and Korea. Moreover, while technology transfer from foreign partners continued to be reinforced, nurturing the capacity for indigenous innovation began to be newly stressed since the 2004 auto industry development policy.[38] To this end, collaborating with foreign partners has been highly emphasized with various conditions for doing business with Chinese auto producers.[39] In addition, to deal with the plummeting sales and overcapacity in the wake of the 2008 global financial crisis, the central government issued a new policy to rejuvenate the auto industry in 2009. The policy encouraged mergers between inefficient auto producers and larger ones in order to enhance market consolidation, and specified subsidies to residents in rural areas for car purchases.[40] In this sense, as the FYPs and auto industrial policies suggest, China's notion of pillar industry for the auto sector had an effect on a set of practices and understandings about how to regulate the sector with long-term strategic value to the national economy.

On the other hand, the historical pathways of evolution with highly decentralized production have led Beijing to suffer from local compliance in terms of various issues, including market entry or local protection. Still,

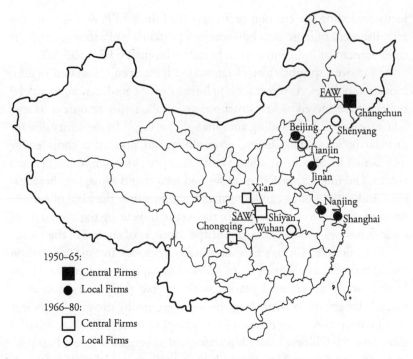

FIGURE 3.2:  Major Auto Assembly Enters China before the 1980s.

Chinese auto firms and manufacturing facilities are spread widely across the country (fig. 3.2), which is partly because the Chinese leadership prior to the reform era was reluctant to concentrate auto manufacturing in one or two regions.[41] As a result, major auto producers have stretched from Changchun to Guangzhou and include most major localities in between, such as Beijing, Chongqing, Shanghai, Hangzhou, and Shiyan. To some extent, such regionalized auto manufacturers had to do with China's history of decentralization during the Great Leap Forward (1957–58), the construction of the "third front" after the Sino-Soviet rift since the mid-1960s as a defense strategy, and the pursuit of a self-sustaining industrial structure by each province in the 1970s.[42] For example, the number of small assembly factories increased dramatically during the Great Leap Forward in 1958. The Sino-Soviet split in the 1960s caused China to relocate its new automobile assemblers from northeast Jilin near the Soviet Union to the inland mountains of northwest Hubei, an unusual location for an auto industry that favors the coastal cities for overseas trade.[43] The Cultural Revolution (1966–76) led to another proliferation of auto assemblers as the central authority lost its control.[44] Such historically shaped regionalization has empowered local governments more than any other factor.

Moreover, as evidenced by the auto industry policies in 1994 and 2004, China's early embrace of foreign capital and technology in the form of JVs also created diverse stakeholders in the sector. Accordingly, the decentralization of manufacturers and the active introduction of foreign collaborative partners are historically specific to China's auto industry, making a set of understandings and practices on how to run those fragmented authorities and producers and satisfy various stakeholders in this particular setting. Hence, despite its strategic value and modernization logic, a horizontal approach (*kuaikuai*) to production and various stakeholders makes the pattern of China's regulation for the auto sector indirect and informal, which I call *soft* regulation from the center.

## *Governing Structure: Decentralized Authorities, Consolidated Power*

Throughout the historical evolution of the sector, the governing structure of the auto industry has remained highly fragmented, both horizontally and vertically. As this section illustrates, however, institutional reforms that stress efficient administration have led to the integration of previously fragmented and overlapping authorities in the planning and ownership agencies at the central and local levels. Still, highly decentralized ownership and the ensuing power of local government ownership constrain the unified regulation of China's auto business. This continuity of vertical fragmentation has promoted the leadership relationship (*lingdao guanxi*, 领导关系) between provincial/municipal governments and local offices of the NDRC and State-Owned Assets Supervision and Administration Commission (SASAC), as local governments hold the rights to appoint their personnel. But the resulting professional relationship (*yewu guanxi*, 业务关系) between central regulators and local offices tends to make central regulation loose and indirect, as central regulators have no official authority over local offices.

In fact, as a comprehensive body, the SPC lacked enforcement power over other central state institutions and state-owned auto enterprises. Furthermore, the equal bureaucratic ranking of the MMI with provincial governments posed a significant obstacle to effective policy implementation in the auto industry.[45] But China's 1998 administrative reform broke new ground by abolishing several ministries that directly managed industries. The former state planning body, the SPC, was transformed into the State Development Planning Commission (SDPC) as a more comprehensive agency. In 2003, the SDPC was renamed as the NDRC. As a core regulator of the auto industry, the NDRC is responsible for long-term planning and industrial policy, technology innovation, and final investment approval.[46] With the state restructuring in 1998, the former MMI was integrated into the State Economic and Trade Commission (SETC);[47] however, when the SETC was dismantled in 2003, its previous authority over industrial policy, market entry, and regulation of investment and technological innovation was moved to the NDRC.[48]

Another function of the MMI, the authority to appoint managers of the central auto firms, was first housed in the SETC, then transferred to the central SASAC on its emergence in 2003. Accordingly, the 1998 restructuring of administration has unified the formerly scattered regulatory authorities at the top, reshaping governing structure of the auto industry in the following respects.

First is the rise of the NDRC as a leading regulator for the auto industry. Its regulatory scope has become more comprehensive than that of its predecessor, the SPC, by integrating the previous authority of the MMI and other defunct industrial ministries. In addition, compared with the SPC, the NDRC has higher bureaucratic status than other ministries or provincial governments,[49] counterbalancing its authority in policy-making decisions and implementations. Thus, the NDRC leads in setting auto industrial policy with the final authority to endorse market entry, new JV investment projects, and domestic partners, which is crucial for Chinese auto producers. Specifically, the Department of Industry Policy under the NDRC acts as the main body that drafts policies for the sector. The department is in charge of analyzing the conditions of industrial development and making policy recommendations for future directions based on national, long-term developmental strategies and goals, as well as monitoring the enforcement of industrial policies.[50] In fact, the 2008 super ministry reform (*dabuzhi gaige*, 大部制改革) restored the industrial ministry, the Ministry of Industry and Information Technology, to facilitate industrial development by making the best use of highly advanced information technology.[51] But the creation of this ministry failed to challenge the NDRC's dominant regulatory authority over auto industrial policy and foreign JV projects. Moreover, with the 2008 global financial crisis, a range of industrial policies for rejuvenating selected sectors, including the auto industry, enhanced the strength of the NDRC.[52]

Second, the creation of the SASAC is another notable move to unify the previously fragmented authority of the auto producers. As an ownership agency, SASAC closely supervises the management of crucial state assets, firms' business decisions through the board of directors, and their personnel.[53] "State asset management" here refers to raising equity capital and competitiveness as well as risk management to prevent loss. Moreover, for effective supervision of central state firms, the policy experiment (*shidian*, 试点) of the SASAC Inspection Group (Guoziwei Xunshizu, 国资委巡视组) was launched in October 2009;[54] inspections are conducted twice a year, involve six central state firms, and generally take two months.[55] Between 2009 and 2014, the SASAC Inspection Group completed twelve inspections for the selected central SOEs, and the working staff increased from three to six people.[56] Under the leadership of the SASAC Party Committee (Guoziwei Dangwei, 国资委党委) and the Inspection Work Leading Small Group (Xunshizu Lingdao Xiaozu, 巡视组领导小组), the SASAC Inspection Group monitors the overall business management of the selected firms, particularly regarding the loss of assets or investment profits, rather than individual corruption issues involving senior managers, which are directly handled by the Central Discipline and Inspection Commission in coordination with the central inspection groups (Zhongyang Xunshizu, 中央巡视组).[57] Some argue that the rise of the SASAC Inspection Group reflects the failed function of the Supervisory Commission (Jianshihui, 监事会) inside SOEs.[58]

Nevertheless, in the auto industry, the SASAC's regulatory oversight remains partial due to the predominance of local state firms in China's auto sector. Indeed, as elaborated in the following, strong local state ownership has circumscribed the direct and formal oversight from the central SASAC, which lacks formal rights to supervise the business of local state firms. With the exception of two central auto firms (FAW and the Dongfeng Group) and three private companies (Geely, Great Wall, and BYD), Chinese auto producers are all local state firms supervised by the local-level SASAC. As a result, the NDRC holds more comprehensive regulatory authority for the auto market than before, but strong local state ownership in the sector limits the scope of SASAC's formal regulation of the local auto producers that dominate the market.

On the other hand, the 1998 administration reform helped to integrate and rationalize regulatory functions at the municipal level into two comprehensive commissions: local offices of the NDRC and the SASAC. In theory, the central NDRC and the SASAC retain no formal leadership over the local-level NDRC and SASAC offices (*yewu guanxi*, professional relationship), because they are organized and directed by provincial and municipal leaders (*lingdao guanxi*, leadership relationship).[59] Local NDRC and SASAC officials, therefore, report directly to their provincial or municipal mayor. For the auto markets, although major projects still require central government approval, support from local authorities is crucial to the success of local auto firms. Moreover, the main concern of the local-level NDRC is to ensure that their business plans favor the development of the local economy. In this regard, local governments do not always strictly implement policies and rules from the center; instead, they may make decisions for their own benefit rather than following national regulations for the sector, except for necessary items that require central government approval. Hence, the problem of compliance sets in when vertical fragmentation looms large. Just like the central SASAC, the local-level SASACs supervise the business management of local state-owned auto producers; after being nominated by the Organization Department of the CCP, top executives and senior managers of local auto SOEs are appointed by the local-level SASACs, which is a significant source of political control.[60]

Indeed, China's central–local dynamics in the auto industry have been studied primarily by focusing on the roles of the local state, which proposed the Shanghai local developmental state or Beijing and Guangzhou laissez-faire local states.[61] However, besides local state ownership, the strong localism that contributes to making central regulation loose is also promoted by the surrounding governing structure featured by administrative nonuniformity across localities for the auto industry. This governing structure certainly contrasts with the case of the telecom sector, as discussed in chapter 4. In general, municipal mayors exert substantial power over the planning, finance, and personnel decisions of local state-owned auto firms, and at least one vice mayor is typically given the task of developing the local auto industry.[62]

But the power of the municipal commissions concerned with planning and economic development varies from city to city. For example, the Auto Industry Leading Small Group (LSG) in Shanghai is under the direct control of the mayor, not the municipal commission, and plays a dominant role in Beijing and Guangzhou.[63] But this is not the case in other major auto cities in China; the auto office in Guangzhou (Guangzhou Auto Industry Office, Guangzhou Qiche Gongye Bangongshi, 广州汽车工业办公室) is subordinate to the Ministry of Machinery and Electronics of the Guangzhou municipal government, and the auto office in Beijing (Beijing Auto Industry Corporation General Office, Beijing Qiche Gongye Gongsi Bangongshi, 北京汽车工业办公室) was affiliated with the Beijing Automotive Industry Corporation (BAIC). Likewise, although the presence and significance of such LSGs differ across localities, the role played by the Auto Industry LSG in Shanghai evinces how deeply party organizations are still involved in managing and supervising the auto industry in coordination with the planning commissions.[64]

## *Property Rights: Dominance of Local State Ownership*

In China, although the concepts of control and governing structure have some reinforcing effects on shaping certain patterns of regulation, the level of ownership is what makes the central regulatory control indirect and informal for the auto market, no matter what kinds of property rights (state or private) predominate. Hence, soft regulation sets in. China's auto sector is dominated by local state ownership, except for the two central state-owned firms (FAW and Dongfeng) and three private companies (Geely, Great Wall, and BYD), making central regulation for the auto market as a whole significantly loose, as the following comparison of central, local, and private auto firms will illustrate. Above all, since local governments—as "owners" of local auto producers—have the legitimacy to share rule-making power with the central government, such shared authority allows local governments to enjoy great leeway in policy implementation. Indeed, rampant local protectionism and price wars among auto producers evidence these realities.[65]

Consequently, even though the central authorities prepare and eventually endorse certain rules and policies for the sector, their implementation and compliance are at the discretion of local (provincial and municipal) governments.[66] This is largely because local authorities may bypass certain policies or rules that run counter to their incentives, unless there are conditions for which central government approval is required. Such leeway in policy implementation is made feasible by strong local state ownership. Rampant local protectionism in China's auto markets during the late 1980s offers a good example. Under the tax regulation that "most net income of enterprises belonged to the government unit that *owned* the enterprise,"[67] the rent-seeking local authorities had huge incentives to protect their own auto producers, leading to high local barriers and regionally fragmented markets. This was certainly against the central leadership's desire to consolidate the market with a small number of national champions. With the reform of the extrabudgetary system that changed net corporate income to enterprise profits, subjecting these enterprises to regular taxation, the issue of local protectionism finally became attenuated.[68]

The creation of the Wuhu-based auto firm Chery offers another example of local authorities' power in the auto industry. By pressuring on the local public security bureau responsible for issuing licenses for local vehicles, the Anhui provincial government established Chery as its local auto firm. In 1999, by illegally using a secondhand assembly line, Chery was able to begin producing passenger cars without approval from the central government. According to one report, the Anhui government "side-stepped Beijing's ban by issuing regulations allowing Chery's cars to be registered as taxicabs."[69] Relatedly, even though major projects, such as those with foreign partners or large-scale investments, still require central government approval from the NDRC,[70] local government support is crucial for the success of Beijing's desires. For example, the idea of merging the SAIC with Nanjing Auto Corporation in late 2007 was actually initiated by the central government.[71] In early 2007, embracing an SAIC–Nanjing Auto merger as a key task, the NDRC visited Shanghai and Nanjing several times to informally coordinate the deal to come.[72] The central leadership wanted the merger to enhance market consolidation and push for the development of an indigenous auto brand. Without cooperation and interest from local leadership,[73] however, this project could not proceed as smoothly as Beijing had planned.[74] The Shanghai and Nanjing municipalities finally agreed to a deal, not because of pressure from the central government but because of the potential benefits that local authorities would derive from the merger. Nanjing Auto Corporation would be relieved of its financial burdens and enhance its manufacturing capacity in terms of technology, business management, and service by learning from the SAIC, whereas the SAIC could make up its commercial vehicle production by taking over Nanjing Auto's successful truck business.[75]

The lack of formal regulatory authority hardly prevents the central party-state from monitoring the business management of major local auto firms. In other words, the sector's strategic significance invites an informal mechanism of regulation directly from the central party-state. In theory, the business of state firms is supposed to be supervised by an ownership agency, such as the SASAC; central state firms are under the supervision of the central SASAC, while local state firms are under the oversight of the municipal SASAC. There is no formally organized channel from the central SASAC to directly oversee the business of local state firms. However, as the case of the SAIC will show, the central party-state deploys an informally organized mechanism of supervision, the so-called central inspection groups, when the sector is strategically important to the national economy and development.[76] Such informal oversight takes place because the central party-state has no formal right to supervise the asset management and direct the business of major local state-owned auto producers. The functions and organization of central inspection groups over major local state-owned auto producers and the mechanism of state regulation over the private auto producer are elaborated further in the case studies of the SAIC and Geely Corporation, respectively.

## Variation Within

Three auto companies, located in different political and economic institutional contexts, are examined here to compare the mechanism and

patterns of regulation. These include the two largest auto SOEs—FAW
SAIC—and one private auto producer, Geely Holding Group. As shown
by the case studies that follow, the central government holds powerful
levers of regulation, regardless of the dominant mode of property rights
or the underlying governing structure. Most notable among these levers
is the NDRC's authority to approve large investment projects, including
overseas JV partnerships, and the party's political supervision over the
appointment of top executives and business management of major auto
producers. What is equally noteworthy is how the type of property right
impacts the form of central regulation even within the auto business.

## CENTRAL FAW GROUP CORPORATIONS: APPROACHING HARD REGULATION

China's leading auto producer, FAW,[77] located in Changchun, Jilin Province, exemplifies centralized regulatory power with strong similarities to
the system of regulation found in infrastructure industries.[78] With more
than 120,000 employees around the world, FAW was established as China's first auto enterprise in 1953.[79] Originally a producer of heavy trucks,
FAW gradually expanded its business line to include light trucks and passenger cars. Its move into the production of passenger cars led to three
major JVs by 2015.[80] At the time I examined the sector, the FAW conglom-
erate (table 3.1) comprised at least twenty-eight wholly owned and eighteen
partially owned subsidiaries, including foreign JVs and companies listed
on stock exchanges.[81] The introduction of a corporate shareholding system
(*gufenzhi*, 股份制) and the creation of boards of directors as advised by
corporation law were expected to have the effect of limiting state interference in business matters. However, shareholding companies do not fully
counteract the Chinese party-state's efforts to maintain control over
crucial state assets; the case of FAW and its JV with Volkswagen illustrates such constraints and highlights the important roles played by China's
resilient Leninist institutions: the NDRC, the SASAC, and the CCP.

FAW is a central SOE, meaning that all of its assets belong to the
central government. In theory, central state ownership makes the central
government responsible for a number of key functions, such as guidance
planning, providing funds, collecting tax revenues, and managing assets
and personnel. As the auto industry's main watchdog, the NDRC designs

Table 3.1
Performance of the FAW Group Corporation

| Year | Gross Industrial Output Value (Current Price) (million RMB) | Investment Amount (million RMB) | Total Assets (million RMB) | Operating Revenue (million RMB) | Pretax Profit (million RMB) | Value Added (million RMB) |
|------|------|------|------|------|------|------|
| 2006 | 17,856,538 | 529,021 | 11,320,331 | 14,916,914 | 1,660,497 | 4,285,569 |
| 2009 | 30,059,347 | 794,475 | 13,149,063 | 20,655,087 | 3,466,070 | 6,605,618 |
| 2012 | 45,317,537 | 2,762,949 | 24,355,661 | 40,770,148 | 6,922,476 | 9,125,839 |
| 2016 | 46,995,036 | n/a | 1,320,401 | 42,685,266 | 4,103,612 | n/a |

Sources: China Auto Industry Yearbook 2007, 8; 2010, 94; 2013, 131; 2017, 119.

national policies for the auto sector[82] and provides macro-guidance for future development in the form of policies for research and development (R&D) and environmental protection, as well as land and supply fees. For example, when FAW, including its subsidiary firms, needs to build new factories or an R&D institute, the NDRC often arranges the distribution of financial resources to help it purchase land.[83] Rather than directly commanding control, the NDRC indicates the direction of business by controlling the allocation of the most important resources, such as finances and land. On the other hand, with the 1998 administrative reform, as industrial ministries were scaled back and the former MMI was downgraded to the level of a bureau, the rights to appoint senior managers of central state firms were eventually transferred to the newly established ownership agency, SASAC.[84]

As elaborated earlier, under the dual leadership of the SASAC Party Committee and the Inspection Work LSG, the SASAC Inspection Group checks any loss of crucial state assets or investment profits for certain selected firms. As of 2015, the FAW had not been listed in the SASAC Inspection Group, but its top executives and senior managers were examined by the central inspection group in 2014.[85] As a result, the former deputy general manager of FAW, An Dewu, was arrested on charges of bribery, and eight other senior managers and the party secretary of FAW and its subsidiaries were warned or had their party membership revoked.[86] Unfortunately, this outcome proved a persistent rumor of long-standing corruption in FAW.[87]

Close examination of FAW also reveals the deeply institutionalized system of personnel management by party organizations, beyond the nominal owner, SASAC. For example, candidates for top offices in FAW are nominated by the party committee inside FAW, and then the Organization Department (OD) of the CCP double-checks their professional backgrounds for any problematic issues. This evaluation process is applied not only to party cadres and government officials but also to senior managers of SOEs.[88] After this precensorship, the OD makes an official recommendation to the CCP Central Committee and the Ministry of Personnel and announces the final endorsement of the State Council. As the appointment of the incumbent FAW president (*zongjingli*, 总经理), Xu Xianping, shows, it was not the SASAC but the OD that held the ultimate power of his appointment.[89] This exhibits how deeply the CCP is involved in personnel procedures and exerts political control over FAW.

In this regard, while the SASAC retains formal authority to appoint top executives and members of the board in FAW, its decision remains largely a rubber stamp. The party's persistent political control over FAW's business management is further illustrated by an examination of the roles of key party members on FAW's board and management team. Bruce Dickson's observation about SOEs in Shanghai seems pertinent for FAW: "To make sure that the party continued to play an active and influential role in SOEs, most SOEs in Shanghai adopted 'internal regulations' requiring that half of the members of the party committee must also be members of the board of directors and that at least one-third of the members of the party committee must be managers with enterprise."[90] A similar situation appears in FAW's JV with Volkswagen. The board of directors (Dongshihui, 董事会) of FAW-VW consists of sixteen members, of whom seven are German and nine Chinese. The JV's chair of the board (*dongshizhang*, 董事长) is FAW president Xu Xianping. Among the nine Chinese board members, four belong to the party committee in Changchun city or Jilin Province.[91] In other words, as long as the majority of Chinese board members are simultaneously members of the party committee, the modern management system of FAW is accountable to the CCP, not the board of directors as corporate governance advises. Figure 3.3 illustrates the regulatory relationship between central authorities and FAW.

Although FAW is central state-owned, it is located primarily, and with a long history, in Changchun. Still, FAW is not just the main system (*zhuti*, 主体) but the driving force (*longtou*, 龙头) to develop the auto industry in the city.[92] The fact that the Changchun municipal government does not own FAW, however, leaves it powerless to appoint firm managers who would pay more attention to how the manufacturer could contribute to the development of the local economy. Its central ownership has also constrained Changchun municipality's influence over FAW's JV partners.[93] Accordingly, Changchun municipal government's role has been confined to creating a "favorable business environment" for FAW in the local economy. By establishing a special office and panel for industry research, as well as allocating RMB50 million annually to a development fund, the Changchun municipal government has tried to

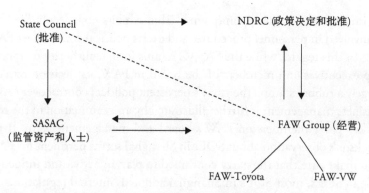

FIGURE 3.3: The Centralized Regulatory Structure of FAW. *Sources:* Based on interviews at FAW headquarters and FAW-VW in Changchun. Interviews no. A(C) 24, October 19, 2005; no. A(C) 25, October 20, 2005; no. A(C) 26, March 21, 2006. The dotted line indicates an informal but powerful channel between FAW and the State Council. Interview no. A(B) 11, January 6, 2006.

create a sound environment for auto industry in the city. Nevertheless, the central government often swamps its efforts.[94] As elaborated in the following discussion of Shanghai's SAIC, the regulatory power of local authorities (including municipal-level commissions) are quite different from FAW—more robust—when there is local ownership. Yet even then, the central government continues to play a crucial role.

## LOCAL SAIC: SOFT REGULATION INSIDE

Shanghai is often viewed as the prime location for the auto business, because of its long-standing competitive edge in machinery, production technology, and auto parts.[95] Moreover, the city's status as a hub of investment and exports has attracted various multinational automakers to set up at least one office there. With the creation of its JVs—with Volkswagen (SAIC-VW) in 1985 and General Motors (SAIC-GM) in 2002—the SAIC has come to establish a comparatively complete production system for passenger cars. As a result, the auto industry has become the engine of Shanghai's economic development.[96] The case of the SAIC, China's largest auto manufacturer (see table 3.2),[97] is particularly notable in that it presents how the central party-state exerts more regulatory control than has often been assumed. The SAIC rightly illustrates the

Table 3.2
Performance of the Shanghai Auto Industry Corporation

| Year | Gross Industrial Output Value (Current Price) (million RMB) | Investment Amount (million RMB) | Total Assets (million RMB) | Operating Revenue (million RMB) | Pretax Profit (million RMB) | Value Added (million RMB) |
|---|---|---|---|---|---|---|
| 2006 | 14,668,751 | n/a | 133,844,725 | 17,503,082 | 2,562,319 | 3,384,048 |
| 2009 | 28,305,136 | 1,432,317 | 25,617,584 | 34,222,980 | 6,219,425 | 6,429,927 |
| 2012 | 48,503,007 | 2,685,288 | 45,016,046 | 62,575,533 | 7,942,997 | 11,703,365 |
| 2016 | 75,520,140 | n/a | 72,443,193 | 93,981,022 | n/a | 18,261,760 |

Sources: China Auto Industry Yearbook 2007, 87; 2010, 101; 2013, 138; 2017, 126.

different pattern of central regulation that appears in locally owned strategic state firms.

MECHANISMS FOR MUNICIPAL-LEVEL REGULATION OF THE SAIC The SAIC is formally owned and supervised by Shanghai's municipal government, which provides it with all-out support. In China, the auto industry serves as an important source of employment and revenue. For example, auto enterprises should pay corporate income taxes equal to 33 percent of their total profits. Of this amount, 60 percent should be remitted to the Ministry of Finance and 40 percent to the municipal government.[98] In practice, the central and local governments each collect 50 percent of tax returns, providing the local government with a strong incentive to invigorate the sector.[99] The Shanghai municipal government consequently has been willing to offer various benefits, such as land or supply fees.[100] Moreover, the Shanghai municipal government agreed to provide the city's auto firms RMB38 billion or more in investment funds by 2010 and to establish a new Center for Strategic Development of the Auto Industry in the Shanghai Academy of Social Science, coordinating with the SAIC.[101]

In contrast to the Changchun municipal government's role in the FAW, the Shanghai municipal government has substantial means for influencing the business of SAIC and its foreign investors. For example, the Shanghai Municipal Development and Reform Commission (SM-DRC), which is subordinate to the Shanghai mayor, is in charge of setting the SAIC's macro-industrial development plan, although such plans must be consistent with national industrial policies. In this way, the SM-DRC, which has the authority to allocate financial and material resources in the city's auto market, is able to exert more direct regulatory control over the business of the SAIC than the central NDRC does.[102] Specifically, in contrast to FAW, the funds for building infrastructure, factories, and R&D facilities are all arranged by the SM-DRC. In return, the commission retains the right to review and approve SAIC's investment projects, except new foreign JVs and investments with projected costs exceeding RMB1.5 billion, which require the State Council's approval. Accordingly, decisions on finance, investment, and technology are first coordinated with the SM-DRC, not the NDRC, as is the case for FAW.

As another local arm of regulation, the Shanghai Municipal SASAC (SM-SASAC) takes formal responsibility for monitoring the SAIC's assets and personnel management. As established in 2004, the SAIC Motor Corporation, subordinated by the SAIC, is responsible mainly for the asset management of the whole SAIC. Therefore, subordinate firms, such as SAIC-VW and SAIC-GM, have to report their balance sheet regularly—including fixed, tangible, and total assets—to the SAIC Motor Corp. After collecting all the information, the SAIC Motor Corporation directly informs the Shanghai Municipal SASAC (SM-SASAC) of the group's financial performance.[103] If necessary—for example, if the SAIC suffered major losses[104]—the SM-SASAC would be expected to communicate with the central SASAC. In theory, though, there is no formal route for the SAIC Motor Corp. to interact directly with the central SASAC; any communication must be conducted through the SM-SASAC.

In addition, in contrast to the obvious direct appointment of FAW's top executive managers by the central government, these same positions in the SAIC are formally appointed by the SM-SASAC. The rationale for this arrangement is again the Shanghai municipality's ownership of the SAIC. Not surprisingly, with respect to the personnel of top executives and senior managers, the party organizations in the SAIC and Shanghai's municipal government are deeply involved. Although the SM-SASAC ultimately endorses the formal nomination, a party committee in the SAIC first recommends nominees, who are then carefully screened by the OD in Shanghai. During the second round, the Shanghai-based party committee reviews successful candidates before referring them to the SM-SASAC (party committee of SAIC → organization department of Shanghai municipal government → party committee of Shanghai municipal government → final endorsement by SM-SASAC). Hence, the SAIC's leadership is ultimately decided by the CCP, not the board of directors.

MECHANISMS FOR CENTRAL REGULATION OF THE SAIC Despite much stronger mechanisms of municipal regulation over the SAIC compared with FAW, the SAIC is not free from the reins of central regulation. While the central leadership has delegated much authority to the Shanghai municipal government to enjoy leeway in managing the local auto industry as a competitive strategy, it maintains indirect influence over business direction and management.[105] First, in terms of business direction, the central government has major levers for large new investments and foreign JV partners, which requires final approval from the center. For example, GM and Hyundai, as partners of Chinese firms, were approved by the central leaders, not by the Shanghai and Beijing municipal governments, for JVs with local firms.[106] Partly because of the highly globalized nature of the sector, foreign capital and technology are indispensable for Chinese auto producers; the lack of local autonomy in choosing their foreign partners is a crucial constraint on local state capacity. Moreover, the central party-state has seemingly applied political criteria to the choice of JV partners, discouraging any great concentration by one or two major foreign automakers or by any nationality of foreign automaker. This policy of what might be called "industrial security" strives to avoid dependence on any single foreign multinational auto company while it leverages foreign firms to help Chinese firms compete.

There is also the issue of local accountability to the center's plans for the strategic auto industry. Local officials and senior executives of local SOEs, such as the SAIC, are expected to act according to central government wishes, because their future promotions will be evaluated around these developmental measures. Some analysts argue that if local interests conflict with national interests, local government and enterprises will bypass central rules related to the development of the local economy.[107] However, this can easily be countermanded, given that the central party-state has the right to appoint mayors who then appoint the top management of SOEs. One senior SAIC engineer pointed to the reality that the SAIC's president lacks professional commitment to develop the firm's technology and innovation. Instead, the executive is more interested in rapid short-term growth to impress central leadership, because such myopic growth raises his chances of promotion. Given that developing an automaker's technology and commercializing it requires at least eight years, the senior SAIC engineer I interviewed argued that the SAIC's top leaders prefer JVs with overseas investors that can provide advanced technology and capital investment to accomplish such short-term business goals.[108] This implies that even though the central government lacks the formal right to intervene in the personnel process of local SOEs (e.g., SAIC), the central party-state's control of personnel remains quite influential.

Second, in terms of business management, the power of local state firms and local governments is constrained by an institutional structure designed by the central party-state. No matter how hard local governments try to enhance their fiscal and corporate governance, they remain local "agents" appointed by the center to effectively implement the central government's wishes.[109] According to one senior manager working in SAIC-VW, "although we are a local JV-SOE owned by the Shanghai municipal government, not the SM-DRC but the central NDRC exerts a critical influence over our long- and mid-term business plan and management. In other words, to be a winner in both domestic and global markets, the industrial, enterprise, and regulatory policies from the center are the most important sources for major local state-owned auto firms in China to refer to, even though their implementation is fragmented."[110] For example, the SAIC's heavy truck business exemplifies a case when the central and municipal governments pursued conflicting objectives. While the Shanghai municipal government had long wanted to build a heavy-duty truck manufacturing base, the SAIC did not pursue this product line because the cost of truck manufacturing in Shanghai seemed too steep. SAIC's behavior was probably due to the fact that this position primarily complied with the aims of the central policy makers, who hoped the SAIC would become a national champion in manufacturing passenger cars, not trucks.[111]

More important, while there are no formally binding relations between the central and local SASAC, the central party-state monitors major local SOEs, including auto, through informal channels. The least known but perhaps most significant informal channel for central oversight over the SAIC is a central supervisory group called the Zhongyang Xunshizu (Central Inspection Group, 中央巡视组).[112] The CCP Central Committee initially proposed the idea of an inspection group in 1996 to combat growing corruption among powerful local cadres (*lingdao ganbu*, 领导干部).[113] In 2003, after a period of experimentation, the *zhongyang xunshizu* was formally announced by the State Council, which aimed to tighten internal party supervision (*dangnei jiandu*, 党内监督), especially of high-ranking cadres whose authority has become considerably concentrated.[114] According to official ordinance, the *zhongyang xunshizu* is responsible for supervising the leading cadres in thirty-one provinces,[115] but the subjects of supervision have been expanded to include the senior managers of local auto SOEs.[116] This informal inspection group oversees business management of the SAIC and other major targeted SOEs because

of these firms' considerable influence on national financial resources and
the number of Chinese auto parts companies.[117] This function is neither
documented in the original official ordinance nor visible in its supervision over the SAIC.[118] According to the interviewees, this *zhongyang xunshizu* consists of six to twelve retired party cadres; its members visit
important, locally owned SOEs and central ones. Their main task is to
oversee balance sheets, asset management, and board meetings. Even
though it is not a formally recognized regulatory institution for auto producers, this centrally organized group monitors whether major local
SOEs misuse any profits; it also reminds them of the central party-state's
desires. Accordingly, these *zhongyang xunshizu* function as nonauthorized
central inspection groups who use their authority for regulation, serving as
an informal "third party" between the state and auto businesses (fig. 3.4).

## PRIVATE GEELY: HAND-IN-GLOVE RELATIONSHIP

In 2017, the private auto producer Geely (table 3.3) ranked as China's top-
selling domestic brand, selling 1.25 million vehicles, an increase of
65 percent over 2016 levels.[119] Geely has grown remarkably since 1997 due
largely to its flexible and independent management compared with that
of state-owned auto producers. Geely is often referred to as one of the
"most innovative enterprises in China" or a "complete vehicle export base
in China."[120] Its total assets as of 2017 reached HKD63,576,[121] and its success has earned it a place in China's top five hundred companies for nine
consecutive years and in the top ten auto manufacturers for eight consecutive years.[122] Given such successful development, a few questions arise.
How does the Chinese central leadership govern private firms in important
industries? Is there any regulatory control from the government? If so, what
means of control are used by the central and local governments? Are the
forms of state regulation different from those in state-owned auto firms?

Considering that Geely's chairman, Li Shufu, is a member of the
ninth Chinese People's Consultative Conference, China's top advisory
body,[123] how do his political ties to the CCP affect how the state regulates the business of a private auto firm like Geely? This case illustrates
that the NDRC, regardless of type of ownership, plays a decisive role in
guiding business strategies and directions for development.[124] Moreover,
while private ownership itself certainly forecloses formal state intervention

FIGURE 3.4: Regulatory Structure of the SAIC: Fragmented Administrative Regulation and Informal Supervision from the Center. SAIC Motor Corporation Ltd. was created by the SAIC Group in December 2004, holding all the assets and business of the SAIC Group. SAIC Motor Corporation Ltd. is expected to "play a strategic role in helping the SAIC achieve its global ambitions." Dotted lines between the central and local NDRC/SASAC indicate nonbinding "advising" authority, whereas dotted lines from the central government to local auto firms show "indirect" central control.
*Sources:* Interviews no. A(SH) 36, March 7, 2006; no. A(SH) 38, March 9, 2006.

Table 3.3
Performance of Geely

| Year | Gross Industrial Output Value (Current Price) (million RMB) | Total Assets (million RMB) | Operating Revenue (million RMB) | Value Added (million RMB) | Sales (million RMB) |
|---|---|---|---|---|---|
| 2005 | 732,003 | 904,497 | 660,000 | 174,152 | 13.30 |
| 2010 | 2,119,270 | 3,409,418 | 2,131,690 | 423,080 | 41.58 |
| 2016 | 20,879,870 | 20,674,077 | 20,879,870 | 5,219,968 | 76.60 |

*Sources: China Auto Industry Yearbook* 2006, 155; 2011, 125; 2017, 148.

from the government, increasing financial support from the NDRC and local authorities—such as the Daqing SASAC or the Shanghai municipal government—has legitimized the state's regulatory control over Geely's business management. In short, the forms of state regulation for Geely are similar to those for local state-owned auto firms—indirect but strong oversight from Beijing.

MECHANISM FOR MUNICIPAL-LEVEL REGULATION OF GEELY In dealing with Geely, local governments employ similar means of control as do state firms—land and investment funds. Because those are the most critical concerns for an auto manufacturing startup in China, support from the local government is the first step, regardless of type of ownership. Indeed, according to the 1994 auto industrial policy, Geely was not even allowed to get into this sector because it was overcrowded with too many companies. However, the multiplier effects of having auto firms, in terms of employment and revenue, offer strong incentives for local authorities to bypass central regulations limiting market entry.[125] This is why, despite the central government's continuous efforts to consolidate the market with a few large auto companies, China still suffers from a glut of more than 100 producers, reaching almost 115 firms in 2012. Geely jumped into the market in 1998 under the support of the Hangzhou municipal government.[126] The Hangzhou Municipal Development and Reform Commission's approval of land served as a significant means of control, affecting Geely's business plans and strategies, in that land is a crucial element for auto producers, enabling them to set up manufacturing factories and launch R&D centers. In China, because land is still in the hands of the government, auto producers cannot obtain land for manufacturing cars without the government's permission and cooperation. Fortunately, Ye Rongbao, vice governor of Zhejiang Province in the mid-1990s, was keen to institute auto manufacturing factories like other local governments had done. Well aware of such local benefits, Li Shufu persuaded the vice governor of Zhejiang, ultimately getting the green light for Geely.[127]

Moreover, such regulatory control over land affects Geely's business direction and plans. For example, when Geely expanded its production base into Taizhou city, the endorsement of the local party secretary was decisive. In this sense, regardless of the auto firm's ownership type, as long as the land is state-owned, its approval right can be used as a lever of state regulation, as this case study exhibits. Moreover, when private companies do business with large public investment concerns, the relevant authorities (local or central) become entitled to oversee their overall business management; if progress is unsatisfactory, the authorities can withdraw investment funds. The investment agreement between Daqing city and Geely in 2013 serves as a good example of this. As detailed later, Geely's acquisition of Volvo required massive investment funds and manufacturing factories for production.[128] Daqing city (specifically the Daqing SASAC), with its own economic interests and strategies, became the second-largest investor, with a 37 percent share of Geely-Volvo.[129] As a major stakeholder, Daqing SASAC, in return, holds the regulatory authority for the business of Geely-Volvo to oversee the firm's production.[130] In other words, Geely's takeover of Volvo provided local governments (Daqing and Shanghai), as major stakeholders of Geely, with legitimate authority to supervise its business management. But this increasing state investment in a private company certainly tends to make the private ownership of Geely somewhat murky.

GEELY'S MECHANISM OF CENTRAL REGULATION Clearly, Geely's successful business to date has much to do with the attention of and support from the central government. The Hu-Wen administration's emphasis on developing indigenous brands (*zizhu pinpai*, 自主品牌) and innovation, in particular, has altered the dynamic for Geely, generating a much more favorable environment for attracting investment funds and acquiring land approval than before.[131] According to the 2009 Plan for Auto Industry Restructuring and Rejuvenation, the Chinese central leadership desired to enhance global competitiveness by restructuring the sector and improving the Chinese brand. At the time, the Party General Secretary, Hu Jintao, and other high-profile cadres encouraged private companies to actively practice a policy of "going out" (*zouchuqu*, 走出去) to acquire advanced technologies and standards, considering Geely the right candidate to do so.[132] For these reasons, the central government directly or indirectly supports Geely in having better access to bank loans and investments from state banks (e.g., Guanghua Bank). This was particularly important after Geely took over Volvo in 2010 when striving to make technological advancements and develop a joint manufacturing system.

Table 3.4
State Subsidies for Geely

|  | 2008 | 2009 | 2010 | 2011 |
|---|---|---|---|---|
| State subsidy (政府补贴) (亿元) | 2.2 | 4.8 | 16.8 | 8 |
| Net profits (亿元) | 4.3 | 12.5 | 13.7 | 15 |
| Share of subsidies for net profits (%) | 51.16 | 38.40 | 122.80 | 53.33 |

*Sources*: Shan, "Fengyong er shanag zizhu"; "Jili konggu qunian zengliyun 138 yiyuan zijin" (Geely had a net profit of 13.8 billion last year, why are funds still so tight?), http://www.022net.com/2011 /7-11/42436321287886-2.html (accessed February 18, 2015).

In fact, regardless of the type of property rights, the acquisition of overseas firms requires not only permission but also massive financial assistance from central leadership, particularly when the Chinese partner is a private company. According to Li Shufu, since acquisition and future operations would cost US$2.7 billion,[133] "several investment institutions participated in the deal making, and a loan syndicate led by the Bank of China financed the purchase."[134] Other reports added that the deal amounted to US$1.8 billion, and "three major Chinese banks, including the Bank of China, China Construction Bank and the Export-Import Bank of China, had agreed to extend loans to Zhejiang Geely Holding Group."[135] One manager working in a Bank of China branch in Zhejiang Province reported that "the bank's Zhejiang and London branches would arrange the loan syndicate to offer Geely nearly USD 1 billion over five years."[136] Relatedly, state subsidies for developing electric vehicles with domestic brands are another source of direct financial support for Geely. As table 3.4 shows, state subsidies for Geely have been increasing since 2008 and peaked when the decision to acquire Volvo was made in 2010.

Some strings are attached to the funds from the center. Above all, such financial support allows central government the legitimate right to supervise the progress and business management of relevant projects.[137] In fact, private ownership prevents the central government from directly exercising any formal regulatory control over Geely, such as its asset management or personnel issues. In terms of business management, there are few channels for the party-state to exert political influence over personnel or asset management.[138] Unlike state-owned auto producers, Geely's assets are managed by the Hong Kong stock market. Inside the firm, there is no party committee as in state firms; instead, the so-called Business

Management Commission (Jingying Guanli Weiyuanhui, 经营委员会) plays a major role in deciding important business projects.[139] As a key managerial body, this commission, consisting of twelve to fifteen members, takes the responsibility for carefully reviewing the firm's business performance and ongoing projects.

Second, the invitation for central oversight resulted from Beijing's strong support for overseas takeovers. Although the Ministry of Commerce is in charge of issuing permits for all major overseas mergers and acquisitions, the final endorsement comes from the NDRC.[140] Geely's remarkable acquisition of Volvo indicates how the central leadership's implicit support played a decisive role in winning the deal. In fact, in its early period of business, Geely had focused on producing and selling low-cost cars in China, targeting ordinary people (*laobaixing*, 老百姓). However, sales of cheap passenger cars in the domestic market quickly plummeted; in the first quarter of 2007, sales were 67,000 units, far below the company's target.[141] To survive in a fiercely competitive market, Geely shifted its business strategy to luxury cars that would be more attractive to Chinese consumers, finally leading the company to bid for its acquisition of Volvo. Overtaking Volvo's entire stock share, Geely aimed to transform Volvo into a wholly owned subsidiary of the Geely Group, so that Volvo's advanced technology and global brand would positively affect Geely's production and sales.[142]

Indeed, competition for the Volvo takeover among local Chinese firms was fierce. According to various sources, more than five auto companies showed interest in the deal, and BAIC competed with Geely until the end. The acquisition of Volvo was indeed very attractive for auto producers and local governments. For auto firms, it offered great access to the advanced technologies and manufacturing systems as well as brand power; for local governments, it promised to boost local employment and revenue, as well as enhancing related markets, such as tires and steel. In effect, after taking over Volvo, the quality of the vehicles and Geely's market power has remarkably improved. Some analysts point to the considerable advantages acquired from Western know-how, such as Geely's "access to the Swedish company's designs and standards as well as the opportunity to develop joint manufacturing systems."[143] Also, such support for Geely was in line with China's new emphasis on nurturing independent innovation and developing domestic brands; as China's indigenous private brand, Geely emerged as a strong candidate for that position. In particular, Geely's development background without a foreign JV partner was impressive enough to attract the central leadership's attention. Beijing's endorsement of Geely to take over Volvo quickly boosted production volume to 200,000 to 300,000 units a year.[144] Perhaps a more interesting question in the near future is how this central endorsement has come to bind the business of the private auto producers.

## *Conclusion*

Despite the highly decentralized ownership and governing structure, the history of China's auto industry development exhibits how its style of market regulation has shifted amid the consistent resilient central regulatory control. Such keen attention from the center can be easily identified by its auto-specific industrial policies (1994, 2004, and 2009) and the FYPs, indicating what concepts and instruments of government control have ruled over the sector. Yet the pattern of central regulation over the auto business is looser than in other strategic industries, such as infrastructure or finance, as the relationship between central regulators (NDRC and SASAC) and their local offices is professional (*yewu guanxi*) without binding authority; the central party-state's implicit use of informal and indirect channels can prevail. The concept of *soft* regulation is proposed to emphasize the characteristics of China's central regulatory control over industries that are strategically important but highly decentralized, such as the auto industry. I cite the dominant ideas on control and mode of ownership, as well as the underlying governing structure, as the factors that make central regulation soft. But this mainly resulted from strong local state ownership and vibrant private auto producers, which clearly limits the formal authority from central regulators. This is why, I argue, what distinguishes China's practices of regulation from those of other advanced economies is the level of ownership (central or provincial/municipal) more than the type of ownership (state or private). The approach of markets-as-institutions is useful in unveiling such diverse and complex rules of the Chinese political economy as China strives to establish the market economy with holding socialist institutions. Indeed, despite market-oriented institutional reforms over the past four decades, we find that the planning and ownership agencies under the leadership of the CCP remain crucial in governing the business of auto markets and firms there.

By comparing two major state firms (one central and one local) and a private auto producer, this chapter presents variations in the sector. The business management (i.e., assets or personnel) of local state-owned or private auto firms is closely supervised by informal and indirect mechanisms of central oversight, whereas the state-owned auto producer FAW is tightly and directly ruled by central authorities and the CCP, reflecting similar regulatory control over the telecom industry, as chapter 4 elaborates.

# CHAPTER 4

## *The Telecommunications Service Industry*

### Hard Regulation

To understand performance, we must explore in depth the way institutions "work," looking at both the consequences of formal incentives and the frequently unanticipated results.

—Douglas North, *Understanding the Process of Economic Change*

China's telecommunications service is another key strategic sector that has not only developed rapidly but also experienced substantial regulatory reform over the decades.[1] Partly because of the early focus on heavy industries, the telecoms industry finally attracted the central leadership's attention in the early 1980s as a candidate for overdue reform, which would equip it with a sound infrastructure for successful industrialization. Indeed, telecommunications service profits increased by 17 percent during the sixth Five Year Plan (FYP; 1981–85), 29.3 percent during the seventh FYP (1986–90), and peaked at 44.4 percent during the eighth FYP (1991–95) (fig. 4.1). Since 1998, the telecoms industry has grown more than 20 percent,[2] and sales value increased from RMB156.2 billion in 1998 to RMB111.576 trillion in 2005.[3] Given the growing importance of the telecoms industry to the national economy, it is an appropriate medium for comparison with the auto manufacturing sector in a way that shows how the Chinese central party-state governs these commonly strategic but very different segments of the economy in terms of ownership and the underlying concepts of control and governing structure.

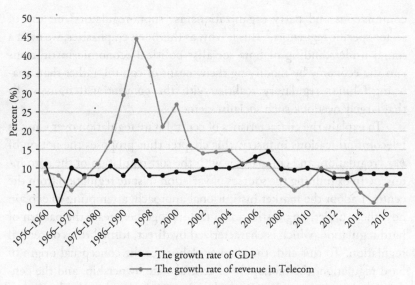

FIGURE 4.1: Growth of China's Telecommunications Industry Compared with GDP, 1956–2016. *Sources: Yearbook of China Communications* 2014 (Zhongguo tongxin nianjian 2014), 35; *Yearbook of China Communications* 2012 (Zhongguo tongxin nianjian 2012), 19; National Bureau of Statistics of China, *China Statistical Yearbook* 2014 (Zhongguo tongji nianjian 2014), 53; National Bureau of Statistics of China, *China Statistical Yearbook* 2015, http://www.stats.gov.cn/tjsj/ndsj/2015/indexeh.htm; National Bureau of Statistics of China, *China Statistical Yearbook* 2016, http://www .stats.gov.cn/tjsj/ndsj/2016/indexeh.htm; National Bureau of Statistics of China, *China Statistical Yearbook* 2017, http://www.stats.gov.cn/tjsj/ndsj/2017/indexeh.htm; National Bureau of Statistics of China, *China Statistical Yearbook* 2018, http://www.stats.gov.cn /tjsj/ndsj/2018/indexeh.htm.

In fact, as in other advanced industrial economies, institutional regulatory reforms have been driven in China's telecoms industry by separating the operator (China Telecom) from the former regulator (Ministry of Posts and Telecommunications, MPT) and establishing a new telecoms regulator, the Ministry of Information Industry (MII). But this chapter argues that the regulatory power of the MII is deeply contested by socialist political-economic institutions, such as the planning and ownership commissions (National Development and Reform Commission [NDRC] and State-Owned Assets Supervision and Administration Commission [SASAC]) as well as various Chinese Communist Party (CCP) organizations. In this respect, one study even names those commissions and party organizations as "supra-regulators" on top of sector-specific regulators.[4] This is why, as this book emphasizes, we need a sound understanding of how socialist political-economic institutions run the economy by modifying their means of control, rather than analyzing China's regulatory realities with the conventional frameworks that largely overlook such socialist elements.

To explain the characteristics of central state regulation over China's telecommunications industry, this chapter thus proposes the notion of *hard* regulation, and compares it with the soft regulation of the auto industry. In examining the sources of variation in state regulation from the center, I adopt the market institutional approach, attempting to explain how these underlying institutional factors together create the pattern of hard regulation, which is characterized by direct, formal rules of central regulation. To this end, the chapter elaborates the conceptual origin of hard regulation, the monopoly of central state ownership, and the centralized governing structure. Particular emphasis is placed on the dominance of central state ownership, which points to how the level of ownership, not state versus private ownership per se, functions as the main factor in drawing up and implementing the varieties of state regulation (hard and soft) for China's strategic industries.

First, various sectors' ties to military and security concerns and their importance to the national economy as the commanding heights are addressed as the conceptual origin of hard regulation. Second, the chapter also points to the bureaucratic origin of Chinese telecoms operators, and explains how it has led to the monopoly of central state ownership in the sector. Moreover, the monopoly of central state ownership in China's telecoms business has advanced the ownership agency of the central state-owned enterprise (SOE), the SASAC, elevating its regulatory authority over the business supervision of telecommunications giants. Compared with the form of central regulation applied in the auto industry, therefore, China's telecommunications business and markets are under the direct and tight supervision of central institutions. Last, as the governing structure of telecommunications regulation has been highly centralized—even before economic reform—local telecoms regulators have no tangible right to make rules and policy decisions. On the business side, the monopoly of central state ownership in the sector has turned local telecoms firms into the local "agents" of central operators.

It is interesting to see how China's regulatory reforms in the sector since the mid-1990s have paradoxically undermined the independent authority of the telecoms regulator (the MII and then the Ministry of Industry and Information Technology [MIIT]), as evidenced by the advancing planning and ownership agencies, such as the NDRC and the SASAC. In addition, as in the case of the auto sector, the chapter points to the continued political oversight of CCP organizations over telecoms business. As well as the recognized roles of the organizations, departments, or party committees inside state firms, particular attention is paid to the Informatization Leading Small Group (LSG) (Xinxihua Lingdao Xiaozu, 信息化领导小组) and the central inspection group, which have been less explored, despite their significant political power in formulating key ideas and monitoring telecom giants.

To develop such arguments, I first examine the state-run monopoly regime to highlight what has changed since the reform. Then I explain the origin and context of regulatory reform that have led the Chinese government to undertake a comprehensive restructuring of the telecoms markets. The chapter proceeds to discuss three sources for making central state regulation *hard* in China's telecoms service industry. It then details one major antimonopoly probe into telecoms giants to show how bureaucratic politics among the central authorities has led to tight state regulation over the telecoms market.

## Telecom Industry's Market Reform Process

### STATE-RUN CONTROL: THE MPT MONOPOLY REGIME

Under the planned economy, China's central government exercised strict control over the investments, production, and sales of telecommunications operators because the maximization of social benefits (not the profits of the operators) was the key goal of telecoms operators.[5] As the telecoms system was exclusively used for semi-military and administrative needs,[6] the state's strict control over service pricing and production capital prevailed, incurring backward technology and insufficient investment capital. With economic reform since the early 1980s, the need to develop infrastructure attracted increasing attention from the central leadership for the posts and telecoms sector, because leadership noted the sector's central and pivotal role in boosting economic modernization and growth.

Particularly, after the Eleventh Third Plenum of the Communist Party Congress in 1992, Deng Xiaoping's emphasis on the development of the basic infrastructure sectors, including telecommunications, shows that the telecoms industry became China's primary focus and one of the central strategic vehicles for economic development.[7] A range of preferential policies was offered to invigorate the sector.[8] For example, corporate tax benefits were given for overseas investments, although the participation of foreign companies as investors in the provision of Chinese telecoms and post services remained highly restricted for security reasons.[9] Above all, by offering various preferential policies, the MPT, which was the only telecoms operator and regulator then, took advantage of various financial resources in developing the sector.[10] Indeed, before the regulatory reform that established the MII by separating China Telecom from MPT in 1997, China's telecoms sector was run by the state monopoly system under the MPT. Because the MPT had dominated the national communications infrastructure by holding the authority of making financial and strategic development plans for the sector until it transformed into the MII in 1997, the power of the State Planning Commission (SPC) remained limited compared with the one in the auto industry. The monopolized system of the sector under the MPT had established low-quality, poor telecoms services that nevertheless levied expensive service charges. Hence, there was a desperate and urgent need to break the monopoly and introduce substantial competition, a need of which the central leadership was well aware.

Accordingly, in 1988, in an effort to inject competition, some related ministries, such as the Ministry of Electronics Industry, the Ministry of Electronic Power, and the Ministry of Railways, asked the State Council to organize a rival service provider.[11] Strong resistance from the MPT delayed the creation of another provider until Deng's southern tour in 1992, which publicized the importance of market competition. In 1993, the State Council finally approved the creation of China Unicom. Following this move, the Jitong Communication Corporation was established as another operator to provide internet services in 1994. Despite more operators in the market, the MPT's resistance and unfair policies favoring its vested interests enabled China Telecom to keep its monopoly. Nevertheless, as the establishment of China Unicom and Jitong reflected, the top leadership recognized the need to introduce more competition in the telecommunications market, which led to implementing successive structural reforms to encourage further market competition. In this regard, it is fair to say that the results of China's efforts to reform and boost the telecommunications markets eventually depended on how to break up MPT's monopoly and create competition by establishing other service providers, even though that competition was carefully orchestrated by the central authorities.

## REGULATORY REFORMS AND CHALLENGES

The transformation of the MPT into the MII and its accompanying market restructuring offered normative and institutional grounds for regulatory reforms in China's telecoms sector. In fact, such reform efforts were driven not only by internal demands and changes but also by external forces, such as the requirements of World Trade Organization (WTO) accession or the global wave of regulatory reform during the 1990s.[12] Internally, in 1998, the restructuring of the administration, which abolished or integrated several industrial ministries, paved the way for establishing a number of regulatory agencies in China's industrial economy.[13]

Externally, the most significant impetus was WTO accession, in that one of the entry requirements for membership was acceptance of the terms of the Basic Telecommunications Agreement,[14] which stipulated the immediate opening of the telecoms service market to foreign investment and specified a maximum ratio of ownership of foreign firms within six years.[15] Although restrictions still loomed large for incoming overseas telecoms giants, these foreign operators were expected to provide fresh impetus to the central leadership to nurture domestic operators to the point that they could compete with the foreign operators. Under such circumstances, regulatory reforms evolved with the following features. Institutionally, the rise of the MII contributed to separating business (China Telecom) from government, as well as reducing bureaucratic tensions between the MPT and the Ministry of Electronics Industry and the Ministry of Railways.[16] Normatively, the creation of competition was greatly emphasized and further encouraged. By completing the separation of China Telecom from the telecoms regulator, the MII no longer interfered with the daily business of telecoms companies.[17]

Again, despite the state's continued efforts to foster competition by restructuring the incumbent firms, the market remained dominated by China Telecom. In the case of mobile services, for example, China Unicom's market share was only 6 percent in 1998, whereas China Telecom's share was 94 percent.[18] In 1999, the MII-led first round of restructuring aimed not to introduce new players but to break up China Telecom because the past creation of new operators had not been successful.[19] In breaking up China Telecom's monopoly, the focus was on how to split it up: horizontally or vertically. A horizontal break-up meant splitting the elephantine enterprise into smaller, local-unit telecom firms by region, allowing China Telecom to maintain its formerly comprehensive services. In contrast, a vertical split highlighted the functional divisions of China Telecom that dominated fixed-line, mobile, satellite, and paging services. By going with a vertical break-up, China Telecom was divided into three companies, each with its own service area: China Mobile (wireless services), China Satellite (satellite business), and a new China Telecom (fixed-line telephone and internet services).[20] Two more basic service providers were launched in 2000: China Netcom and China Railcom, which were designed to compete with China Telecom, but their target services were different. China Netcom operated the internet service, IP telephony, and other value-added services; China Railcom was in charge of local and long-distance fixed-line services.

Nevertheless, because China Telecom still accounted for more than 90 percent of the market share of local network services, China Netcom and China Railcom lobbied for a second break-up of China Telecom.[21] A number of pundits advised that introducing new carriers or improving the regulatory mechanism would be more effective, but the State Council insisted on the MII-led second-round split of China Telecom into China Telecom and China Netcom, which merged with the former China Netcom and Jitong Communications in 2001. Both provided fixed-line services; while China Telecom was mainly in charge of the southern provinces (including lucrative Guangdong and Shanghai, as well as Tibet and Gansu), China Netcom provided services in the northern regions that encompassed Beijing, Tianjin, and Liaoning.[22] There were mounting concerns suggesting that such continuous break-up schemes would fail to usher in meaningful competition unless the telecoms service price was allowed to be set in open-market competition and private and overseas companies were free to enter China's domestic market and do business and compete with incumbent operators.

By allowing operators to provide fixed and mobile services in May 2008, the government once again carefully orchestrated the market structure with three players: China Mobile, Telecom, and Unicom. According to the original plan, the former fixed carrier, China Netcom, came to be integrated into China Unicom, which retained the GSM wireless network; the Unicom-run CDMA mobile service would be transferred to the dominant fixed operator, China Telecom; China Mobile would take over the other small fixed-line operator, China Railcom.[23] The rationale appeared to leverage the overall competitiveness of the operators by merging relatively weaker operators in fixed and mobile markets with stronger firms. In fixed and mobile services, one carrier (such as China Mobile and Telecom) nearly dominates the markets, so the need to balance competition is growing. In effect, as the three operators come to provide fixed and mobile services, it is largely expected that not only will the formerly biased competition be adjusted but that consumers will be able to enjoy more choices and perhaps lower fees.[24]

In short, China's overall process of regulatory reform in the telecoms industry has unfolded by breaking the monopolized power of MPT as the operator and regulator, as well as by managing competition by merging and breaking up operators. Consequently, the newly restructured regulator, the MII, emerged; market competition among operators remains dynamic but closely orchestrated by the central regulatory authorities. Likewise, the reform confronts new challenges on how to keep this managed competition and market restructuring in the near future.

## Conceptual Origin of Hard Regulation

China's tight control over the telecoms industry is concerned with the sectoral characteristics of the natural monopoly as well as its distinctive historical pathways of development. Beyond China, a natural monopoly industry, such as telecommunications, often invites the state's close market regulation to foster and keep fair competition in the markets by breaking up the previous monopoly. Yet because of the sensitivity of network sectors, China's top leadership has favored managed competition within a limited number of operators. Moreover, telecoms' significance as the heart of the national economy and its ripple effects on overall economic modernization and growth offers some legitimacy to the central leadership's tight regulation through direct and formal institutions. Such regulation, called hard regulation, for the telecoms service business highlights different patterns of state regulation than what is found in the automobile markets.

Equally important in shaping the concept of hard regulation is China's historical pathways of telecoms sector development. Before reforms, because semi-military and administrative needs were prioritized, the posts and telecoms sector was locked under the direct leadership of the CCP, the government (specifically the MPT), and the military, in combination.[25] Under the planned economy, the telecoms industry served mainly the CCP and the military. Although telecoms operators were named as enterprises (*qiye*, 企业), they were actually governed by military rule.[26] The military's direct leadership over telecoms operators was particularly strong during the Cultural Revolution.[27] However, China's early primacy of heavy industry as a development strategy and security concerns from the Soviet Union's threats resulted in unbalanced state investment, which in turn was responsible for the backward nature of the telecommunications infrastructure prior to reforms (table 4.1). Likewise, the military's longtime direct rule of the telecoms industry over the past three decades has had substantial effects on shaping China's concept of control over the sector: tight central regulation through direct and formal measures.

With reforms, the increasing importance of sound infrastructure industries, including telecommunications, rapidly emerged among the central leadership, and such perceptions on strategic sectors were clearly documented in the Five-Year Plans.[28] For example, the sixth FYP (1981–85) put great emphasis on posts and telecommunications as a strategic key sector, noting it as central to the national economy. In so doing, the role of political elites in reminding Deng Xiaoping of the priority of developing this backward sector deserves to be noted, given its potential economic payoffs.[29] In the 1980s, Bo Yibo, who previously had been responsible for telecommunications policy, became an outspoken advocate

Table 4.1
State Investment for the Telecommunications Industry from the Fifth
to the Eighth Five-Year Plan

| | Investment in Fixed Assets of Posts and Telecoms (billions RMB) | National Investment in Fixed Assets (billions RMB) | Average Growth Rate of Fixed Assets of Posts and Telecoms (%) | Proportion of Investment in Fixed Assets of Posts and Telecoms to National Investment in Fixed Assets (%) |
|---|---|---|---|---|
| Fifth Five-Year Plan (1976–80) | 19.08 | 3,300 | 7.33 | 0.60 |
| Sixth Five-Year Plan (1981–85) | 58.87 | 5,352 | 32.98 | 1.10 |
| Seventh Five-Year Plan (1986–90) | 201.98 | 12,468 | 25.38 | 1.62 |
| Eighth Five-Year Plan (1991–95) | 2,423.89 | 36,726 | 75.46 | 6.60 |

*Sources:* National Bureau of Statistics of China, *Zhongguo tongji nianjian*, 1998, 186; Wu, *Zhongguo tongxin fazhan zhilu*, 470–71.

for telecommunications development in high-level central leadership meetings and asked that the MPT have better access to investment funds and foreign exchange.[30] The determined intervention of the political elite was a contribution to promoting the strategic significance of the telecommunications industry in the early reform era.

After the mid-1980s, various preferential policies were offered.[31] For example, in 1986, control of service pricing was moderated, and for provincial governments, including municipal and autonomous regions, the State Council endorsed the collection of additional taxes on long-distance calls and telegrams.[32] Such support and weight on the development of infrastructure industries had been consistently sought throughout the eighth (1991–95) and ninth FYPs (1996–2000). The telecommunications sector's strategic significance was once again stressed at the tenth FYP (2001–5).[33] More recently, with the fast development of the internet and social media platforms, Chinese authorities have taken various measures to tighten censorship, such as blocking global social networks and portal services, including Facebook, Twitter, and Google; installing the so-called Great Firewall; and deleting politically sensitive news or posts on the internet. In particular, a new cyber-security law that came into effect on June 1, 2017, increased "censorship requirements, mandated data local-ization, and codified real-name registration rules for internet companies, in addition to obliging them to assist security agencies with investigation."[34] In this regard, the central party-state's tight regulation of telecoms ser-vice seemed inevitable to censor sensitive subjects from the public.

## Governing Structure: Fragmented Centralization

Governing structure, as the rules that underpin power relations among the authorities and state-business relations in the sector, is another source of creating hard regulation in China's telecoms service business. In this section, I examine administrative uniformity in the organizational struc-ture of the telecoms industry to highlight China's hierarchically central-ized governance. Then I emphasize how, in the context of centralized reg-ulation, regulatory reform has paradoxically undermined the independent authority of the telecoms regulator compared with the MPT era. This oc-curred because more state agencies became involved in governing Chi-na's telecoms service markets, and the regulatory authorities became frag-mented and overlapped at the central level. Consequently, the overlapping has become a barrier to the independent function of the telecoms regula-tor. Both NDRC's recent antimonopoly probe of giant telecoms opera-tors and SASAC's investigation into the behavior of telecoms firms' top executives illustrate how China's rising power of planning and ownership commissions has come to challenge the telecoms regulator but firmly su-pervised the telecoms giants at the top.

### ADMINISTRATIVE UNIFORMITY

The administrative uniformity in telecoms governance is a good indica-tor of China's hierarchically centralized rules of regulation[35] in that ad-ministrative uniformity does not take place by accident but by careful design and coordination from the supra-provincial authority.[36] As figure 4.2 shows, since 1955, the structure of provincial telecoms regulators and government institutions has become consistently similar, "despite both inherent heterogeneity among Chinese provinces and the increased economic autonomy accorded to the provinces during the reform era."[37] During the MPT regime (1949–97), the geographical and administrative structure of government was organized into three levels. At the central level, the MPT guided and supervised the overall industry. Local offices of the MPT, known as Posts and Telecommunications Administrations (PTAs), were organized at the provincial and municipal levels.[38] Under the leadership of provincial/municipal PTAs, Posts and Telecom Bureaus were set up at prefectural levels. Under the logic of dual leadership (*shuangzhong lingdao*, 双中领导), the PTAs were administered by both the central MPT and local governments simultaneously.

However, all revenues from telecoms services were first collected by the MPT, then redistributed to each PTA, while the MPT kept much of this revenue.[39] In this way, the MPT could exert powerful regulatory control over local telecoms bureaus, making them "essentially provincial-level MPTs with parallel bureaucratic and economic interests."[40] Such administrative uniformity continued to exist during the MII and MIIT era; the provincial-level Communication Administration Bureau (*tongxin guanliju*, 通信管理局) under the leadership of the Telecom Administration Bureau (*dianxin guanliju*, 电信管理局) of the MII, responsible for implementing MII policies, coordinated the relationship between the overall development of the sector and local economy issues and administered the oversight of telecoms firms across localities.[41] While the MII formulated the rules and policies for the overall telecoms markets, their actual enforcement was administered by the local telecoms regulator, the provincial-level Communication Administration Bureau.

Because this bureau was structurally tied to the MII, local telecoms regulators were actually no more than "agents" of the MII by following its directions. In China's administrative system, these vertical bureaucracies are called lines,[42] and they can shape the leadership relationship between the MII and its local offices.[43] Because this relationship involves binding authority, tight and formal regulation over the local telecoms market is directly exercised. Such an organizational structure continued after the MII was restructured into the MIIT with the 2008 super-ministry

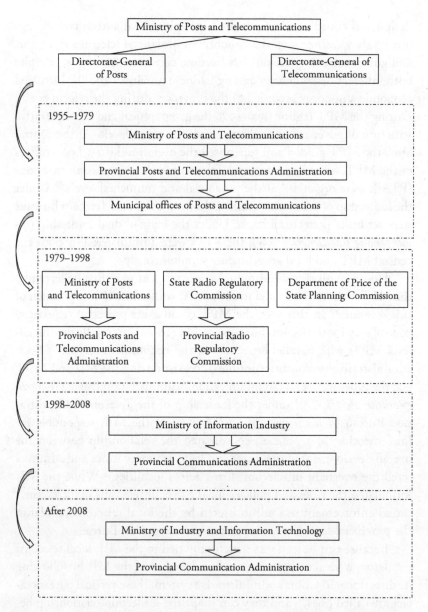

FIGURE 4.2: Evolution of the Organizational Structure of China's Telecom Regulation. *Source:* Mou (2011: 104).

reform. In this regard, even though the level of ownership remains central, the governing structure is not simply the derivatives of the monopoly of central state ownership, having some effects on reinforcing hard regulation from the center.

Indeed, Beijing's goal was very clear: the central leadership wanted to make the best use of information technology to accelerate industrial development and expected national information security to be better protected by integrating related ministries.[44] However, because the new MIIT has to deal with other industries (i.e., electronics or machinery) as well as information-related ones, telecoms regulation has come to attract less attention than it did during the MII regime. This raises a big question of who actually hold the most authoritative power to regulate the business of the telecoms industry.[45] Nevertheless, what has remained unchanged is administrative uniformity, indicating the persistent rules of central regulation. As the local telecoms regulator, the Communication Administration Bureaus in the provincial, municipal, and autonomous regions are responsible for the following four tasks: (1) implementing national policies, rules, and laws on the administration of the telecoms industry; (2) approving local telecoms business and administering local telecoms service fees and quality; (3) coordinating economic and service relations among telecoms firms; and (4) coordinating telecoms and information security.[46] Even though the MII was restructured into the MIIT, there has been little change in power relations between the central and local authorities; the provincial Communication Administration Bureau still acts as an agent of the principal MIIT (specifically the Telecoms Administration Bureau).

## THE PARADOX OF REGULATORY REFORM: MORE REFORMS, LESS INDEPENDENCE

Compared with the auto industry, the SPC hardly held a dominant position in dealing with the telecoms market and development policies; rather, the MPT, as a regulator and operator, enjoyed independent authority over the sector.[47] The regulatory reform in China's telecoms service sector that established the MII by separating the operator from the MPT has paradoxically undermined the increasingly independent function of the MIIT because of the overlapping authority of the central planning and ownership commissions. Although such overlapping authority would make central regulation tighter by having more watchdogs, reform efforts to enhance competition and separate telecom business from government has made the telecoms regulator more vulnerable to government bodies than before. Indeed, after the MII was newly established, the past various rights of the MPT were divided into other government bodies (i.e., the functions of network construction for postal administration) or telecoms firms. Such sharing of authority with other agents has actually promoted the shifting power relations between the telecoms regulator and state commissions (such as the SPC, later the NDRC or SASAC) regarding the authority for the service pricing and asset management of telecoms firms.

With respect to service pricing, first the overlapping authorities of the planning commission have challenged the independent function of the telecoms regulator. During the MPT regime, the SPC was responsible for the pricing policy of the national economy and formulated the principal guidelines, while the MPT specified the details of how to manage pricing for the telecoms sector. Back then, there was no supervising mechanism to ensure whether the MPT's pricing management was in line with SPC guidelines.

PLANNING AGENCY IN TELECOM REGULATION The 1998 government restructuring that established the MII and the restructuring of the SPC into the State Development Planning Commission (SDPC) brought about much change in regulatory dynamics (table 4.2).[48] It was particularly no-

Table 4.2
Comparison of the Telecommunications Regimes

|  | Before Reform | 1998–2008 | After the 2008 reform |
| --- | --- | --- | --- |
| Operator | MPT | Six telecom firms | Three telecom firms |
| Regulator | MPT | MII, NDRC, and SASAC | MIIT (Bureau of Telecom Management), NDRC, SASAC |
| Owner | Government | SASAC and shareholders | SASAC and shareholders |

*Sources*: Interviews no. T2, December, 7, 2005; no. T3, December 7, 2005; no. T7, December 19, 2005; no. T9, December 20, 2005; no. T12, January 20, 2006; no. T16, February 9, 2006; no. T17, February 9, 2006; no. T21, February 21, 2006; no. T23, April 22, 2008; no. T25, April 29, 2008.

table that the pricing bureau and the pricing supervision bureau (Jiage Jianchasi, 价格检查司), responsible for establishing telecoms pricing policies and managing them, were set up under the jurisdiction of the SDPC.[49] In this way, the planning agency as another regulator has become formally and directly engaged not only in formulating telecoms pricing policies as in the MPT era but also in supervising pricing. To some extent, this shows how China's planning agency exerts more regulatory power over the sector than before and, most important, challenges the independent function of the telecoms regulator.

In effect, the SDPC's right to adjust the pricing for telecoms services has been a serious and direct constraint to the MII.[50] After the SDPC was restructured into the NDRC in 2003, the Pricing Bureau (Wujiaju, 物价局) under the NDRC and its local offices was authorized to monitor the pricing competition of telecoms operators in close collaboration with the telecoms regulator and its local offices. When necessary, the NDRC holds public hearings.[51] For instance, in February 2008, after hours of debate and public hearings, the MII and NDRC jointly announced "a price cut on mobile roaming service charges of between 54 percent and 73 percent, depending on locality."[52] Meanwhile, the director of the Pricing Bureau of the NDRC said that "the NDRC and the MII will work to fix a definite timetable,"[53] aiming to push forward the implementation of a one-way (caller-pay) charging system.

Such overlapping authority has intensified bureaucratic infighting between the planning agency (the NDRC) and the telecoms regulator (MIIT), as evidenced when the NDRC attempted to apply the antimonopoly law against two telecoms giants in 2011, claiming they were engaging in price discrimination by abusing their dominant market status. As explored later in this chapter, this was a remarkable step in that without prior consultation with the MIIT, the NDRC invoked the antimonopoly law against the two telecoms giants, China Telecom and China Unicom. Likewise, compared with the MPT regime, the MIIT's regulation over the telecoms market has become fragile because it has to negotiate with the NDRC regarding service pricing and other policies.[54]

OWNERSHIP AGENCY IN TELECOMS REGULATION SASAC's growing role in the telecoms business is another source undermining the independence of the telecoms regulator from the government, particularly in terms of the following aspects: market restructuring (*chongzu*, 重组) and the supervision of asset management and personnel of the telecoms giants. As Margaret Pearson notes, "the idea that regulation is consistent with the promotion of competition is highly relevant in China's strategic industries, since a main goal of regulators is to structure competition rather than passively to oversee it."[55] This contention helps us explain how SASAC's role in restructuring the telecoms market is part of state regulation.[56] One may argue that SASAC undertook market restructuring for the telecoms sector because it is the ownership agency for central state-owned telecoms giants. However, it should be noted that before SASAC emerged in 2003, MII had actually designed and conducted the first- and second-round market restructurings in 1999 and 2002, respectively. Hence, *chongzu* is not the intrinsic right to an ownership agency; rather, it can also be performed by the regulator.

Moreover, some changes in the norms of telecoms regulation (*dianxin jianguan*, 电信监管) have also been remarkable since the latest restructuring. In the first and second rounds, the main concern was to create competition in the market by breaking up China Telecom's long-held monopoly. To this end, between 1999 and 2002, the MII split China Telecom to create China Mobile, Netcom, Railcom, and Satcom.[57] As the 2008 *chongzu* showed,[58] the norm shifted to manage competition by reinforcing three oligarchies, Mobile, Telecom, and Unicom (fig. 4.3),[59] not to end China Mobile's dominant position, which is close to a monopoly.[60]

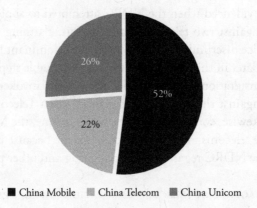

China Mobile ■    China Telecom ■    China Unicom ■

FIGURE 4.3: Revenue Share of China's Basic Telecommunications Services, 2015. *Source:* Lin, Lu, and Chen, "Reform and Development of Basic Telecommunication Service," 61.

Some argue that genuine competition is possible only by breaking up China Mobile, which tends to monopolize the market because the mobile service is rapidly replacing the fixed-line one.[61] Yet China's top leadership strongly prefers to keep the most profitable and competitive China Mobile going, believing this not only makes China Mobile globally competitive but that it raises the level of other domestic operators.[62]

In short, when regulatory functions broadly refer to "the supervision of markets" by promoting competition and monitoring business management, the MII was the main regulatory agency that carried out market restructuring twice—in 1999 and 2002—by merging and separating the existing operators. Yet the SASAC-led market restructuring in 2008, which generated the current three telecom giants, illustrates how regulatory reforms in China's telecoms service sector have empowered the SASAC, while relatively enfeebling the MIIT.

Second, the SASAC's growing meddling in telecoms regulation is also seen in its roles of asset and leadership supervision, which have aimed to secure crucial state assets from any loss or transfer to private or overseas ownership.[63] Prior to the advent of the SASAC in 2003, in fact, the management of the assets and personnel of telecoms operators was directly and entirely supervised by the MPT.[64] Although the MPT had monopolized regulatory control over the asset management and personnel of the operators, the newly restructured MII had to share authority with other agencies, such as the Ministry of Finance or the Ministry of Railways, as new telecoms firms entered the market.[65] Thus, regulatory supervision could no longer be monopolized by the MII as the MPT had done. Furthermore, since the creation of the SASAC in 2003, the SASAC's Bureau of Financial Supervision and Audit Evaluation has taken charge of overseeing telecoms firms' finance and budget management after the operators' reports.[66] Generally speaking, the boards of directors draw up their own budgets.

China's central state-owned telecoms firms should report their total assets, revenue, net profits, and asset management to the SASAC.[67] In this way, the SASAC monitors the telecoms firms' financial transactions in conjunction with the Ministry of Finance because these transactions account for a significant share of state assets (table 4.3). In doing so, the SASAC reviews the operators' large-scale investment plans to ensure appropriate and efficient use of assets and to prevent overlaps or unnecessary

Table 4.3
Telecommunications Firms' Share of Central State Assets, 2010

| | Total Assets (million RMB) | Net Assets (million RMB) | Total Revenue (million RMB) | Net Profits |
|---|---|---|---|---|
| Central SASAC | 244,275 | 95,665 | 167,769 | 8,523 |
| Centrally-owned telecom firms | 17,128 | 8,785 | 8,813 | 1,672 |
| Share (%) | 7 | 9.2 | 5.3 | 19.6 |

*Notes:* These revenues and net income are "reported" to, not possessed by, the SASAC. The data of telecom firms are collected from China Telecom 2010 financial reports, the China Unicom 2010 financial report, and the China Mobile 2010 financial report.

*Sources:* Data for the Central SASAC are from *Zhongyang qiye 2010 niandu zongti yunxing qingkuang* (The operating situation of central enterprises in 2010), http://www.sasac.gov.cn/n1180 /n1566/n258203/n259490/13864252.html.

investments in telecoms, which could bring about a loss of state assets. The SASAC then reviews whether the investment conforms with the national development plan and the firm's long-term strategy.Indeed, in 2006, the SASAC reconfirmed its absolute control (*juedui kongzhili*, 绝对控制力) over the telecoms industry, as well as six other key sectors, all of which closely relate to the national economy and security.[68, 69]

As table 4.3 shows, the operators' significant contribution to state assets and their strong central state ownership together have enabled the SASAC to have legitimate rights over the business of the telecoms market. Likewise, the SASAC focuses on supervising "the *business* of centrally-owned telecoms firms" (fig. 4.4), while the MIIT regulates overall IT (including huge electronic manufacturing) and is not confined to basic telecoms services.[70] In this regard, even though the MIIT's scope of telecoms regulation is broader than the SASAC's, its regulatory authority is not necessarily superior to the SASAC, which holds direct and considerable clout for telecoms operators.

THE CCP IN TELECOM REGULATION The CCP's political oversight over the business of strategic industries is undeniably prevalent but remains relatively less analyzed. As deeply embedded supervisors in both government and business, various party organizations in the telecoms industry for-

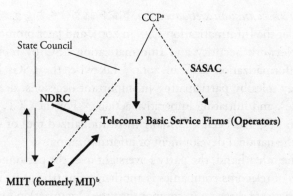

FIGURE 4.4: Monitoring the Business of Basic Telecommunications Service. [a]This refers to the Central Standing Committee of the Political Bureau and Organization Department. [b]After the 2008 administrative reform, the former MII was transformed into the Ministry of Industry and Information Technology (MIIT), and the Bureau of Telecommunications Administration under the MIIT is mainly responsible for regulatory function. *Sources*: Based on the author's interviews in Beijing (December 2005; January–February 2006; April–May 2008).

mally and directly oversee the policy making and rules of the sector, as well as the business management and personnel of the operators.

The CCP's supervision over telecoms policies and rules has been carried out through the Informatization LSG (Xinxihua Lingdao Xiaozu, 信息化领导小组),[71] which studies national development strategies and guides the direction to pursue.[72] Its initial effort to lead the building of an integrated national economy and information system established the National Economy and Information Management LSG (Guojia Jingji Xinxi Guanli Lingdao Xiaozu, 国家经济信息管理领导小组) in 1986. With the rapid growth of the telecoms sector over the 1990s, the central leadership decided to set up the Informatization Work LSG (Xinxihua Gongzuo Lingdao Xiaozu, 信息化工作领导小组) in 1999, and renamed it the Informatization LSG under the leadership of the premier in 2001. Moreover, as the tenth FYP (2001–5) illustrated, China's emphasis on informatization toward industrialization further reinforced the roles and authority of the Informatization LSG to guide the sector by coordinating competing policies and interest groups. Because of the increasing severity of the information security problem in China, the National Network and Information Security Coordination Small Group (*guojia*

*wanglu yu xinxi anquan xietiao xiaozu,* 国家网路与信息安全协调小组) was
set up under the Informatization LSG in 2003, and later promoted as the
Central Network Security and Informatization LSG by replacing the
former Informatization LSG in 2014.[73] Likewise, the LSGs have been
playing key roles by participating in important decisions, dealing with
main issues, and initiating imperative actions.[74] For the CCP, the Informatization LSG has been a formally institutionalized tool of regulation
to guide the national development of informatization.

On the other hand, the party's oversight over the personnel and top
executives of telecoms companies is another major part of its regulatory
job, and there are three main components: the Organization Department
(OD), the party committee inside the firms, and the central inspection
groups.[75] First, as to the personnel of the central SOEs, including all telecoms operators, the OD and SASAC reserve the right to nominate and
appoint top executives. Whereas the SASAC lists this as one of its key
responsibilities on paper,[76] the OD acts on the authority of the party's
*nomenklatura* system, a key instrument of the CCP's control over leadership selection.[77] According to *nomenklatura* logic, which "only lists the
most important position,"[78] telecoms firms' top executives are appointed,
removed, and rotated by the OD. Because the OD does not have suffi-
cient information about candidates and firms, it considers the SASAC's
"suggestions" (*jianyi,* 建议) seriously.[79] Some even claim that the OD's
personnel authority is close to perfunctory in that the SASAC is better
informed about candidates through its direct oversight (*jiandu,* 监督).[80]
Nevertheless, SASAC's suggestions have no binding force; the ultimate
nominator, the OD, may appoint other candidates beyond the SASAC
list.[81] Second, if the OD acts as the party's external mechanism of political oversight, there is the party committee inside the firms.[82] As examined in the case of the auto industry, the party committee is a highly
political organization,[83] whose main task is to supervise the behavior of
party members and firm operation and ensure that the policy directions
and desires of the party leadership are in line with business management.
For the latter, the party secretary of the committee inside the firm is often the chairperson of the board of directors for all telecoms operators.[84]

For example, the party secretary of the former China Netcom (which
merged into China Unicom in 2008),[85] Zhang Chunjiang, confirmed that
"my job is to ensure that the direction of our Communist Party is upheld

within China Netcom."[86] In fact, China Netcom under Zhang's leadership spearheaded the reform of corporate governance, creating a model for other large state firms by strengthening its board of directors and clarifying the roles of the firms' party committees in business management. This demonstrates that such reform efforts are not necessarily designed to dilute the party's political clout in corporate governance. Instead, even though China, with listings in overseas stock markets, has introduced the Western type of modern corporate governance (i.e., a board of directors) at least in form, members of the board all but belong to the party committee.[87] In other words, these are internationally listed telecoms operators that are controlled by the party-state.

Last, by organizing a specialized inspection group (*xunshizu*), the CCP tries to directly monitor the behavior of top executives in leading state firms, including telecoms giants. Such an effort partly reflects the limits of the SASAC and other party organizations in effectively monitoring top executives. Relatively independent from both government and firms, these centrally organized inspection groups carry out intensive, focused supervision of targeted key state firms as well as provincial leaders and state institutions.[88] Here the difference from the auto industry comes from the legitimacy of the inspection groups' supervision. Because these centrally organized inspection groups hold legitimate authority for monitoring their business management and top executives, their supervision over telecoms giants is formally and directly exercised.

In contrast, such centrally organized inspection groups lack the legitimacy to directly oversee the business and personnel of the local state-owned major auto producers. Hence, their supervision remains informal. The corruption issue among telecoms giants surfaced when several China Mobile senior executives were found to be involved in major corruption scandals. In 2009, as a result of a probe by the central inspection arm of the party, China Mobile's former vice chairman Zhang Chunjiang was fired on suspicion of embezzlement.[89] The central inspection group undertook a close review of three giant telecoms firms in 2011.[90] Another set of central inspection groups uncovered corruption by two senior executives of the China Unicom Corporation Group in 2013.[91]

China's telecoms regulation thus contributes to unveiling power relations between the OD and the SASAC concerning leadership selection and appointment in central SOEs and confirms how, despite such enthusiastic reform efforts, the party's system of political checks remains durable without substantial modifications. Likewise, the hard form of central regulation prevails in the telecoms markets, not through the telecoms regulator (as in the MPT regime) but by the contested authorities at the central level, including the paradoxically languishing telecoms regulator (the MII, later the MIIT) and socialist political-economic institutions, such as the NDRC, SASAC, and the CCP.

## Dominance of Central State Ownership: Growing Out of the Ministry

Although the underlying concepts of control and governing structure have some reinforcing effects on creating a *hard* or *soft* form of central regulation, central state ownership plays a leading role in enabling the central authorities to exercise tight regulatory control over the telecoms giants directly and formally. "Property rights" refer to "rules that define who has claims on the profits of firms,"[92] but this leaves questions regarding the state's role in encouraging competition, directing investments, and supervising the markets in general. The dominant mode of property rights thus may have an effect on the manner and extent to which the state acts in the market and defines power relations between constituencies in and around market actors. Above all, strong central state ownership in China's telecoms services sector tends to legitimate the rights of central authorities to directly manage and formally oversee the business of telecoms firms, making both firms and regulators lethargic at the local level. In other words, local telecoms operators are nothing more than local offices of the firms because their business plans, management, and personnel are all mandated from their headquarters in Beijing. More important, in contrast with auto companies, telecoms operators have grown out of the ministries. Before the rise of the MII, the General Bureau of China Telecom (Zongguo Dianxin Zongju, 中国电信总局) in the MPT was the main body for managing the telecoms business.

In theory, the MPT was supposed to serve as an administrative body for the sector, but its frequent and direct engagement in business management, including overseeing the assets and personnel of the General

Bureau of China Telecom, was substantial in reality.[93] To ameliorate such duplicated authorities of the MPT as regulator and operator, China Telecom (originally named the Directorate General of Telecommunications) emerged by separating business management from the MPT under the principle of separating government from enterprise (*zhengqi fenkai*, 政企分开) in 1995.[94] Another bureacratic origin is found in the case of China Unicom, whose creation was engineered by the former Ministry of Electronic Industry, the former Ministry of Electricity, and the Ministry of Railways.[95] Such bureaucratic origin of incumbent telecoms operators has left two significant legacies to the sector: one is that this allows the telecoms ministry (MII/MIIT) to maintain regulatory oversight over the business management of telecoms operators and their revenue intake. The other is that central state ownership became the dominant mode of ownership as telecoms operators were established, first by separating existing functions from the ministries and then by merging and breaking up incumbent operators.

The monopoly of central state ownership in the telecoms industry advanced the regulatory power of the SASAC, the ownership agency of all three telecoms operators, to directly supervise their business management and personnel and orchestrate the market structure in 2008. For example, Shanghai China Telecom is under the leadership of the SASAC via the headquarters of China Telecom; the Shanghai-based SASAC has no formal rights to supervise its performance in the market. Both locally based telecoms firms and local telecoms regulators (such as Telecommunication Administration Bureaus) act according to the directions and mandate of central authorities or the headquarters of telecoms firms, and little choice is allowed for local authorities to influence major rules and policies. As a result, the dominance of central state ownership in this sector has generated a highly centralized regulatory system with direct and formal authority (hard regulation) in the following three aspects. First, rule-making power is not shared with local authorities but concentrated at the center, even though fragmentation and overlapping of the authorities at the top remain challenging. Second, policy implementation strictly proceeds from the central authorities and regulatory agencies, such as the MIIT, NDRC, and SASAC, without leaving much leeway. Last, the means of business supervision are accomplished through formal rules and organizations, contrasting with the case of the auto industry.

Despite the WTO agreement on the gradual opening up to private and foreign investors,[96] nonstate firms are still hardly seen in the telecoms service business. As this lack of nonstate capital saves the central authorities from the trouble of negotiating on rules and policies with various stakeholders, the exercise of tight and direct regulation from the center is likely to be much more feasible. The following case of antimonopoly probing presents how the NDRC challenges the authority of the MIIT by leading the supervision of the telecom giants' market monopoly and unfair competition. Still, the dominance of central state ownership leads the central authorities to exert tight regulation through direct and formal measures (hard regulation) over the telecoms giants.

## The Politics of Antimonopoly

The antimonopoly investigation of the telecoms giants as of 2011 presents how China's steady reform efforts over the previous two decades paradoxically undermined the independence of the telecoms regulator, the MIIT, from the government, while advancing its traditional but modernized state planning commission, the NDRC. As noted already, the MIIT and the NDRC hold the regulatory authority to set service pricing (*zifei*, 资费); particularly, the NDRC Pricing Bureau still participates in setting the prices of the overall economy as in the era of the planned economy.[97] Because of concerns about the loss of crucial state assets, the SASAC is also involved in supervising the monopolistic activities and business of the telecoms giants, in an attempt to inhibit vicious competition.[98] Yet the SASAC lacks legal authority when telecoms giants break the rules that prohibit monopolistic activities (not the monopolistic position itself) in markets.[99] Likewise, compared with the MPT regime, the planning and ownership agencies (such as the NDRC and SASAC), which are symbols of China's enduring pursuit of a socialist market economy, are undermining the telecoms regulator's independence from other government bodies by sharing its conventional boundaries. The 2011 antimonopoly probing into telecoms giants points particularly to the empowered NDRC over the MIIT in managing market competition.

In China, the rise of the antimonopoly regime seems to have introduced new rules to the telecoms markets. The antimonopoly regime consists largely of three elements: antimonopoly law, the norm of disciplining anticompetition behavior, and state agencies in charge. In August 2007, after thirteen years of protracted review, China's National People's Congress finally approved the antimonopoly law (*fanlongduanfa*, 反垄断法)[100] that aimed to prohibit overheated market concentration and other monopolistic practices (not status) by private and state-owned business alike through price fixing and collusion.[101] This law, which came into effect in August 2008, was expected to advance the Chinese economy toward a market-oriented system, while moving away from the legacies of a planned economy in which less competitive giant SOEs could easily enjoy the privileges of vast and unchallenged monopolies.[102] China's antimonopoly law particularly warned giant SOEs against harming fair competition by abusing their monopolistic market status.

The antimonopoly investigation began with a report from China Tietong to the NDRC in June 2011, claiming that China Telecom and China Unicom tried to monopolize the internet broadband market by abusing their dominant position.[103] With Tietong's report, the NDRC, the leading state agency in the enforcement of the antimonopoly law, made a preliminary conclusion that the telecoms giants had abused their position regarding service charges.[104] China's antimonopoly law, in effect, stipulates that "a business operator having market dominance is prohibited from treating equally qualified trade counterparts differently in terms of transaction price or other conditions without legitimate reasons."[105] According to the government department responsible for the pricing issues of antimonopoly laws, these operators were trying to "keep competitors out of the Internet access market by demanding prohibitive prices for leasing their networks."[106] Indeed, China Telecom and China Unicom together accounted for more than two-thirds of the broadband internet market in 2011. Their dominant position enabled them to demand higher prices than their competitors. The newly approved antimonopoly law considers such behavior to be price discrimination based on market monopoly. For a careful investigation of this case, the NDRC consulted the MIIT, the Legal Affairs Office of the State Council, and the Supreme People's Court in October 2011. Although the opinions from these institutions were somewhat different, they commonly judged that decisive evidence indicating monopolistic behavior by the telecoms companies was absent, and they emphasized the need for careful deliberation.[107] At the outset, the NDRC actually planned to make a final decision after hearing from the SASAC and had already engaged in much discussion with the telecoms firms; both parties agreed to resolve the issue amicably.[108]

Despite such underlying negotiations and consultations, on November 9, the NDRC made public its investigation of China Telecom and Unicom without final coordination with the SASAC and the MIIT. According to the NDRC, "the two operators breached anti-monopoly regulations and [it] was preparing to slap the two firms with combined fines of eight billion RMB."[109] Indeed, this was a rare high-profile move against major state firms.[110] Soon after, China Telecom and China Unicom submitted a written counterargument to this initial assessment. The companies acknowledged the charges and made efforts to improve their broadband services by providing lower prices with a faster network, so the NDRC finally decided to suspend its antimonopoly probe, based on its evaluation results.[111] According to a clause of the system of "manager approval" (*jingingzhe chengren zhidu*, 经营者承认制度) within the antimonopoly law, the case can be closed if corporate entities (violators) acknowledge a matter of violation and accept a government request for modification.[112]

This probe was particularly remarkable in that the NDRC, without final consultation with the MIIT or the SASAC, moved on making its investigation public, claiming the firms' abuse of market monopoly.[113] As pointed out earlier, the NDRC's surprising announcement of antimonopoly notices to China Telecom and Unicom in November 2011 did not disappoint such an expectation and sent a strong signal regarding the shift in how competition in China's telecoms market would be regulated. Above all, this antimonopoly investigation suggests how the underlying normative and institutional elements in China have led to a waning telecoms regulator while advancing the state planning agency. Normatively, this antimonopoly investigation is manifested when the Chinese state begins to use legal measures rather than administrative ones in disciplining market competition, ultimately controlling the pursuit of business interests and autonomy. Institutionally, the power of the NDRC within the fragmented and overlapping institutional structure at the center shows how a so-called supra-regulator, with more comprehensive authority than the telecoms regulator, can be proactive in overseeing market competition on a legal basis, eroding the independence of the government's role as telecoms regulator.

In fact, prior to the enactment of the antimonopoly law in 2008, the State Council set up two administrative bodies: the Anti-Monopoly Commission (*fanlongduan weiyuanhui*, 反垄断委员会) and the Anti-Monopoly Enforcement Structure (*fanlongduan zhixingjiegou*, 反垄断执行结构) to supervise the monopolistic behavior of firms (see figure 4.5).[114] The Anti-Monopoly Commission involves fifteen government ministries, including the NDRC, MIIT, SASAC, and Ministry of Commerce, which is responsible mainly for drafting policies on antimonopoly-related issues and assisting the enforcement of antimonopoly probing. Substantial investigation of antimonopoly activities is undertaken by the Anti-Monopoly Enforcement Structure, organized by the NDRC, the Ministry of Commerce, and the State Administration of Industry and Commerce. In particular, the NDRC probed monopolistic pricing. In this regard, the MIIT and the SASAC, despite their membership of an antimonopoly commission, have little influence in the process of anti-monopoly probing. As figure 4.5 shows, the institutional structure of the antimonopoly

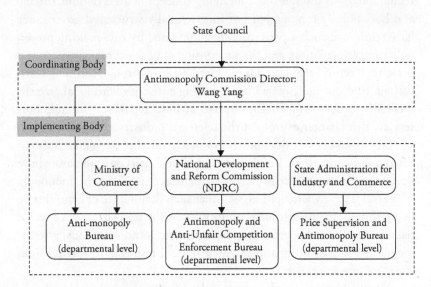

FIGURE 4.5: China's Antimonopoly Regime. *Sources:* Moning, "Fanlongduan fali 'jingji xianfa' youduoyuan," 45.

regime places the NDRC at the core as both policy maker and enforcement body, while incapacitating other regulatory authorities of the SASAC and the MIIT. Moreover, while the NDRC focuses on nurturing fair market competition, the sound financial performance of state firms is the key concern for the SASAC. Such conflicting interests caused telecoms giants to be squeezed between the NDRC and the SASAC. According to some Chinese pundits, because telecoms firms are under big pressure from the SASAC regarding business performance (i.e., raising assets or profits), their monopolistic acts on internet service pricing are perhaps inevitable.[115]

## Conclusion

The central authorities' tight regulation over the lucrative telecoms industry is far from surprising, given its importance to national economy and security in China. Still, it is notable how the wholly centralized state ownership (level of ownership) of the telecom operators has created *hard* regulation, even though the underlying concept of an economic lifeline and horizontally fragmented but hierarchically structured governance have reinforced such a pattern. When measured by rule-making power, policy implementation, and the supervision of business management and personnel, central regulation is exercised directly through formally institutionalized mechanisms without sharing authority with local governments. In accounting for the sources of hard regulation for telecoms service, this chapter examined the telecoms industry's longtime ties to military as well as security and economic concerns as the increasing censorship indicates. Then I reviewed how China's telecoms operators have grown out of the ministries, making the telecoms giants the monopoly of central state ownership. I argued that such dominance of central state ownership and administrative uniformity in the telecoms service sector has contributed to undermining the legitimate authority of local governments in policy making and implementation, resulting in vertical lines (*tiaotiao*) of governance.

Finally, I have pointed to the paradox of regulatory reform in China's telecoms service industry as the most notable result, in that the regulator's independence from government was better ensured before the regulatory reform. In other words, the horizontal fragmentation at the central level would not just disturb the independent function of the telecoms regulator from other planning and ownership agencies but also frustrate the coordinated policy adoption and successful implementation of important rules, as the antimonopoly probing in 2011 evidences. Interestingly, this also means such overlapped authorities at the top contribute to harden central regulation over China's telecoms market and business through multiple regulators' direct and formal supervision.

# CHAPTER 5

## Beyond China

### State Regulation in a Socialist Market Economy

> Whatever the result, discussion of the Chinese and Vietnamese
> reforms and their true nature must continue, even if it is impos-
> sible to decide what to call the system now prevalent.
>
> —Janos Kornai, *From Socialism to Capitalism*

In the 1990s, China's attitude of actively embracing market forces and global integration, as well as its introduction of remarkable market-oriented institutional reforms, led observers to believe the country was shifting from a planner to a rational and minimalist state in governing its economy.[1] Heavy emphasis on state-owned enterprise (SOE) reforms that closed a number of inefficient SOEs and the pursuit of "separating government from enterprises" sent strong signals to the world of China's notable steps toward a market-oriented economy. However, recently, particularly after Xi Jinping took office in 2013, we have seen the introduction of resilient but modified planning and ownership commissions, with various party organizations on top of other industrial regulators. Particularly remarkable is the increasing trend of party organizations having a tighter hold in regulating the business of foreign companies, especially regarding the operation of their business and investment decisions. According to one senior executive whose company is doing business in China, "some foreign firms were under 'political pressure' to revise the terms of their joint ventures with state-owned partners to allow the party final say over business operations and investment decisions."[2]

What we actually learn from China is that first, regulation and state planning are not incompatible, and second, there are varieties of state regulation, just as there are varieties of capital, actors, and markets. As the chapters in this book have elaborated, since 1993, China's efforts to undertake institutional reforms have ultimately aimed to enhance the efficiency and productivity of SOEs that dominate the heart of the economy under the state's macro-guidance. Therefore, the Chinese economy, under the vision of a "socialist market economy," is still centered on the state planning agency responsible for macro-regulatory control and state ownership mainly serving the vested interests in power, not the public.

My findings suggest that China has been reformulating the goals and function of state planning, generating types of regulation that are distinctly different from regulation in other liberal market economies. Moreover, China's historical endurance in its selective approach to industrial modernization has promoted a multilayered industrial structure.[3] Such varieties of state regulation show how early scholarly efforts that attempted to capture China's internal dynamics and complexities through a single theoretical framework and parsimonious accounts were exceedingly limited in explaining the dynamics of China's many political economies.

This concluding chapter begins by revisiting the importance of formal and informal Leninist institutions for the study of Chinese political economy, as well as the sources of variations in China's market regulation from the center, highlighting the significance of the level of ownership that actually determines the central state regulation as soft or hard. To test my findings, I examine other strategic industries. By comparing China to Vietnam, the chapter also examines whether the findings from the practices of Chinese regulation can have general explanatory power in the regime of a socialist market economy. I discuss more broadly why Chinese practices matter to the study of regulation and how to approach the subject of regulation, which has been dominated by theories and practices from advanced industrial economies. Based on the findings of this study, the book concludes with some prospects concerning China's future of economic governance.

## Remaking Socialist Institutions for Market Regulation

How does China regulate a socialist market economy that is persistently pursued? In this book, I have strived to answer this key question by tracing the historical evolution of political-economic institutions and comparing two different strategic sectors as empirical cases. By taking continental Europe's (Germany and France) approach, this book defines regulation as a general government tool to control the economy and society, implying all modes of state intervention. Thus, industrial policy and five-year plans (FYPs) serve as important means of regulation in the Chinese context.

This book has examined how China's deeply seated socialist political-economic institutions, such as planning commissions, state ownership, and the Chinese Communist Party (CCP), remain central to governing its economy by modifying their roles in the past command economy. Focusing on guiding and indicating the macro direction of development rather than setting narrow targets to accomplish, China's planning agency, the National Development and Reform Commission (NDRC), has been transformed into a kind of supra-regulator by maintaining key control over large-scale investments, market entry, pricing, and overseas partners in joint-venture projects. The automobile and telecoms sectors offer empirical explanations for how the goals and tools of regulation from the state planning commission have evolved and made variations across sectors. In this process, although coordination mechanisms and means of regulation have changed over the course of economic reform, the Chinese party-state formulates the plans for regulating the markets, rather than commanding them.

While the planning agency supervises the overall policies and macro-economy, the state ownership agency, the State-Owned Assets Supervision and Administration Commission (SASAC), takes part in supervising the business of key state firms, closely monitoring their asset management and the personnel of leading state firms in most strategic sectors. The widely known Organization Department or the Party Committees inside SOEs as well as the Leading Small Groups (LSGs) and central inspection groups illustrate how various party organizations still penetrate government and business (domestic and foreign) and even exercise more powerful political control over them. Analysis of the actual practices of both the LSGs' supervision and the central inspection groups responsible for monitoring the performance of leading cadres and state firms evidences how, in spite of four decades of market-oriented reforms, various party organizations remain deeply engaged in China's regulatory governance.

Another potential contribution to the field of Chinese political economy would be to reveal my findings on the varieties of state regulation
across strategic industries. Indeed, it is hardly surprising to see that the
central party-state's regulation exists when the strategic value of the sector is high. Still, what is remarkable is that even though the common
strategic importance invites central regulatory control, there are variations
in how central regulatory control is enforced. As elaborated in chapter 2,
China's consistent pursuit of a selective approach to industrialization during the Mao era and to economic modernization since Deng has generated a tiered industrial structure that marks different levels of openness
to the market forces and institutions. It would be odd to expect that a
single type of regulation exists in running the highly diverse and complex systems of the economy. This book argues that this is why the market
institutional approach that disaggregates markets as institutions is useful
for analyzing China's complex regulatory realities. Indeed, as my empirical case studies in chapters 3 and 4 evidence, the dominant mode of
ownership (level of ownership) along with the concepts of control and
governance structure are important sources for establishing the varieties
of state regulation across China's strategic industries.

By comparing two strategic but very different sectors—automobiles
and telecommunications—I propose both a soft and a hard form of regulation. China's automobile industry shows that highly decentralized
political (strong local authorities) and economic institutions (dominant
local state ownership) are not necessarily immune to central regulatory
control. That is, when the sector has been developed by strong local powers under decentralized ownership and globalized business with foreign
investors, the exercise of central regulation tends to be indirect and informal. The concept of *soft* regulation is proposed here for strategic but
decentralized industries in China. On the other hand, the telecoms service industry is governed entirely by central state ownership under the
vision of the commanding heights, through which tight and direct central regulation is enforced through highly concentrated formal institutions. I call this pattern *hard* regulation to highlight the differences in
the underlying institutions of soft regulation (table 5.1). In short, variations in China's state regulation evidence how it would be futile to emphasize that either growing market forces or the resilient strong hand of
the state is key to the mechanism of operating the Chinese market

Table 5.1
Linking Ownership, Concepts, and Governing Structure

| Industry | Dominant Mode of State Ownership | Concepts of Control | Governing Structure |
|---|---|---|---|
| Automobile (soft regulation) | Local | Pillar industry, but regionalized production and opening to nonstate capital (private, foreign) | Decentralized authorities (*kuaikuai*) Central-local regulators: professional relationship (*yewu guanxi*) |
| Telecommunications (hard regulation) | Central | Commanding heights; closed to nonstate capital; absolute central state ownership | Fragmented centralization (*tiaotiao*): overlapping central-local telecom regulators: leadership relationship (*lingdao guanxi*) |

economy, for such an approach often simplifies inherent diversities and complex realities, leading observers to overlook many political economies within China.[4]

## APPLYING TO OTHER STRATEGIC INDUSTRIES

My findings from a comparative case study of automobile and telecoms services show that what actually plays a major role in forming soft or hard regulation is the level of ownership (that is, the dominant mode of state ownership, rather than the state or private ownership itself). Exploring other strategic industries, including financial services, energy, airline, and steel, confirms the level of ownership as the main factor in establishing whether the central party-state regulation is hard or soft (table 5.2). What is equally important to note is that this does not necessarily mean both the dominant view on control and longtime governing structure cannot be simply seen as a derivative of ownership; instead, there are some reinforcing (not causal) factors inherent in each pattern. For ex-

Table 5.2
Central Regulation over China's Strategic Industries

| | Banking | Securities | Oil | Electric power | Airlines | Steel |
|---|---|---|---|---|---|---|
| Concepts of control | Absolute central control | Favoring central leadership (CSRC) | Absolute central control | Encouraging marketization | Strict central regulation | Strong central directives and restrictions |
| Governing structure | Centralized | Decentralized | Centralized | Double fragmentation | Centralized (CAAC) | Decentralized |
| Dominant mode of state ownership | Central | Local | Central | Local | Central | Local |
| Type of central regulation | Hard | Soft | Hard | Soft | Hard | Soft |

ample, China's banking and securities sectors show how the difference in ownership establishes a variation in central regulation, as well as their preferences for how regulation and governing structure reinforce each pattern.

FINANCE: BANKING AND SECURITIES In the banking sector, for example, all of China's major commercial banks are central SOEs (*yangqi*, 央企), and their local branches are ultimately managed by the headquarters and supervised by the China Banking Regulatory Commission (CBRC) in coordination with the Ministry of Finance in Beijing.[5] While local authorities oversee the financial markets under their jurisdiction, the rules and policies they refer to are designed by the central regulators. In particular, the CBRC's highly focused authority stems from its strong professional expertise.[6] In fact, such centralized governing structure and ownership have a lot to do with China's long pursuit of absolute control over the finance sector since Mao, as elaborated in chapter 2. Hence, tight and direct regulation from the central party-state via formal rules and procedures (hard regulation) is applied. Compared with the securities markets, the importance of the level of ownership is notable.

In terms of the concepts of control, as in other financial sectors, the central leadership's absolute control is emphasized. In fact, because of the potential conflicts between local governments and the relatively weak regulatory knowledge at the local level for complex financial issues, strong preference for central regulation prevails, even when local governments hold legitimate authority for overseeing local securities markets.[7] In contrast with the banking sector, various locally oriented financial institutions in China's securities markets, including private capital management companies or credit and financing guarantor companies, as well as the provincial governments, are entitled to manage their own financial affairs.[8]

Nevertheless, not only does the Chinese Securities and Regulatory Commission (CSRC), armed with professional expertise, hold the power to set the ground rules and policies, but these guidelines, supported by the Ministry of Finance, bind the regulatory activities of provincial governments.[9] However, because China's securities markets are dominated by various small local or private credit- and capital-management companies, the CSRC's regulatory control remains indirect through its provincial offices. In this way, central regulation for the securities markets emerges from a strong preference for Beijing's oversight and the CSRC-centered governing structure. However, the strong presence of local state ownership makes it soft.

ENERGY: OIL AND ELECTRIC POWER China's energy sector exemplifies how the governing structure functions as a reinforcing factor in making soft or hard regulation. The business of China's oil industry, which is monopolized by three large central SOEs, is directly supervised by several central authorities, including the NDRC, the SASAC, and the Ministry of Environment Protection under the long-held concept of absolute control due to concerns of national economic security. Indeed, the monopoly of central state ownership enhances the legitimacy of direct and tight central regulation for the oil sector, but the vertically and horizontally integrated governing structure also deserves to be noted. In governing the oil industry, the NDRC not only plans major projects but also has important regulatory authority to approve and oversee oil pricing and environmental protection; as a result, the local authorities implement the decisions made in Beijing.[10] In this way, such a centralized structure of governance enables the central authorities, such as planning or ownership agencies (NDRC or SASAC), to directly and strictly regulate the market and business of national oil corporations through formal rules and procedures.

On the other hand, the case of the electric power sector is notable in two aspects. First, the electric power sector shows that China's energy sector is not always under direct and strong central regulation as is often assumed; second, strategic significance and strong local state ownership do not necessarily lead to soft regulation as in the automobile industry. In terms of ownership, the governing structure, and concepts of control, the electric power sector is clearly different from the oil industry. Under the vision of marketization, the authority for regulatory reform in the electric power sector between 2006 and 2015 has been delegated mainly to provincial governments, allowing for project approval (e.g., wind energy).[11] Besides, there are large central SOEs in the sector, and their subsidiaries are present across the regions. There are also numerous provincial SOEs, so the dominant mode of ownership in China's electric power sector is local (precisely, provincial) state ownership.[12] Given that the local governments play important roles in intraprovince power generation, allocation, and investment,[13] the central regulation for the markets and business of electric power firms is inevitably limited. Furthermore, because its governing structure is fragmented not only vertically but also horizontally, the central authorities face difficulty in coordinating and enacting Beijing's policies because they suffer from exerting regulatory control over local state-owned electric power firms.[14] Unlike the securities market, where soft regulation is practiced through the CSRC despite strong local and private firms, central regulation for the electric power sector remains in question.

AIRLINE AND STEEL After several state efforts to restructure the market and to enhance the efficiency of the airline sector since 1980,[15] the big three central SOEs (Air China, China Southern, and China Eastern) emerged as the leading carriers after the early 2000s.[16] Still, the airline sector's overall market structure remains highly fragmented, with numerous local carriers because of local governments lobbying for the center. Under such circumstances, there was a breakthrough when the Civil Aviation Administration of China (CAAC) came to have considerable leverage over regulation, including pricing, investment approval, and overall planning for the sector. This allows the central government to directly oversee the market and the business of the big three carriers and strictly monitor the safety of carriers across localities.[17] Likewise, even though China's airline industry is featured as an SOE oligopoly, with the big three central SOEs,[18] tight central state regulation is not likely to occur without the concentrated regulatory authority of the CAAC.

Such a role of the governing structure in reinforcing a soft or hard form of regulation is also found in another strategic industry: steel. Although there are some large central state-owned steel companies, China's steel industry is dominated by a number of local SOEs. Such strong local state ownership has undoubtedly empowered local authorities to make their own policies and rules, as well as supervise their compliance of local steel SOEs.

Nevertheless, the central government maintains regulatory control over the steel sector by requiring local governments to make their plans and rules under the boundary of the national steel industry's policies. Just like the automobile sector, the 2005 steel industry policy and the 2009 steel rejuvenating plan (following the global financial crisis in 2008) show

how Beijing values its strategic importance to the national economy. The NDRC, which formulates both national (e.g., Made in China 2025) and industry-specific policies, regulates the steel market and business by using industry policies and rules regarding foreign investment restriction as a means of control. Above all, China's industrial steel policies are not simply guidelines the local authorities can bypass. Rather, they serve as the binding rules with which all steel producers must comply.[19] For example, according to Article 23 of the 2005 steel industry policy, foreign companies are not prohibited from having a controlling stake in Chinese steel producers.[20] Despite such powerful tools of regulation from Beijing, strong local state ownership and the resulting delegated authority across localities make the central regulation of the steel markets and business loose and indirect. Hence, *soft* regulation applies.

In short, a review of China's other strategic industries shows that although the level of ownership (central or provincial/municipal) is key to making central regulation soft or hard, the governing structure and ruling conceptions over ideal control are not simply derivatives of ownership, as they have some reinforcing effect on making each pattern. An examination of other strategic industries reveals how the central party-state oversees the business of leading sectors and how the kind of governance structure and concepts of control relate closely to the dominant mode of ownership.[21] For example, the vision of absolute control often comes down to the monopoly of central SOEs, which shapes the vertically integrated structure of governance. By the same token, strong local state ownership and the resulting delegated authority tend to limit Beijing's direct and strict exercise of regulation over fragmented markets and the business of large local SOEs.

## Beyond China: Regulation in Vietnam's Transitional Economy

This study compares China with Vietnam to see whether China's selective approach to reform and the varieties of state regulation are compatible with broader socialist practices found in other transitional economies. Vietnam and China are often treated as more alike than different in their formal institutional composition,[22] because Vietnam has adopted similar pathways of reform armed with the vision of a socialist market economy.[23] Since the 1980s, while marketization and state restructuring have been proceeding apace in China and Vietnam, "there is never a single compulsory course in the strict sense," as Janos Kornai noted.[24] In other words, these countries are not converging on the idealized model of regulation and even allow for customary national variations; China and Vietnam appear to build up their own regulatory regimes, which are distinct from other advanced industrial economies, to maintain the party-state's political control over key sectors.[25] As for China, Vietnam's ultimate goal is to create a socialist market economy through economic renovation and reform (*doi moi*).[26] This is in sharp contrast to establishing a liberal market economy, as advocated by leading international institutions, such as the Organisation for Economic Co-operation and Development, the World Bank, and the World Trade Organization.[27]

## SELECTIVE APPROACH TO MODERNIZING INDUSTRIES

Before *doi moi*, particularly during the 1950s, China's influence on Vietnam's path to socialism was stronger than the Soviet Union's influence on China. According to one study, "since 1950, Chinese advisers had come and provided brotherly guidance, not only for the army but also in the strategic concept of socialism and concrete policy, such as the agricultural tax."[28] Although there is some debate among Vietnamese intellectuals on the extent of China's influence, my field research in Hanoi confirms numerous signs that Vietnam benchmarked the reform experiences of China. Among these are China's vision of a socialist market economy and the gradualist and experimental approach to key public policies.[29] In this regard, Vietnam's pursuit of a socialist market economy was also mobilized by the desire to enhance the efficiency and productivity of the state ownership-centered economy, while maintaining macroeconomic stability.

Moreover, while Vietnam has attempted to combine state intervention (mainly in the form of state planning) and market-oriented incentives and rules,[30] its notion of a socialist market economy has induced a selective approach to regulating the scope and depth of reform. As in

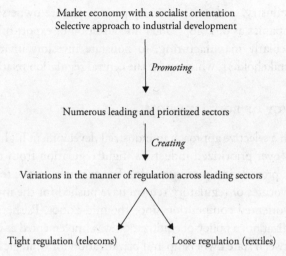

Market economy with a socialist orientation
Selective approach to industrial development

*Promoting*

Numerous leading and prioritized sectors

*Creating*

Variations in the manner of regulation across leading sectors

Tight regulation (telecoms)    Loose regulation (textiles)

FIGURE 5.1: How Does Vietnam Regulate Its Market Economy with Socialist Characteristics?

China, there are some highly prioritized industries, such as natural resources or networks, that remain state-owned.[31] Indeed, the Vietnamese leadership also strives to control the process of the reforms rather than embrace the market forces unilaterally across sectors.[32] Accordingly, while some highly prioritized sectors, including heavy industries (i.e., cement, steel) and natural-resource-based industries (i.e., crude oil, electricity) are under tight regulation through state ownership, other export-oriented sectors (i.e., textiles and garments) have been rapidly liberalized (fig. 5.1).[33]

Similar to China, such a selective approach to regulating the scope and means of the reform has led to creating variations in the manner of state regulation across sectors. For example, under the policy of *doi moi*, the agriculture sector, formerly the dominant sector of the Vietnamese economy,[34] has become privatized through gradual reform, including allowing farmers to go beyond the contract system and transfer land under certain circumstances.[35] In addition, according to Vietnam's fourth FYP (1996–2000), the development of light industries, including textiles, garments, and footwear, was also encouraged as newly selected priority sectors, mostly for export, a field in which Vietnam has a comparative advantage because of low labor costs. This early openness to private and foreign investors was the predominant view in Vietnam's textile and garment industry, and resulted in 83 percent private ownership out of 6,000 companies as of 2016.[36] Such liberalization of export-oriented sectors, particularly manufacturing, to nonstate investors invited diverse groups of stakeholders, which made the central regulation relatively loose.

## THE POLICY OF EQUITIZATION

While such a selective approach to industrial development highlights state ownership over prioritized industries, tight regulation from the central party-state prevails in those industries. For example, in the telecoms industry, advocates of regulatory reform have pushed for the introduction of market-oriented competition since the mid-2000s. Rather than full-scale privatization, a policy of equitization was implemented as an adapted reform between state ownership and privatization for strategically important prioritized sectors.[37] With the policy of equitization, the government maintains ownership as the largest stakeholder, enabling political influence over state firms, while nonstate actors as the newly emerging shareholders are expected to bring about efficiency and transparency in the business management of leading state firms.[38]

As China has adopted corporatization rather than privatization as the second-best institution to secure crucial state assets,[39] Vietnam has not immediately moved to privatization either; rather, it has adopted the policy of equitization[40] in reforming the state-owned enterprises of prioritized industries.[41] In this way, Hanoi has been better able to mobilize capital investments and enhance efficiency and transparency of equitized state firms by introducing shareholding enterprise systems without losing political influence over those leading sectors. In the telecoms sector, two large mobile firms, Vinaphone and Mobiphone, were equitized in 2006 and soon after, respectively.[42] However, the state's regulatory oversight of the firms was not shared with nonstate stakeholders.

Consequently, under the policy of equitization, Vietnam has been seeking to enhance the efficiency and productivity of SOEs, while serving the interests of those in power by keeping the state's significant ownership in equitized firms.[43] To avoid resistance from the group of vested interests, such political consideration is crucial. Compared with other export-oriented prioritized sectors (textiles or garments), the nature of state regulation is direct and tight; the varieties of state regulation are thus identified across Vietnam's strategic industries. Like China, efforts to build a market economy with socialist characteristics and the resulting selective approach are the underlying driving forces of Vietnam's economic innovation and reform. As Douglas North points out, such meta-institutions are important for understanding the process of economic change and governance, and Vietnam is not an exception.[44]

## LIMITED AUTHORITY OF SOCIALIST INSTITUTIONS

Despite Vietnam's similar socialist vision and institutional adaptation,[45] it differs from China in one important aspect: the fragile regulatory authority of Vietnam's planning agency and the Communist Party over the business of leading sectors. This is partly a result of Vietnam's relatively weak socialist underpinnings,[46] ideologically and institutionally, as the country remained divided until 1975. It was even said that "the socialist planned economic structure had never taken root in the south. In fact, objections to the central leadership's effort to extend socialism southward helped to stimulate the economic reform."[47] This is in contrast with China, where the government is ultimately subordinate to the CCP.[48] As discussed earlier, in China, various party organizations have played key roles in monitoring the government's compliance. These organizations include the premier, ministries, and regulatory agencies, as well as the state firms through the party groups (*dangzu*) or, more recently, the central inspection groups (*zhongyang xunshizu*). But this is hardly seen in Vietnam, at least not formally.[49]

Moreover, Vietnam lacks the corresponding party organizations that retain the authority to exert political influence over the government and state firms. For instance, a Vietnamese Communist Party (VCP) statute (Article 24) stipulates that "each government agency with three or more active party members must form a party chapter [*co so dang uy*]. If an agency has a large number of VCP members, it can subdivide its chapter into party cells."[50] Yet there are substantial differences between the party groups in China and a party chapter in Vietnam in terms of responsibilities and authorities. Whereas the primary responsibility of Vietnam's party chapter is educating and overseeing its own members, the party groups (*dangzu*) in China are responsible for helping the CCP oversee the compliance of government and state firms with the party's lines, principles, and policies. Indeed, those party groups inside state firms exercise political control over personnel and business management. This is also missing in Vietnam, where a party chapter or party cell is not structured inside a firm or holds the authority to supervise the business of a state firm. In other words, a party chapter in Vietnam fails to stipulate its authority over the organization in which it is housed.[51]

Another difference can be found in the power of the planning agency. During the transition from a planner to regulator as the market-oriented reform deepened in China, the state planning commission maintained the authority to regulate the economy by crafting FYPs (macro-level) and various industrial policies (micro-level) that specify strategic or pillar industries. As a result, China's planning agency regulates the overall markets, based on a concrete assessment of available resources and consolidated strategies. In Vietnam, however, the Ministry of Planning and Investment (MPI, formerly the State Planning Commission) does not have such authority to formulate long-term national socioeconomic development plans or industrial policies. The MPI's roles focus on undertaking the implementation of FYPs within the framework of Vietnam's Socio-Economic Development Strategy.[52] Moreover, the Ministry of Industry and Trade handles the implementation and supervision of industrial plans and strategies. Consequently, the MPI has little authority to make plans for regulation.[53] Perhaps this is why there are overlapping efforts and too many leading or prioritized industries in Vietnam.

## Regulation for a Socialist Market Economy

Influenced by countries with advanced and successful industrial economies under a democratic regime, the study of regulation often assumes a clear-cut line between government and business, in which an independent regulator ensures fair competition. Privatization is considered the most desirable avenue for breaking up a monopoly and promoting fair competition, ultimately toward a liberal market economy. As this book shows, the Chinese practices add another layer to the field of regulation in general in terms of the underlying norms and institutions that grew out of its own historical experiences. In this sense, we need a more inclusive definition of regulation to better explain how China actually regulates its economy, rather than narrowly confining such a definition to the authoritative rules of the ministerial agencies that monitor and enforce compliance.

To be sure, as Xi Jinping claimed in the Eighteenth and Nineteenth Party Congresses, China is seeking to establish a socialist market economy in which state planning, state ownership, and the CCP remain central and resilient in governing the market-oriented economy. In fact, the significance of national tradition and historical pathways has been raised in studies of regulation in advanced industrial economies. According to Steven Vogel, "governments have undertaken reforms that reinforce distinctive national trajectories based on different underlying ideas about the appropriate role of the state in the market and on structural features of the political economic context. Common pressures for reforms are mediated by national institutions. In other words, change is carried out along distinct and well-established (national) institutional paths."[54]

If we take an example from the United States, independent regulators had their origin in the US model of regulation, and it reflects the deeply rooted aspects of US political-economic society in which a laissez-faire state (the minimalist state in the market) is desirable and highly valued; the independence of a regulatory commission from both government and industry is always emphasized. This model of independent regulator has been diffused over the European continent, but its actual practices in Europe have been modified, even though the institutional form appears to be somewhat similar. For example, in Germany and France, "the tradition of state intervention and state sponsorship as well as support of cartels, often realized in the ministerial direction of major industries, means that both regions have faced problems of extricating bureaucratic and sectoral interests from the regulatory era."[55] Despite the importance of national traditions and domestic context, those advanced industrial countries largely share their ultimate goals of regulation: a liberal or coordinated market economy.

This is not the case in China, where market institutions are ultimately the party-state's tools to establish a socialist market economy. This reminds us of Charles Lindblom's classic study, which points to the possibility of separating the concept of markets from that of ownership, arguing that private ownership is not a prerequisite condition for the market system, and public ownership is thus not incompatible with the market economy.[56] In other words, there are alternatives to the market system, such as a socialist market economy where public and private, that is, mixed ownership, exists. Indeed, after numerous consultations and studies at the central level since the late 2000s, China has considered introducing mixed ownership to enhance the efficiency, productivity, and transparency of large state firms by injecting private capital into them. In this way, private firms can obtain more opportunities to collaborate with relatively stable, large-scale state firms, and the state can remain the largest shareholder. In addition, the continued emphasis on state ownership in key strategic industries indicates the enduring mechanism of bureaucratic coordination amid the advancing market forces in China.

Moreover, we used to categorize national types of regulation, such as the US model of an independent regulator, and the German or French models, which accept mixed economies and state intervention. In this book, my findings on the varieties of state regulation within China suggest going beyond such a static approach. China's inherent complexities resulting from its pursuit of a socialist market economy have created a tiered industrial structure accompanying distinct regulatory control across sectors and tiers. As chapter 2 elaborated, China's transition from a planned to a market economy has gradually proceeded in terms of depth and scope. To minimize the potential costs resulting from the market transition and maintain the party-state's leadership throughout marketization, the Chinese central leadership has envisioned a selective approach, creating a tiered industrial system where the ideal conception of control and property rights is distinctively applied.[57] In tandem with the tiered system of industrial economy, the varieties of state regulation have emerged in China.

Likewise, China's practices exhibit the limited mileage of the conventional approach that highlights an independent regulator and privatization as ideal institutions for promoting fair competition in the markets, serving the public good. What is more, Xi's leadership during his first five years made it clear China is not willing to follow such orthodox policies. The Nineteenth Party Congress in November 2017 confirms that Xi's China is striving to build its own socialist market economy for a new era. This leaves us important questions relating to how existing studies can embrace the political-economic realities of a socialist market economy and refine the theory of regulation in general.

## Future of China's Economic Governance

Scholarly consensus has not yet been reached with respect to the future trajectory of China's pathways and outcomes. The extensive web of different arguments and projections indicates considerable difficulty in accounting for China's dynamic experiences and complex realities. That is, depending on the focus of the subject, including location and time period, we may reach somewhat contrasting conclusions. Among these contrasting arguments, some optimistic views suggest that Chinese governance will ultimately be integrated into the liberal market order.[58] Therefore, China's ascent will not be a threat to the West because China will play the West's game, not its own. According to Edward Steinfeld, for example, despite its unique pathways and physical realities, China is likely to follow the trajectories of the West and other developed East Asian countries, such as Japan, South Korea, and Taiwan, through a process of institutional outsourcing. According to this logic, as China has become deeply integrated into global political-economic systems since the 1990s (particularly after its World Trade Organization membership), it is inevitable it would make its domestic institutions compatible with globally accepted rules and institutions. Indeed, China has attempted to modernize its industrial structure and governance of national champion companies through institutional reform, such as promoting corporate governance.[59] Consequently, the country's deep integration into global production and the world market has gradually but irreversibly helped it learn how to play the West's games, even though some peculiar features remain resilient.

Nevertheless, what is missed here is that China's outsourced institutions have been consistently contextualized to accommodate the vested interests in power while embracing market-oriented rules and institutions. In other words, China has been proactive in learning and benchmarking institutions from advanced industrialized countries, but such outsourced institutions from overseas firms and countries appear similar only in form;

their actual practices have been substantially modified and adapted to accommodate China's socialist political-economic realities, including the state planning and ownership agencies as well as the CCP. Politicized corporate governance under the power of party organs, or a resilient NDRC would be good examples illustrating the limited merit of the institutional outsourcing perspective.[60]

Recent trade conflicts between the United States and China have also evidenced China's significant integration into international institutions (particularly the World Trade Organization), and rule-based norms have hardly led to the liberal market system advanced market economies advocate; rather, the world is likely to evolve with two systems: a liberal market economy and a socialist market economy. In fact, the deep underlying source of trade conflict is not a trade deficit but China's assertive industrial policy, such as Made in China 2025. The US leadership perceives that such state-backed policies in China and government subsidies to promote advanced technologies pose a threat to the United States' predominance over China.[61] This is why issues such as forced technology transfer, poor protection of intellectual property rights, and massive state subsidies are central to the issue of trade conflicts.

Since China's membership in the World Trade Organization in 2001, the country has taken advantage of free trade and access to global markets, while restricting foreign companies from accessing its own markets. This is particularly remarkable in the field of high technology, where the trio of Baidu, Alibaba, and Tencent was able to successfully win over such global competitors as Google, PayPal, and Amazon, which are either blocked or have restricted access to the Chinese market. There is increasing pressure for strategic industries, including new energy and electric vehicles, artificial intelligence, and information technology, to share key technology and produce goods through joint ventures with Chinese partners. The United States and a number of European countries point to China's such "unfair" play, which they say is no longer tolerable. Therefore, it is fair to argue that China's deep integration into the liberal international order and institutions has failed to make the country play according to the West's rules. Rather, China is acting according to its own rules, a trend that has become particularly noticeable since Xi assumed leadership.

In this regard, a trade war between the United States and China is likely to be just the beginning of competition and tension, in that the ultimate systems the two great powers advocate are inherently different (a liberal market economy versus a socialist market economy). Above all, large state-owned firms, including financial institutions, and various organizations of the CCP in business, which are central to successfully running a socialist market economy, are the root of political-economic institutions for the People's Republic to maintain power and legitimacy. Hence, although China can reach a temporary compromise with the United States in terms of more market-oriented rules and institutions and further liberalization of the financial and service sectors, this compromise will be short-lived as the interests of China's socialist market economy far outweigh the dictates of a liberal market economy.

Indeed, there was already an argument that Chinese capitalism became far more statist over the 1990s by shifting from rural-based entrepreneurial capitalism during the 1980s.[62] Although China's global integration and the corresponding institutional reforms have accelerated since the 1990s, Huang Yasheng pays more attention to domestic dynamics, such as the changing leadership since the Tiananmen Square crackdown, the downfall of rural-based leadership (i.e., Zhao Zhiyang or Wan Li), and the rise of the mostly urban-based leadership (i.e., Jiang Zemin or Zhu Rongji).[63] Moreover, Shanghai, from which both Jiang and Zhu originated, reflects a history of heavy-handed interventionism by the state, an urban bias, and a biased liberalization in favor of foreign direct investment over indigenous small-scale private firms.[64] Given this leadership orientation and shifting focus of development, Huang argues that "in the 1990s, though not reverting back to central planning, China began to adopt policies and practices that favored the more state-controlled urban areas. During this period, China made notable progress in reducing the ideological stigma associated with the private sector."[65] In this sense, the current Chinese economy is a commanding-heights economy in which state-led capital exerts more influence on the economy than do market forces.[66] However, as I have elaborated in this book, either state-led capitalism or the market-driven economies all remain partial in accounting for China's layered and complex realities of political economy. By disaggregating the markets as institutions, therefore, this book suggests that commanding-heights economies and market-oriented economies coexist across industrial tiers, because the dominant mode of state ownership (the level of ownership) together with the underlying governing structure and concepts of control are largely different across the tiers, which are combined distinctively. Because there are variations in the manner of state regulation, neither state-led capitalism nor market-driven economy suffers from offering an overall account of China's inherent complexities.

The question, then, is how the Chinese party-state will make the best use of the market forces and mechanisms to establish a socialist market economy in which state actors are also market actors. My arguments for the varieties of state regulation, the CCP's continued political monitoring of the business of key sectors, and the resilient state planning for regulation provide much insight for incoming Chinese paths and prospects. Particularly, the primacy of state ownership and regulatory control of strategically important enterprises is an issue that looms large in the near future. To be sure, at the Eighteenth Third Plenum of the Party Congress as of 2013, although General Party Secretary Xi declared the importance of the market's decisive roles in the distribution of resources as well as the introduction of mixed ownership to reform the state sector, the central status of state ownership and the accompanying party's political control over China's key state firms were hardly altered.[67] For example, "the central government via the SASAC retains ownership of large state enterprise groups that dominate key sectors, including the heart of the national economy (*jingji mingmai*) and pillar sectors,[68] making significant profits. When large local state firms are included, almost 70 percent of China's top 500 enterprises were state-owned in 2007 and still remain around 60 percent as of 2015."[69]

Moreover, "when SOEs go public, the state typically retains a majority holding so that they in some ways appear to be market actors while still also being part of the state sector."[70] In the case of central SOEs, which include the largest and most profitable state firms, the central government (specifically SASAC), as the largest shareholder, owns more than 70 percent of the stakes of fourteen central SOEs; in 2014 the state held more than 50 percent of the shares of sixty-three central SOEs (table 5.3). This is why the type of state firm is probably more important than the declining gross industrial output or number of SOEs, as Nicholas Lardy argued.[71]

Table 5.3
Chinese State as the Largest Shareholder of Central State Firms, 2014

| Stake share | Above 70% | 50–69% | Below 49% | N/A |
|---|---|---|---|---|
| Number of firms | 14 | 49 | 34 | 16 |

*Sources*: *Guowuyuan guoyou zichan jiandu guanli weiyuanhui* (国务院国有资产监督管理委员会) http://www.sasac.gov.cn/; refer to Appendix 2 for other sources.

Another implication this book points to is the CCP's empowerment in shaping the Chinese practices of market regulation. In recent times, the advancing CCP under Xi's leadership has confirmed this book's findings and China's future prospects.[72] The party's political supervision over the business of strategic industries is particularly intense through formal or informal channels. As this book clearly shows, central inspection groups, the finance and economy LSG, and the informatization LSG serve as China's distinct measures of regulatory control. In one meeting with top executives of the country's largest companies in 2016, Xi made it clear that "the Chinese Communist Party has the ultimate say over state companies . . . the party's leadership in SOEs is a major *political* principle, and that principle must be insisted on."[73]

In so doing, Xi established the Central LSG for Comprehensively Deepening Reform (Zhongyang Quanmian Shenhua Gaige Lingdao Xiaozu, 中央全面深化改革领导小组)[74] to coherently and consistently facilitate the overall plans, coordination, and implementation of the reforms. This LSG, headed directly by Xi, acts as a superior political body for bureaucratic coordination, reflecting the central party-state's visions, concerns, and anxieties about the depth and scope of future reform.[75] In this regard, the manner and scope of the CCP's regulatory control over major business are likely to become crucial in understanding Chinese-style regulation. In effect, the reform of the economic system is the main task for the Central LSG for Comprehensively Deepening Reform, and its key function lies in ensuring desirable government–market relations.[76] Therefore, the Chinese party-state is likely to step up its deepening of economic reforms without relinquishing the leadership of state ownership and the CCP in regulating the commanding heights. The markets' decisive roles are likely to be limited to nonstrategic sectors, as this book suggests; the emphasis on private capital, including foreign capital or market forces, hardly implies the arrival of a market-driven economic system. Instead, the growth and successful business of private firms in China is not likely to bring about the retreat of state firms and the CCP's political oversight of them, given that the party's proactive supervision in business, particularly foreign firms, is even accelerating under Xi's leadership.

# APPENDIX I

## Research Methods

The major source of data for this study of the Chinese state's regulation of the business of China's automobile and telecommunications sectors is extensive interview data from central and local officials, firms, scholars, journalists, and consultants over an eight-year period (August 2005–July 2006, April–May 2008, April and August 2011, May and July 2012). In each sector, interviews were conducted with general and senior managers of firms, including foreign joint ventures, as well as officials and scholars who were involved in policy making or consultation. By returning to the field in 2008, 2011, and 2012, I confirmed the data collected in my initial interviews. When important policy changes or new points were raised by interviewees, new information was used to test or reconfirm earlier findings. As a foreign researcher, I experienced some difficulty getting access to senior managers of firms in the telecommunications sector (compared with the auto sector) due to security reasons. Often, interviewees declined to comment on the questions I asked. In such cases I had to rely on accounts from Chinese journalists who reported on the business management of telecommunications firms and their relations with the authorities.

Although the structure of interviews was open-ended, I tried to keep the conversation within the boundaries of my key concerns by raising relevant questions. Prior to interviews with government officials and some renowned scholars, I prepared by reading their articles or interviews with Chinese newspapers and journals. I began with general background questions on the sector, government policies, growth strategy, and so on. Drawing on some secondary resources, I gave interviewees an idea of my understanding and waited for their responses. This was an effective way of inducing them to elaborate on ambiguous and complex decision-making processes and their implementation.

In searching for the central government's political and economic influence on local and private automobile firms, my questions focused on identifying the tools of control and the mechanisms each central government employed. For example, (senior) managers in the central automobile state-owned enterprise, the First Auto Works (FAW), were asked about preferential policies from the central and local government to promote large auto business groups, relationships with both central and local governments, relationships with foreign joint venture partners, and the roles and significance of automobile industrial policies in doing business. In asking questions about the existence of political control from the Chinese Communist Party over the business, I was very cautious and waited until interviewees became relaxed and appeared to be willing to talk with me.

For the automobile industry, the most important and interesting interviews came from conversations with local entrepreneurs. Their responses contrasted sharply with officials and scholars in Beijing. In particular, regarding the role and influence of the central party-state on the local auto business, scholars and officials in Beijing emphasized that the center offered only a macro policy direction, whereas information from managers in local firms enabled me to better understand the mechanism of central regulation in China's local auto industry. I asked general and senior managers in private automobile companies about market competition with leading state firms, the effects of automobile industrial policy on a firm's business development, the existence of preferential policies from local governments, and the future plans of private automobile firms. From interviews with entrepreneurs from different firms, I learned how automobile industrial policies and regulations actually work at the enterprise level. As the interviews proceeded, I accumulated different viewpoints across institutions (both academic and business) and localities, which provided valuable comparative insights as well as more sources for future interviews. In addition, interviews with a senior partner of a consulting firm were particularly fruitful, in that the interviewee had rich experiences with Chinese automobile firms, including their joint venture partners. He introduced me to a number of Chinese managers with whom he had worked as a partner in the past. This became an invaluable asset for expanding my network in the field.

I was fortunate to be able to obtain interviews with both Chinese and foreign managers. My interviewees included representatives from the China FAW Group Corporation, FAW-Volkswagen, and China Auto Industry Research in Changchun; Shanghai Automotive Industry Corporation (SAIC) Group, SAIC-General Moters, SAIC-Volkswagen, Chery Enterprise Shanghai Office, Geely Auto International Corporation, *Shanghai Automotive News*, Shanghai Academy of Social Sciences, and A.T. Kearney (auto consulting firm) in Shanghai; Geely Automobile Enterprise Group in Hangzhou and Taizhou; and Guangzhou-Honda in Guangzhou. I also spoke to representatives of Beijing-Hyundai Automobile Enterprise, Daimler-Chrysler Auto Enterprise, and *China Automobile News* in Beijing. Valuable information and insights concerning China's automotive industry policies and regulation were collected from interviews with government officials working in the Department of Industry and Economy of the National Development and Reform Commission (NDRC).

Although interviews were my major source of data collection, I also attended annual automobile conferences and forums in Shenyang (November 2005) and Beijing (April 2006). These participatory events were good opportunities to observe how government officials and firm managers communicate with each other and whether ideas from business are considered in government policy. Even though most firms in the automobile sector are state owned, I observed that through these conferences, government and business have the opportunity to explain how certain policies are adopted. I also heard responses from automobile firms. Most important, these events provided an excellent network for future interviews, which is the most difficult but critical part of field research in China.

For the telecommunications industry, my interviews focused on understanding the regulatory relationships among the Ministry of Information Industry (MII) (later the Ministry of Industry and Information Technology), the NDRC, and the State-Owned Assets Supervision and Administration Commission (SASAC), as well as the tools of control over telecommunication firms. Since all telecom service firms are central state-owned, interviews were conducted largely in Beijing, where the headquarters of these firms are located. There I paid more attention to relationships between the MII and its local bureau. Managers among the telecom operators were asked about the regulatory power of the MII over the telecom markets and business, tools for managing competition, and the existence of political pressure from the Communist Party or other authorities in doing business. I asked officials and scholars about the definition and goals of regulation (*jianguan*) in mainland China; the division of regulatory authorities among the MII, the NDRC, and the SASAC; the causes of weak local telecom regulation; any tools of control from the Communist Party; and how and who holds the leading regulatory authority to manage competition in the telecommunications markets.

Because of limits imposed on foreign researchers to access telecom service firms, I relied on interviews with Chinese officials and scholars working in government research institutions or universities. In addition to telecom firms such as China Unicom, China Mobile, and Putian Telecoms, research institutions and universities I drew responses from included the Development Research Center of the State Council (specifically, the Department of Enterprise Research), the Chinese Academy of Social Sciences (CASS) Research Center for Regulation and Competition, the CASS Center for Informatization Study, the CASS Institute of Industry and Economy, the CASS Institute of Law, MII China Academy of Telecoms Research, and Beijing University of Posts and Telecommunications.

In total, I conducted 103 interviews in China across seven cities. Each interview ranged from one and a half to two hours in length. The breakdown was: automobile sector, fifty-seven interviews, eighteen firms; telecommunications sector, thirty-three interviews, three firms, and five research institutions; state–business relations in general, twelve interviews, six research institutions and universities. I coded the interviews to ensure confidentiality. The first letter in the interview number indicates the sector (A for automobile, T for telecommuncations) and then the location (B for Beijing, C for Changchun, G for Guangzhou, H for Hangzhou, SH for Shanghai, and SY for Shenyang). The date of the interview follows. To supplement data from the interviews, I referred to information from statistical yearbooks, government internal reports, newspaper reports, and scholarly journals. As the Chinese automobile and telecommunications markets have become central in global competition, various reports and data from media and research institutions have become available. I used those published sources whenever necessary and available.

# APPENDIX 2

## Limits of Previous Studies on Regulation

### VIEW FROM MAINLAND CHINA

Since the early 1990s, the subject of regulation (*jianguan*, 监管) has become popular among Chinese scholars and officials as a consequence of the internal economic reform and the external influence of the global move toward regulatory reform. However, the main concern in mainland China was to highlight how the notion and practices of Chinese regulation are distinct from those of advanced market economies, even though China has arguably benchmarked its institutions and policies, as detailed earlier. When "regulation" refers to an important way a government rules an economy,[1] "Chinese regulation" implies the modified goals and manners of coordination (*xietiao*, 协调) in governing the economy, not entirely replacing its bureaucratic coordination with market forces.[2] Hence, the party-state remains central in the market, but the primacy of regulatory mechanisms has shifted to market coordination. This conceptual clarification is important in that it also affects the ensuing institutional backdrop and responsibilities of regulatory agencies. Particularly, as regulatory agencies are in charge of both policy making and supervision, the authorities often overlap, which ultimately limits the independent work of regulators.[3] Nevertheless, overall views in mainland China largely tend to be divided into two groups. Those who give more credit to the effects of the institutionalization of regulation suggest that the separation of government from business has been enhanced, thanks to the rise of regulatory agencies and the emphasis on their independent oversight.[4] Others note deficiencies in the legal and administrative systems[5] and their exercises that accompany principles of accountability and transparency in markets.[6] Some pay more attention to obstacles to the practice of regulation when the reforms result in redistributing vested interests of large state-owned enterprises and leading state agencies. Particularly, political meddling from the party and ongoing sticky state–business relations were expected to ultimately constrain the independent functions of the regulators.[7]

## THE LIMITS OF THE NEOLIBERAL APPROACH

Heavily influenced and developed by the experiences of the advanced liberal economies (especially the United States and the United Kingdom), the neoliberal approach to (economic) regulation considers a government's primary task to be fostering successful markets. This requires creating accompanying institutions, such as property rights, laws, rules of exchange, and, most important, independent regulators from industry and political organs (such as the executive or legislature).[8] Independent regulators are responsible mainly for creating a level playing field among incumbents and new entrants to promote fair competition. Normatively, this neoliberal approach presents a clear preference for a low degree of state intervention in markets, aiming to evenly enforce fair rules of competition and protect consumers' interests through price regulation. In other words, like sports referees, the regulators focus on promoting fair competition among market players, rather than promoting specific players and sectors.[9] In so doing, the antitrust law is underscored and considered as a core policy component against incumbents' monopolistic behavior and a measure of consumer protection against hazards and fraud. Likewise, states that favor this neoliberal type of regulation attempt to achieve such goals not by state intervention but by independent regulators and legal rules.

During the 1980s, the United Kingdom and the United States were prime examples of the neoliberal approach to regulatory reform. Regulatory policies were designed to actively promote competition, sometimes favoring new entrants over incumbents, and to be relatively blind to what particular firms entered the market and in what numbers.[10] In this process,

institutional formality and hierarchy in the governing system were enhanced throughout the reforms;[11] furthermore, a substantial increase in
bureaucratic resources ensured compliance with the rules.[12] Accordingly,
the neoliberal approach to regulation often tends to be simplified as a
state retreat from the markets because of its strong emphasis on privatization and liberalization as tools to promote a deregulated, freer market.
However, as the United Kingdom's typical neoliberal approach shows, the
rise of multilayered regulatory institutions and the increasing formaliza-
tion of codes of behavior resulting from regulatory reforms testify to
how regulatory policies for freer markets paradoxically require more
rules.[13] What we have learned from the experiences of the neoliberal type
of regulation is that the state constructs and enforces market rules.

As noted, with the global wave of regulatory reform, the idea of the
regulatory state has become an increasingly popular subject of debate
among scholars of the Chinese political economy.[14] Internally and externally, there have been enough reasons to examine the neoliberal type of
regulation in the context of China. Internally over the 1990s, market-
oriented institutional reforms have led to a number of regulatory agencies across infrastructure and financial sectors and the modernization of
corporate governance.[15] Moreover, the 1998 streamlining of bureaucracy,
an initiative that abolished industrial ministries, was often considered a
major step in departing from a planned economy toward a market-oriented
one.[16] This was partly because such rationalization of bureaucracy that
abolished a range of industrial ministries from the planned economy is
likely to reshape the state–business nexus by divesting the sticky ties of
the past between government and state-owned firms across industrial sectors.[17] Some have even boldly argued that "China has made real progress
toward making the Chinese state into a regulatory state suited to a func-
tioning market economy."[18]

In debating the rise of the regulatory state in China, scholars in this
group have referred to the closing of a number of industrial ministries
and economic bureaus through the reforms of 1998 and 2003 and the formation of the regulators responsible for encouraging and monitoring fair
competition in the market. In this manner, the institutional design of
regulators and a normative emphasis on competition and transparency
in the markets were regarded as important steps toward a market-oriented
but socialist market economy. Other major indicators—the introduction

of public hearings over utility prices, competitive bidding for public projects, and the auction of land or mineral resources—although sometimes limited, were notable subjects of discussion. Such changes were expected to give rise to a buyer's market as a new mechanism for governing the markets and contributing to a more transparent business environment.[19] In this way, some scholars have argued, the sticky ties between government and state enterprises decreased, eventually leading to the separation of government from firms (*zhengqi fenkai*, 政企分开 703).[20]

Paradoxically, effective market regulation is perceived to mandate a more active state in markets. To some extent, this offers justification for more hierarchy among the bureaucratic authorities, including the reorganization of the National Development and Reform Commission as a macro-economic supra-regulator, and the rise of the State-Owned Assets Supervision and Administration Commission since the early 2000s.[21] Externally, the global move of regulatory reforms and its impact on Chinese officials and intellectuals has certainly influenced the design of administrative restructuring and state enterprise reforms.[22] Moreover, China's commitment to open domestic markets and enhanced transparency with its membership in the World Trade Organization (WTO) have encouraged Chinese practitioners to search for a middle ground that promotes market liberalization under the party-state's close supervision.

Nevertheless, this conventional window reveals undeniable limits in accounting for China's complex system of regulation in that it fails to integrate resilient socialist political-economic institutions, such as state planning and the deeply embedded party organizations, into the model. How those institutions affect the creation of a market for competition and constrain the independent function of regulators would determine their validity in explaining the systems of Chinese regulation. Some early studies point to those inherent constraints of the model. For example, Margaret Pearson notes that even though China's central leadership has rationalized its administrative structure, established regulatory bodies, and separated government from business, these institutional reforms have yet to lead to a remolding of the Chinese party-state into a globally advised regulatory governance system. Drawing on six case studies of infrastructure and financial service industries, Pearson contends that the independent functions of regulatory institutions are constrained by continued state ownership, the power of comprehensive state commissions, and party organs. Normatively, market-oriented competition is encouraged, but the state carefully orchestrates the playing field and number of players, favoring a "small number of dominant, state-chosen and state-owned players to protect the party-state's considerable financial and social interests in these key assets."[23] Hence, "managed competition" sets in, as seen in the commanding heights' sectors.[24]

In studying the system of Chinese regulation, China's political realities, such as the Chinese Communist Party's (CCP) invisible but powerful role in government and state firms, should not be dismissed. Yet studies that use the neoliberal approach remain flawed by being largely muted on how the CCP actually exercises its political supervision over the regulators and the regulated, as well as how party organizations coordinate with newly emerging regulators when the reform challenges their vested prerogatives. Those questions remain unanswered. Some argue that the party's mobilizing capacity is declining because of its ideological downfall and rampant cadre corruption;[25] it is fair to say that the CCP still dominates and engineers the leadership of government and state enterprises by controlling the personnel. Based on a factional framework, Victor Shih's exhaustive study on China's financial system and inflation control presents compelling accounts on how the CCP has remained central in regulating inflation and monetary policies over the reform era.[26] Particularly, since the beginning of Xi Jinping's leadership, the remarkable advance of various party organizations sufficiently endorses such an observation. In this regard, the key question should be: what forms of regulation are emerging, particularly in strategic industries where vested political and economic interests are heavily focused, and how are they distinct from the orthodox model of regulation?

## THE LIMITS OF THE STATIST APPROACH

The statist approach to economic regulation contrasts sharply with the neoliberal one, normatively and institutionally. Normatively, statist regulation places the roles of the state at the core, so that competition in markets is carefully orchestrated and managed to promote a limited number of firms in strategic industries, rather than prioritizing consumers' interests and welfare.[27] Under this logic, countries that seek statist regulation allow for substantial government intervention in designing markets, managing competition, and steering specific sectors. In doing so, the government often supports particular companies with a range of preferential policies, such as industrial policies and state subsidies. Such policies are favored for enhancing the international competitiveness of those selected actors and making them national champions.[28] Consequently, the statist approach tends to discourage excess competition, which may lead to lowered profits of selected candidates for the national champions. Compared with the neoliberal approach, regulatory institutions in the statist approach tend to be highly centralized (less fragmented at the top); it is particularly notable that "cross-functional comprehensive agencies play a powerful role in designing the rules of markets and policies."[29] Because the ministries act as regulators, ministerial discretion becomes predominant. Moreover, a historically strong bureaucracy and close ties between government and industry also tend to hinder the independent function of regulators. Being relatively free from political checks from the legislature, regulators in the statist approach are apt to be less accountable to public interests and more concerned with expanding their own authority.[30]

For example, the Japanese experience shows how historically strong, formerly comprehensive ministries resisted the transfer of their authority over industries to newly set-up regulators.[31] As a result, regulatory reform in Japan during the 1980s was often leveraged by ministries trying to expand their authority by governing approval for market entry. Besides providing subsidies, the Japanese state carefully orchestrated the structure of the market to limit overheated competition and sought to foster national champions. For China, the resilient or even more empowered comprehensive state commissions, industrial policies, and the desire to make national champions echo core elements of this statist approach to regulatory reform and regulation.[32] By studying China's behavior in the WTO, Roselyn Hsueh has analyzed how the central government has exercised its regulation over foreign direct investment and the liberalization process across sectors to meet dual goals: complying with WTO commitments and maintaining control over key strategic sectors.[33] To this end, Hsueh argues that China uses a bifurcated strategy that centralizes its regulation over strategic sectors while decentralizing decision making to local authorities and encouraging private investment for less strategic sectors.[34] Despite this notable analysis, Hsueh's study remains largely silent on the political roles and influence from various party organizations in the central government and industry.

In this regard, when we think of the subject of regulation in Chinese political economy, it is important to note why and how China's experience deviates from the statist approach, despite its strong state hand. Particularly, because the statist approach to regulation is grounded largely on advanced liberal-market economies (such as Japan or France), it is devoid of socialist political-economic institutions, such as a planning bureaucracy or the Communist Party. As a result, the statist approach, just like the neoliberal one, fails to properly explain how those resilient socialist institutions have complicated and even reproduced statist efforts in establishing regulatory institutions for a market-oriented economy. For example, Tsai and Cook point out that Chinese regulation has been sought as an endogenous institutional replacement without system failure to minimize the potential costs of the privileged cadres and their opposition.[35] Although the conventional statist approach has focused on aspects of the state's capacity in policy making and implementation as the unitary actor, China's political system and its sheer size offer somewhat inherently different initial conditions that actually discourage the central government from carrying out policies and enforcing the rules coherently and unilaterally.

On the other hand, although not dismissing the enduring impacts of Leninist institutions on policy making and implementation, Gregory Chin notes that "in the regulation of China's strategic industries, especially those with large-scale foreign invested projects, the roles of the party and the state bureaucracy continue to be tightly interlinked."[36] Indeed, its emphasis on the Leninist institution, particularly the State Planning Commission and its relational ties with the CCP, certainly benefit students of political economy beyond China. But China's study still seems to falter in providing the overall mechanism of the party's market regulation, in that the CCP often exerts its commanding power through informal institutions and channels as well as formal ones. In a similar vein, another recent analysis on two strategic industries (telecommunications and aviation) from Sarah Eaton aptly points to the advance of the state, highlighting the ideational origin behind the market reform rather than institutions or interests to explain why different initial points and procedures of reform in the telecoms and aviation sectors could end up with similar results in a market structure dominated by central state-owned enterprises.[37] The key issue is not the advance of the state per se but how the advance of the state unfolds differently in terms of scope and the manner of control across industrial sectors and tiers, which generate variation in the patterns of the advanced state in regulating markets.

Others hold that China's decentralized system of authority is likely to produce increased rent-seeking and predation.[38] According to this logic, the party-state's capacity to mobilize and monitor agents has declined substantially. The rampant corruption of local cadres evidences the issue of governance deficit. Some even hold that the Chinese state has been turned into a decentralized predatory state,[39] a view that emphasizes the dark side of statist economic regulation. For example, Minxin Pei argues that China's gradual reform strategies, which aim to secure the party-state's political control confronting institutional and legal reforms, have provided the ruling elites with the leeway to co-opt emerging business elites. This, in fact, enables party officials to protect their political prerogatives. Pei argues that the East Asian development state is exceptional in that the "helping hand" does not turn into predatory practices, while the Chinese state has always had much potential to become a "grabbing hand" for rent-seeking opportunists because of decentralized political authority and property rights.[40]

The view of a decentralized predatory state tends to overstate the effects of the decentralization policy in the following respects. First, in theory, even though there is a high correlation between decentralized property rights and rampant predation, local agents do not always have the incentives to strip assets. This is because the loss of state assets will critically affect the future tenure of local officials. Top executives of major local state firms are appointed directly by the central state in coordination with party organizations. Hence, the decentralization of property rights in China does not necessarily result in decentralized predation. Second, administrative decentralization is certainly inclined to weaken the central party-state's capacity to enforce policies and rules from the center and monitor local cadres and their compliance. Instead, the center strengthens the macro-level regulatory control of "strategically important issues."[41] As Christopher Hood and colleagues note, "the lessening of regulation at one level may be accompanied by re-regulation at another."[42] Given that most important business projects in China still require central approval, decisive authority continues to be in the hands of the central party-state, even though much decision-making authority has been delegated to local officials.

Such dichotomous approaches that stress the predominance of either the role of the state or market forces are flawed in explaining China's multifaceted political economies. This is partly because of the murky boundaries between state and market, which have developed out of more than four decades of economic reform, and the fact that resilient socialist legacies, such as the planning agency, party organizations, and state firms, have contributed to them. Why are there murky boundaries between state and market in China, accompanying lingering socialist political-economic institutions? How has such a macro-backdrop given rise to variation in the method of state regulation, even among strategic industrial sectors?

As was elaborated in chapter 2, this book first attempted to present how China's vision of establishing a socialist market economy since Deng has accelerated its tiered industrial structure by distinguishing the depth of marketization across sectors, accompanying the planning agency and party organizations, including leading small groups or the party committee to ensure political checks.[43] In other words, China's pursuit of creating a socialist market economy provided an ideological background and justification to maintain state planning, public ownership, and the CCP amid the market-oriented reform. But as elaborated in chapter 2, it has been a strategically selective challenge as to where and to what extent such socialist institutions should run the economy, giving rise to the tiered industrial structure and varied patterns of regulating these institutions. For example, the party committees (*dangweihui*, 党委会) inside state firms often exert an invisible but powerful effect on making decisions relating to personnel and monitoring business management under the direct leadership of the central party leadership.

Yet political economy scholars of regulation, which is based largely on the experiences of liberal market societies, have failed to incorporate or dismiss those crucial political-economic realities into the models; this is why conventional approaches have struggled to analyze how the practices of Chinese regulation deviate from others. Indeed, as noted earlier, some recent studies on Chinese political economy have found that rising market forces and liberalization efforts have invited close regulatory control from the central party-state for strategic industries.[44] Adding to those findings, this book emphasizes that there are many complexities and variations in the manner of central state control, even over strategic industries. Furthermore, I argue that China's tiered industrial structure, which has grown out of the planned economy, should be a subject of serious consideration. Informal institutions prevail in Chinese politics, economy, and society, and the CCP still runs them for political oversight. Hence, to better understand and explain China's regulation practices, one needs to approach them from the inside out, rather than the outside in, because China has been and will be persistently pursuing its own way.

In that sense, how the CCP uses its levers of political control over the regulators and the regulated should be taken seriously.[45] Another study suggested that the CCP's control and the roles of party organs in regulatory agencies are perhaps the least understood elements of China's political economy.[46] Focusing on the finance industry, for example, Sebastian Heilmann analyzed how party organs actually have an effect on economic regulation in China. According to his findings, the centralization of financial market regulation and supervision in the late 1990s could have been achieved through the party's personnel authority and political supervision.[47] The creation of the Central Financial Work Commission enabled the party leadership to effectively centralize financial regulation and closely supervise the performance of senior executives in financial firms and state financial regulatory bodies. Rather than passively accepting its declining monitoring capacity, the CCP has actively confronted the changing environment, trying to maintain its power over personnel and supervision, which remains the most powerful lever of political control over the business of state firms.

# APPENDIX 3

## *Interview Lists*

### *General*

1. Institute of Political Science, CASS, no. G1, April 28, 2008
2. School of Government, Beijing University, no. G2, April 29, 2008
3. CASS, no. G3, May 8, 2008
4. Renmin University, no. G4, May 8, 2008
5. NDRC, no. G5, May 9/12, 2008
6. Chinese Public Administration Society, no. G6, May 5, 2008
7. Chinese Public Administration Society, no. G7, May 1, 2008
8. DRC, no. G8, August 9, 2011
9. Center for Chinese Economics, Beijing University, no. G9, July 20, 2012
10. CASS, no. G10, July 19, 2012
11. SCMP, no. G11, July 19, 2012
12. DRC, no. G12, May 4, 2012

## Automobile

BEIJING

1. Institute of Industrial Economics, CASS, Beijing, FDI, manufacturing industry, no. A(B) 1, August 31, 2005

2. Institute of Industrial Economics, CASS, Beijing, automobile industry, no. A(B) 2, September 6, 2005

3. Institute of Industrial Economics, CASS, Beijing, retail industry and finance, no. A(B) 3, September 27, 2005

4. Institute of Industrial Economics, CASS, no. A(B) 4, November 1, 2005

5. Beijing Automobile Investment Co., Ltd., no. A(B) 5, November 10, 2005

6. DRC, Industrial Economics Research Department, I, no. A(B) 6, November 17, 2005

7. Hyundai Qiche Touzi Youxian Gongsi, no. A(B) 7, November 18, 2005

8. Hyundai Qiche Touzi Youxian Gongsi, no. A(B) 8, November 18, 2005

9. Beijing Auto Investment Co., Ltd, no. A(B) 9, November 22, 2005

10. *Beijing Qing Nian Bao* (Beijing Youth Daily), no. A(B) 10, November 30, 2005

11. DRC, Industrial Economics Research Department, no. A(B) 11, January 6, 2006

12. DRC, Technical Economics Department, no. A(B) 12, February 15, 2006

13. Industrial Economics Research Department, no. A(B) 13, February 15, 2006 (II)

14. Beijing Auto Investment Corporation, no. A(B) 14, February 17, 2006, II

15. CASS, no. B(A) 15, February 21, 2006

16. CASS, no. B(A) 16, February 21, 2006

17. Beijing Auto Investment Corporation, no. A(B) 17, February 22, 2006

18. Daimler-Chrysler (China) Ltd., no. A(B) 18, February 23, 2006

19. Reporter (China), *Automotive News*, no. A(B) 19, February 25, 2006

20. DRC, no. A(B) 20, March 24, 2006

21. Reporter, *China Automotive News*, no. A(B) 21, April 27, 2006

22. BAIC-FOTON (北汽福田车股份有限公司), no. A(B) 22, April 29, 2006

23. DRC, no. A(B) 23, April 30, 2006

CHANGCHUN

1. Auto Industry Research (*Qiche Gongye Yanjiu*), no. A(C) 24, October 19, 2005
2. China FAW Group Corporation, vice manager, no. A(C) 25, October 20, 2005
3. FAW-VW, no. A(C)26, March 21, 2006

SHENYANG

1. Fraunhofer Institute for Production Systems and Design Technology in Germany, no. A(SY) 27, November 29, 2005

SHANGHAI

1. SAIC-GM, no. A(SH) 28, February 27, 2006
2. Kolbenschmidt Shanghai Piston Co., no. A(SH) 29, February 28, 2006
3. United Automotive Electronics System Co., Ltd. (UAES), a JV of Robert Bosch GmbH and Zhong-Lian Automotive Electronics, no. A(SH) 30, March 1, 2006
4. SAIC, no. A(SH) 31, March 1, 2006
5. Institute of National Economy, Shanghai Academy of Social Science, no. A(SH) 32, March 3, 2006
6. Fudan University, no. A(SH) 33, March 3, 2006
7. Reporter, *Shanghai Automobile News*, no. A(SH) 34, March 6, 2006
8. SAIC-GM, no. A(SH) 35, March 6, 2006
9. SAIC Corporation Limited (上海汽车集团股份有限公司), no. A(SH) 36, March 7, 2006
10. Chery (奇瑞) Shanghai KOWIN Automotive Components Co. Ltd., no. A(SH) 37, March 8, 2006
11. SAIC-VW, no. A(SH) 38, March 9, 2006
12. Geely Holding Group (吉利股份集团), no. A(SH) 39, March 9, 2006
13. A. T. Kearney (Shanghai) Management Consulting Co. Ltd., no. A(SH) 40, March 10, 2006

14. SAIC-SSangyong SUV China Project Team, no. A(SH) 41, March 17, 2006
15. SAIC-GM, no. A(SH) 42, April 25, 2006
16. American Axle & Manufacturing (AAM), no. A(SH) 43, April 26, 2006
17. SAIC-SSangyong SUV China Project Team, no. A(SH) 44, March 18, 2006

### HANGZHOU AND TAIZHOU

1. Geely Holding Group Corporation, Hangzhou Headquarters Office, no. A(H) 45, March 14, 2006
2. Geely Holding Group Corporation, Hangzhou Headquarters Office, no. A(H) 46, March 14, 2006
3. Geely Holding Group Corporation, Taizhou Office, no. A(T) 47, March 15, 2006
4. Geely Holding Group Corporation, no. A(H) 48, March 15, 2006

### GUANGZHOU

1. Guangzhou-Honda Automobile Co. Ltd., no. A(G) 49, March 31, 2006

### BACKUP INTERVIEWS

1. DRC, no. A(B) 50, May 2, 2008
2. Journalist, no. A(B) 51, May 7, 2008
3. SAIC, no. A(SH) 52, March 28, 2011
4. Geely International Corporation, no. A(SH) 53, March 31, 2011
5. *Shanghai Daily*, no. A(SH) 54, April 1, 2011
6. DRC, no. A(B) 55, April 26, 2011
7. SAIC-VW, no. A(SH) 56, April 29, 2011
8. Fudan University, no. A(SH) 57, July 12, 2012
9. SAIC-VW, no. A(SH) 58, July 13, 2012

# Telecommunications

1. Institute of Industrial Economics, CASS, no. T1, September 5, 2005, I
2. Beijing University of Post and Telecommunications, no. T2, December 7, 2005
3. Beijing University of Post and Telecommunications, no. T3, December 7, 2005
4. Business Reporter, *Beijing Daily Messenger*, no. T4, December 9, 2005, I
5. Business Reporter, *Beijing Daily Messenger*, no. T5, December 12, 2005, II
6. Beijing University of Post and Telecommunications, no. T6, December 15, 2005
7. Department of Economics, Beijing University, no. T7, December 19, 2005
8. China Unicom, Beijing, no. T 8, December 20, 2005
9. Institute of Industrial Economics, CASS, no. T9, December 20, 2005, II
10. Department of Economic Management, BUPT, no. T10, January 17, 2006
11. Enterprise Research Institute, DRC, no. T11, January 19, 2006
12. Institute of Industrial Economics, CASS, no. T12, January 20, 2006
13. Institute of World Economics of Politics, CASS, no. T13, January 23, 2006
14. Center for Informatization Study, CASS, no. T14, January 24, 2006
15. Institute of Law, CASS, no. T15, February 7, 2006
16. Research Center for Regulation and Competition, CASS, no. T16, February 9, 2006
17. Department of Department Strategy & Regional Economy, DRC, no. T17, February 9, 2006
18. Enterprise Research Department, DRC, no. T18, February 9, 2006

19. Putian Telecoms Co. Ltd., no. T19, February 16, 2006
20. Allwant Technology Co. Ltd., no. T20, February 16, 2006
21. China Academy of Telecommunication Research, MII, no. T21, February 21, 2006
22. CASS, no. T22, April 28, 2006

### BACKUP INTERVIEWS

23. CASS, no. T23, April 22/24, 2008
24. Journalist, no. T24, April 23, 2008
25. Beijing University, Dept. of Govt, no. T25, April 29, 2008
26. Institute of Quantitative & Technical Economics, CASS, no. T26, April 29, 2008
27. Industrial Regulation and Competition Research Center, CASS, no. T27, May 8, 2008
28. DRC, no. T28, May 5, 2008
29. CASS, no. T29, May 14/15, 2008
30. CASS, no. T30, April 26, 2011
31. SCMP journalist, no. T31, July 20, 2012
32. DRC, no. T32, July 21, 2012
33. CASS, no. T33, July 18, 2012

# Notes

## 1. How Does China Regulate a Socialist Market Economy?

1. Feng, "Chinese Tech Groups."

2. According to Ming Xia, given that "the Party commands, controls and integrates all other political organizations and institutions in China," the term "party-state" "accurately captures China's political reality." See Xia, "The Communist Party of China."

3. According to Curtis Milhaupt and Wentong Zheng, Jack Ma, the cofounder of Alibaba Group, was ranked second among politically connected entrepreneurs at China's top ten internet companies. His party-state affiliation is Zhejiang Province's People's Political Consultative Conference. See Milhaupt and Zheng, "Beyond Ownership," 222.

4. Oertel, "Why the German Debate."

5. Milhaupt and Zheng, "Beyond Ownership."

6. Regulation is defined here as a general government tool used to control the economy and society. Hence, regulation encompasses all modes of state intervention in economic and social life. In this context, regulation is a means to steer the economy rather than passively oversee the market in terms of pricing or competition.

7. National Bureau of Statistics of China, *China Statistical Yearbook*.

8. Kornai, *The Socialist System*, 91–95; Naughton, "China's Distinctive System," 455.

9. The economic reform in 1978 set off the process of dismantling the system of central planning, but the relationship between ministries and major state sectors was not reformed until the 1990s. See Pearson, "Governing the Chinese Economy," 719, 727; Naughton, *Growing Out of the Plan*; and Steinfeld, *Forging Reform in China*.

10. Yang, *Remaking the Chinese Leviathan*; Pearson, "The Business of Governing Business"; Pearson, "Variety Within and Without"; Heilmann, "Regulatory Innovation by Leninist Means"; Yeo, "Between Owner and Regulator."

11. Fligstein, *The Architecture of Market*, 32–33.

12. China's economy consists of three tiers: top, middle, and bottom. Industries at the top tier include those most strategic to the national economy and security, such as

finance, petroleum, and power. A selective approach to managing industries was first proposed by Sun Yafeng in the 1950s and actively implemented in the 1970s. See Sun, "Ba jihua he tongji"; and Sun, "Lun jiazhi." More recent accounts refer to Ernst and Naughton, "China's Emerging Industrial Economy," 35–59; Naughton, "China's Distinctive System"; and Pearson, "Variety Within and Without."

13. Hood, Scott, James, and Travers, *Regulation inside Government*, 3. On the creation and implementation, as well as the politics of regulation over the process, refer to Carrigan and Coglianese, "The Politics of Regulation."

14. Majone, "The Rise of the Regulatory State in Europe."

15. Vogel, *Freer Markets*; Moran, "Review Article."

16. Gilardi, "Institutional Change in Regulatory Policies."

17. Jordana and Levi-Faur, "The Politics of Regulation," 3–4.

18. Particularly during the 1990s, regulation and the regulatory state in advanced industrial countries, such as the United Kingdom, the United States, Japan, and Europe, were topics of interest. Studies include Majone, "Rise of the Regulatory State"; Majone, *Regulating Europe*; Vogel, *Freer Markets*; McGowan and Wallace, "Towards a European Regulatory State"; and Eisner, *Regulatory Politics in Transition*.

19. Similar points are addressed in Vogel, "Why Freer Markets Need More Rules," 342.

20. Yang, *Remaking the Chinese Leviathan*; Pearson, "Business of Governing Business."

21. In Chinese, the term "public good" (*gonggong wupin*) is used to address the societal /collective good under command control. I regard the public good during the planned economy as the societal/collective good. See Liang, *Zhongguo gonggong wupin*, 68; Liu, *Zhongguo jingji zhuanxing*; Wang, "Woguo gonggongpin tigei."

22. Tsai, "Adaptive Informal Institutions"; Tsai, "Solidarity Groups, Informal Accountability"; Kennedy, "Comparing Formal and Informal Lobbying Practices."

23. Vogel, *Freer Markets*; Majone, *Regulating Europe*; Majone, "Rise of the Regulatory State."

24. Liang, *Zhongguo gonggong wupin*, 115–16.

25. Liang, *Zhongguo gonggong wupin*, 69.

26. Liang, *Zhongguo gonggong wupin*, 69, 116.

27. Wu, *Understanding and Interpreting*, 25.

28. Vogel, "Why Freer Markets Need More Rules."

29. Office of the United States Trade Representative, Executive Office of the President, "Findings of the Investigation into China's Acts, Policies, and Practices Related to Technology Transfer, Intellectual Property, and Innovation under Section 301 of the Trade Act of 1974," Office of the President, United States, March 22, 2018, 24. https://ustr.gov/sites/default/files/Section%20301%20FINAL.PDF.

30. Office of the US Trade Representative, "Findings of the Investigation into China's Acts," 19.

31. Office of the US Trade Representative, "Findings of the Investigation into China's Acts," 19.

32. Office of the US Trade Representative, "Findings of the Investigation into China's Acts," 36.

33. Martina, "Exclusive: In China."

34. Martina, "Exclusive: In China."

35. Martina, "Exclusive: In China."

36. Naughton and Tsai, *State Capitalism, Institutional Adaptation.*

37. Party Secretary Xi Jinping emphasized this at the 18th Party Congress. See Cheng and McElveen, "Pessimism about China's Third Plenum"; Li, "Plenum Insight."

38. Yang, *Remaking the Chinese Leviathan*; Pearson, "Governing the Chinese Economy"; Pearson, "Business of Governing Business in China"; Pei, *China's Trapped Transition*; Breslin, "Capitalism with Chinese Characteristics"; Heilmann, "Regulatory Innovation"; Heilmann, "Policy-Making and Political Supervision"; Yeo, "Between Owner and Regulator"; Yeo and Pearson, "Regulating Decentralized State Industries."

39. Yang, *Remaking the Chinese Leviathan.*

40. Pei, "China's Governance Crisis"; Pei, *China's Trapped Transition*; Pei, "The Dark Side of China's Rise."

41. Pearson, "Variety Within and Without"; Pearson, "Governing the Chinese Economy"; Pearson, "Business of Governing Business in China"; Yeo, "Between Owner and Regulator"; Yeo and Pearson, "Regulating Decentralized State Industries."

42. For further discussion on the limits of neoliberal and statist approaches, refer to Appendix 2.

43. Similar points are emphasized in other studies; see Tsai, "Adaptive Informal Institutions"; Tsai, "Solidarity Groups"; Dickson, *Red Capitalists in China*; Dickson, *Wealth into Power.*

44. Recited from Barma and Vogel, "Economic Sociology," 118.

45. Polanyi, *The Great Transformation.*

46. Fligstein, *Architecture of Market.*

47. Vogel, *Freer Markets.*

48. Meyer and Rowan, "Institutionalized Organizations."

49. Fligstein, *Architecture of Market*, 32–33. I do not examine rules of exchange here because my case studies indicate that rules of exchange are not a source of variation in regulation.

50. Arrighi, *Adam Smith in Beijing*, 43.

51. Arrighi, *Adam Smith in Beijing.*

52. Ernst and Naughton, "China's Emerging Industrial Economy."

53. Ernst and Naughton, "China's Emerging Industrial Economy," 42–47.

54. Ernst and Naughton, "China's Emerging Industrial Economy," 47.

55. Ernst and Naughton, "China's Emerging Industrial Economy," 47.

56. Pearson, "Variety Within and Without."

57. Pearson, "Variety Within and Without."

58. Fligstein, *Architecture of Market*, 34.

59. Fligstein, *Architecture of Market*, 34.

60. Milhaupt and Zheng, "Beyond Ownership."

61. Milhaupt and Zheng, "Beyond Ownership," 676; Lee, *Specter of Global China*, 4.

62. Fligstein, *Architecture of Market*, 35.

63. Fligstein, *Architecture of Market*, 35.

64. Sun, "Ba jihua he tongji fangzai"; Sun, "Lun jiazhi"; Chen, "New Issues since the Basic Competition," 21–22.

65. Fligstein, *Architecture of Market*, 28.

66. Guven, "Reforming Sticky Institutions," 265.

67. Guven, "Reforming Sticky Institutions." The significance of the size of China is discussed extensively in Chung, *Centrifugal Empire*, 3–6.

68. Lieberthal and Oksenberg, *Policy Making in China*; Thun, *Changing Lanes in China*; Kennedy, *Business of Lobbying in China*; Moore, *China in the World Market*; Segal and Thun, "Thinking Globally, Acting Locally"; Steinfeld, *Forging Reform in China*; Chung, "The Political Economy of Industrial Restructuring"; Pearson, "Business of Governing Business in China."

69. They include armaments, electrical power and distribution, oil and chemicals, telecommunications, coal, aviation, and shipping. "China Defines Key National Economic Sectors."

70. Pillar industries include machinery, automobiles, IT, steel, base metals, chemicals, land surveying, and research and development. See Breslin, "Government-Industry Relations," 37.

71. Yang, *Remaking the Chinese Leviathan*; Pearson, "Business of Governing Business in China"; Heilmann, "Regulatory Innovation"; Andrews-Speed, Dow, and Gao, "The Ongoing Reforms to China's Government."

72. For more details, refer to Appendix 2. In designing the research for this book, I felt that positivism was a leading direction to pursue, but I must address the potential drawback of this tautology because the modes of central regulation—the dependent variable—and key independent variables such as property rights are closely connected. Persuasiveness is the most important criterion, for pertinent arguments may overcome such methodological criticism. See Chung, *Centrifugal Empire*, 14. The empirical implications of the theory are explored through the comparative case studies.

73. Here, "strategic industries" means sectors that make crucial fiscal or developmental contributions to the national economy. Strategic industries are largely but not always under the state sector, and some, such as the automobile sector, have mixed ownership.

74. Thun, *Changing Lanes in China*; Segal and Thun, "Thinking Globally."

75. For more theoretical discussion on the limits of conventional approaches, refer to Appendix 2.

## 2. The Evolution of China's Multifaceted Industrial Regulation

1. Feigenbaum, "A Chinese Puzzle."

2. North, *Understanding the Process*, 78.

3. Kirby, "Continuity and Change"; Bian, *Making of the State Enterprise System*; Bian, "Explaining the Dynamics of Change."

4. North, *Understanding the Process*, 73.

5. Bian, "Explaining the Dynamics," 208.

6. Bian, "Explaining the Dynamics," 208.

7. Kirby, "Continuity and Change"; Bian, "Explaining the Dynamics."

8. For an extensive discussion on the Soviet role in the PRC's economy during the 1950s, see Naughton, "Pattern and Legacy," 233–34.

9. Teiwes, "Chinese State," 133.

10. Teiwes, "Chinese State," 133.

11. Naughton, "Pattern and Legacy," 233.

12. Wu, *Understanding and Interpreting*, 38.

13. Mao, "On the Ten Major Relationships," 272–76.

14. State Council, "Guanyu gaijin jihua guanli tizhi de guiding"; Sun, "Woguo sangye jihua guanli," 56.

15. Wu, *Understanding and Interpreting*, 46–47.

16. Wu, *Understanding and Interpreting*, 46.

17. Naughton, "Pattern and Legacy," 237.

18. Wu, *Understanding and Interpreting*, 51; Mao, "Eighteen Issues."

19. Wu, *Understanding and Interpreting*, 52.

20. Naughton, "Pattern and Legacy," 243.

21. Naughton, "Pattern and Legacy," 244.

22. Chai, *China: Transition*, 32.

23. Ma, *Xiandai zhongguo jingji shidan*, 158–59.

24. Chai, *China: Transition*, 32.

25. Chai, *China: Transition*, 32.

26. Chai, *China: Transition*, 32.

27. Sun, *Selected Works*, 367.

28. Mo, *Sun Yefang chanye*, 73.

29. Wu, *Understanding and Interpreting*, 37. During the 1960s and 1970s, Wlodzimierz Brus, an exponent of the Polish school of market socialism, advocated combining planning with market mechanisms. Brus divided economic decision making into three tiers: macroeconomic decision making, enterprise decision making involving local issues, and decision making on the economic activities of households and individuals. According to Brus, if decision making was centralized in the first tier (macro–decision making) and the second tier (enterprise decision making) but decentralized at the third tier, the model was a centralized model (i.e., the Soviet model); if decision making was centralized at the first tier but decentralized at the second and third tiers, the model was decentralized (i.e., Eastern European countries); Wu, *Understanding and Interpreting*, 5–16.

30. He, Wang, and Wu, "Guanyu jihua tiaojie he shichang"; Liu and Zhao, "Lun shehuizhiyi jingji," 49; Fan and Zhang, "Shehuizhuyi jingji zhong"; Liu, "Luelun jihua tiaojie," 8.

31. Hsu, "Political Economy of Guidance Planning," 45.

32. White, *Riding the Tiger*, 46; Wu, "Zhidao xing jihua tanlun," 5–6.

33. Liu and Zhao, "Lun shehuizhiyi jingji zhong."

34. He, Wang, and Wu, "Guanyu jihua tiaojie"; Hsu, "Political Economy of Guidance Planning," 383.

35. State Planning Commission (SPC), "Guanyu gaijin jihua tizhi"; Zhou, *Dangdai Zhongguo*, 189.

36. Naughton, *The Chinese Economy*, 92. Because the Chinese leadership failed to rationalize a planned economy through the mid-1980s, particularly regarding prices and financial relations, partial reform occurred. As a result, the autonomy of certain enterprises was expanded and the dual-track system combining planning and market forces evolved. See Yang, "Governing China's Transition," 442.

37. Naughton, *Chinese Economy*, 90.

38. Naughton, *Chinese Economy*, 90.

39. Qian, "How Reform Worked in China," 14–19.

40. Naughton, "Market Economy."

41. Naughton, "Market Economy," 150; Lau, Qian, and Ronald, "Reform without Losers."

42. Ma and Cao, *Jihua jingji tizhi*, 147.

43. Ma and Cao, *Jihua jingji tizhi*.

44. White, *Riding the Tiger*, 76.

45. See, for example, Solinger, *China's Transition from Socialism*.

46. Chung, "Reappraising Central-Local Relations," 9.

47. Naughton, "Market Economy," 153–54.

48. Zhou, *Dangdai Zhongguo de jingji*, 186, 190–91; Fan and Zhang, "Shehuizhuyi jingji zhong"; Hu, *Quanmian kaichuang shehuizhuyi*, 18.

49. Liu, "Luelun jihua tiaojie," 8.

50. This principle was generally from the late 1970s to the mid-1980s. See Ding, "Jixie gongye shixing," 8; Liu and Zhao, "Lun shehuizhiyi jingji zhong"; Liu, Hu, and Yu, "Jihua he shichang"; Fan and Zhang, "Shehuizhuyi jingji zhong"; He, Wang, and Wu, "Guanyu jihua tiaojie"; Liu, "Luelun jihua tiaojie"; Wu, "Zhidao xing jihua tanlun."

51. *Zhongguo Gongchandang Zhongyang Weiyuanhui*, 55.

52. Chen, "New Issues since the Basic Competition."

53. Zhou, *Dangdai zhongguo de jingji*, 191–92; Ding, "Jixie gongye shixing sanzhong"; Naughton, "China's Experience of Guidance Planning," 743. Similar points are raised by Chen, "New Issues since the Basic Competition," 21–22.

54. Zhou, *Dangdai Zhongguo de jingji*, 191–92.

55. Chai, *China: Transition*, 54.

56. Chai, *China: Transition*, 54.

57. This point is discussed in Lardy and Lieberthal, *Remaking the Chinese State*.

58. Chai, *China: Transition*, 54.

59. Chai, *China: Transition*, 40.

60. SPC, "Zhonghua Renmin Gongheguo"; Xiang and Zhang, "Zhongguo chanye zhengce," 19–20.

61. Naughton, *Wu Jinglian*, 353.

62. Naughton, "China's Experience," 744; Rutland, *Myth of the Plan*, 28; Estrin and Holmes, *French Planning*.

63. Naughton, "China's Experience," 760.

64. Liu, *Zhongguo shi ge wu*, 572.

65. Ma and Cao, *Jihua jingji tizhi gaige*, 231–32; Shi, Yang, and Huang, "Changing Pattern of Development," 97.

66. Heilmann and Melton, "Reinvention of Development Planning."

67. Liu, *Zhongguo shi ge wu*, 584.
68. Liu, *Zhongguo shi ge wu*; Huang, "Guojiajiwei zai xin shiqi," 45.
69. Huang, "Guojiajiwei zai xin shiqi," 45.
70. Huang, "Guojiajiwei zai xin shiqi," 45.
71. Liu, *Zhongguo shi ge wu*, 584.
72. Huang, "Guojiajiwei zai xin shiqi," 45.
73. Ma and Cao, *Jihua jingji tizhi gaige*, 239.
74. Ernst and Naughton, "China's Emerging Industrial Economy"; Pearson, "Variety Within and Without."
75. Naughton, "Market Economy," 153.
76. They include Xue, "Shehuizhuyi jingji de jihua guanli," 21–23; Xue, *Zhongguo shehuizhuyi jingji*, 91–122; Luo, "Guanyu jihua jingji," 44–45; Ma, "Guanyu jingji guanli tizhi."
77. Lee, *Industrial Management and Economic Reform*, 175; emphasis added.
78. Wu, *Understanding and Interpreting*, 83.
79. Wu, *Understanding and Interpreting*, 196.
80. *Guanyu guoyou qiye gaige he fazhan ruogan zhongda wenti de jueding* (Decisions on several important issues regarding reform and development of state-owned enterprises), Fourth Plenary Session of the 15th CCCPC, 1999, http://www.people.com.cn/GB/shizheng/252/5089/5093/5175/20010428/454976.html; Wu, *Understanding and Interpreting*, 88.
81. Compared with the reforms of the 1980s, there was a major shift toward a well-regulated competitive market, departing from an emphasis on particularistic contracting. See Naughton, "Political Economy of China's Economic Transition," 119.
82. Clarke, "Corporate Governance in China"; Tenev and Zhang, *Corporate Governance and Enterprise Reform*, 5–28; Yeo, "Contextualizing Corporate Governance."
83. Heilmann and Melton, "Reinvention of Development Planning"; Cheng, "Zhongguo gaoceng lingdao."
84. One of the most comprehensive studies is Brodsgaard and Zheng, *Chinese Communist Party in Reform*.
85. Li, "Zhongyang caijing lingdao xiaozu xiankai"; Li, "Jiemi zhongyang caijing lingdao xiaozu," 27.
86. Naughton, "SASAC Rising."
87. Wu, "Xiaozu zhengzhi yanjiu"; Cai, "Zhongyang caijing lingdao xiaozu."
88. Kim, "Leading Small Groups," 123.
89. Cheng, "Zhongguo gaoceng lingdao xiaozu."
90. Zhang, "Dangnei lingdao xiaozu changyu," 10–11.
91. Zhang, "Dangnei lingdao xiaozu changyu," 11.
92. Chen Yun proposed the abolition of the Finance and Economy Commission because its works overlapped with the CFELSG. See Cheng, "Zhongguo gaoceng lingdao xiaozu."
93. Cheng, "Zhongguo gaoceng lingdao xiaozu."
94. Heilmann, "Regulatory Innovation by Leninist Means," 5; Zou, *Zhongguo zhongyang jigou yanse shilu*, 206–7.
95. Li, "Juemi zhongyang caijing lingdao xiaozu," 1.

96. Zhang, "Chen Yun yu zhongyang."
97. Cao, "1958 nian yu 1962 nian."
98. Cai, "Zhongyang caijing lingdao xiaozu."
99. Cheng, "Zhongguo gaoceng lingdao," 33–34.
100. Cheng, "Zhongguo gaoceng lingdao," 35.
101. Cheng, "Zhongguo gaoceng lingdao," 33.
102. During the period 1998–2003, Hua Jianmin served as the head of Zhongcaiban and as the associate head of the SDPC. Under Premier Zhu Rongji, the State Economic and Trade Commission, not the SDPC, was the most powerful state economic agency.
103. Cai, "Zhongyang caijing lingdao xiaozu"; Cui, "Zhongyang caijing lingdao xiaozu," 49.

## 3. The Auto Industry: Soft Regulation

1. "Chinese Automaker Hoping for Revival."
2. State Council Secretariat, "Qiche chanye tiaozheng."
3. State Council of the PRC, "Made in China 2015 Strategy."
4. 2004 FAW Annual Report, First Auto Works Group, Changchun.
5. Zhongguo qiche gongye xiehui, *Zhongguo qiche gongye gaige*, 25.
6. Zhongguo qiche gongye xiehui and Zhongguo qiche gongye zixun weiyuanhui, *Zhongguo qiche chanye chengzhang zhanlue*, 35.
7. Zhou et al., *Dangdai Zhongguo de jingji tizhi gaige*, 227.
8. Zhongguo qiche gongye xiehui, *Zhongguo qiche gongye gaige*, 26.
9. Zhongguo qiche gongye xiehui and Zhongguo qiche gongye zixun weiyuanhui, *Zhongguo qiche chanye chengzhang zhanlue*, 38.
10. China Association of Automobile Manufacturers & China Automotive Technology and Research Center, *China Automotive Industry Yearbook* (2012).
11. The large assemblers included FAW, Second Auto Works, and the SAIC. The three smaller ones were Beijing Jeep, Guangzhou Peugeot, and Tianjin Auto.
12. Segal and Thun, "Thinking Globally, Acting Locally"; Thun, *Changing Lanes in China*; Brandt and Thun, "The Fight for the Middle"; Pearson, "Variety Within and Without," 33.
13. Zhongguo qiche gongye xiehui, *Zhongguo qiche gongye gaige*, 27.
14. Zhongguo qiche gongye xiehui and Zhongguo qiche gongye zixun weiyuanhui, *Zhongguo qiche chanye chengzhang zhanlue*, 39.
15. Zhongguo qiche gongye xiehui and Zhongguo qiche gongye zixun weiyuanhui, *Zhongguo qiche chanye chengzhang zhanlue*, 39.
16. Heilmann and Melton, "The Reinvention of Development Planning."
17. Industries include electronics, chemicals, machinery, telecommunications, construction, transport, and petroleum. Liu et al., *Zhongguo shige wunian jihua yanjiu baogao*, 25.
18. *Qiche gongye chanye zhengce* (March 12, 1994), http://www.people.com.cn/GB/qiche/25959/34162/34165/2540192.html.
19. *Qiche gongye chanye zhengce* (March 12, 1994).

20. Article 2, *Qiche gongye chanye zhengce* (March 12, 1994).

21. Article 2, *Qiche gongye chanye zhengce* (March 12, 1994).

22. Qu, "Chaogan gongshi jiandu."

23. Interviews with senior managers of SAIC-VW, no. A(SH) 38, March 9, 2006; no. A(SH) 55, April 29, 2011; no. A(SH) 57, July 13, 2012. See Appendix 3 for interview information.

24. Interview with a SAIC-VW senior manager in Shanghai, no. A(SH) 38, March 9, 2006. The difference is found between Chinese scholars and entrepreneurs: while scholars in general devalue the role of auto industrial policy, most entrepreneurs, working in state-owned and private enterprises, underscore its necessities and roles.

25. "Qiche chanye fazhan zhengce" (May 21, 2004), chapter 10, http://www.miit.gov .cn/n1146285/n1146352/n3054355/n3057292/n3057308/c3577031/content.html.

26. "Qiche chanye fazhan zhengce" (May 21, 2004), chapter 13.

27. "Qiche chanye fazhan zhengce" (May 21, 2004), chapter 13, article 44.

28. "Qiche gongye chanye zhengce" (March 12, 1994), chapter 6.

29. Qu, "Chaogan gongshi jiandu."

30. "Qiche chanye tiaozheng he zhenxing guihua" March 20, 2009, http://www.gov .cn/zwgk/2009-03/20/content_1264324.htm.

31. "Qiche chanye tiaozheng he zhenxing guihua" (March 20, 2009), chapter 2, article 4.

32. Cao, Pan, and Wu, "Woguo qiche chanye butong," 2–3.

33. "Qiche chanye tiaozheng he zhenxing guihua" (March 20, 2009), chapter 4.

34. Bradsher, "China's Embrace of Foreign Cars."

35. Qu, "Chaogan gongshi jiandu."

36. Johnson, *MITI and the Japanese Miracle*; Evans, *Embedded Autonomy*; Kohli, *State-Directed Development*.

37. *Qiche gongye chanye zhengce*, March 12, 1994.

38. "Qiche chanye fazhan zhengce," May 21, 2004.

39. Thun, "Industrial Policy, Chinese-Style," 471.

40. "Guowuyuan yuanze tongguo qiche."

41. Harwit, *China's Automobile Industry*, 37.

42. Harwit, *China's Automobile Industry*, 37; Sit and Liu, "Restructuring and Spatial Change," 657; Marukawa, "Why Are There So Many," 172.

43. Sit and Liu, "Restructuring and Spatial Change," 657–58.

44. Sit and Liu, "Restructuring and Spatial Change."

45. Lieberthal and Oksenberg, *Policy Making in China*; Huang, "Between Two Coordination Failures."

46. Shi and Zhi, "Woguo qiche chanye zhengfu," 3.

47. Zhongguo qiche gongye xiehui and Zhongguo qiche gongye zixun weiyuanhui, *Zhongguo qiche chanye chengzhang zhanlue*, 42.

48. Yang, *Remaking the Chinese Leviathan*, 40.

49. Yeo, "Between Owner and Regulator"; Pearson, "Governing the Chinese Economy"; Pearson, "Variety Within and Without."

50. See http://cys.ndrc.gov.cn/jgsz/default/html (accessed February 11, 2006).

51. Interview no. T 26, April 29, 2008.

52. Zhang, "Shida chanye zhenxing jihua chuqi"; Naughton, "Understanding Chinese Stimulus Package," 8–9.

53. Yeo, "Between Owner and Regulator"; Pearson, "Governing the Chinese Economy," 720.

54. Guoziwei Xunshiban, "Li Rongrong chuxi guoziwei."

55. Jiang, "Guoziwei xunshizu jinzhu."

56. Jiang, "Guoziwei xunshizu jinzhu."

57. F/N 87; Han, "Jiji zuohao xunshi gongzuo."

58. Zhao and Ren, "Guozi jianguan ruhe zaiyifa zhiguo," 39.

59. One entrepreneur working in Guangzhou-Honda did claim that the NDRC in Guangzhou remains the agent of the central NDRC, even though in principle there are no direct relations between the central and local NDRC and SASAC. Interview no. A(G) 48, March 31, 2006.

60. Huang, "Between Two Coordination Failures," 555.

61. Thun, *Changing Lanes in China*.

62. Especially during the 1980s, the efforts of vice mayors greatly contributed to the development of the auto industries in Shanghai, Beijing, and Guangzhou, especially Beijing vice mayors Jiang Zemin and Wu Yi in the late 1980s, Shanghai vice mayors Huang Ju and Wu Bangguo in 1985, and Guangzhou vice mayor Xie Shihua in 1985. Harwit, *China's Automotive Industry*, 55–57.

63. See Thun, *Changing Lanes in China*, 110–17, 151–55; Harwit, *China's Automotive Industry*, 55–57.

64. Thun, *Changing Lanes in China*, 110–17.

65. Wedeman, "Crossing the River," 70–82.

66. Correspondence with Jian Sun (June 2006), vice president of A. T. Kearney Greater China, Shanghai Office.

67. Wedeman, "Crossing the River," 81; emphasis added.

68. Wedeman, "Crossing the River," 81.

69. Liu and Yeung, "China's Dynamic Industrial Sector," 544.

70. NDRC's approval at the central level is now required for investments by Chinese companies exceeding US$300 million in the resources sector and for investments exceeding US$100 million in the nonresources sector. These thresholds are ten times those set out in the 2004 rules. Provincial-level NDRC approval is required for all investments by Chinese companies below the thresholds mentioned above, with one important caveat. If an investment is made by a central state-owned enterprise under the direct control of the SASAC, provincial NDRC approval is not needed and the central SOE can make its own decision. See http://www.nortonrosefulbright.com/knowledge/publications /49739/a-new-combination-of-going-global-and-welcoming-in (accessed April 26, 2018).

71. Yu, "Shanghai qiche nanqi hezuo"; Zhang, "Shanghai nanqi hebing neimu."

72. Yu, "Shanghai qiche nanqi hezuo."

73. The SAIC decided to take over the Nanjing auto groups not simply because of the central government's implicit pressure, but rather because this merger could provide the SAIC with an excellent opportunity to be the national champion by complementing its relatively weak commercial vehicles, such as light trucks and buses. Author's interview in Shanghai (July 2011).

74. Zhang, "Shanghai nanqi hebing neimu."

75. Xinkuaibao, "Dijiuhui: Shang-Nan hezuo."

76. Yeo and Pearson, "Regulating Decentralized State Industries"; Yeo, "Complementing the Local Party Discipline."

77. Unless otherwise specified, FAW denotes First Auto Works Group Corporation (*Zhongguo Diyi Qiche Jituan*), not individual firms within its shareholder structure, such as FAW-VW or FAW Xiali.

78. For studies on regulatory mechanisms of China's infrastructure industries, refer to Pearson, "The Business of Governing Business"; Pearson, "Governing the Chinese Economy"; Pearson "Variety Within and Without"; Yeo, "Between Owner and Regulator."

79. FAW profile on official website, http://www.faw.com/aboutFaw/aboutFaw.jsp?pros=Profile.jsp&phight=580&about=Profile (accessed February 26, 2015).

80. FAW Group Corporation's first JV partner was Volkswagen in 1991. Subsequently, FAW signed JV agreements with Toyota in 2002 and Mazda in 2005, http://www.faw.com/aboutFaw/aboutFaw.jsp?pros=/international/volkswagen.jsp&phight=600&about=FAW-Volkswagen (accessed February 26, 2015).

81. FAW profile page, http://www.faw.com/aboutFaw/aboutFaw.jsp?pros=Profile.jsp&phight=580&about=Profile (accessed February 26, 2015).

82. They include three key auto industrial policies: *Qiche gongye chanye zhengce* (Auto Sector Industry Policy), 1994; *Qiche chanye fazhan zhengce* (Auto Industry Development Policy), 2004; and *Qiche chanye tiaozheng he jinxing guihua* (Auto Industry Adjusting and Enhancing Plan), 2009.

83. Interview no. A(C) 25, October 20, 2005.

84. "Zhongyang qiye gongwei."

85. Gui, "Xunshizu zhiqi xiaoshou fubai"; "Yiqi-dazhong liuren weifan."

86. Gui, "Xunshizu zhiqi xiaoshou fubai"; "Yiqi-dazhong liuren weifan."

87. Zhao and Ren, "Guozi jianguan ruhe zaiyifa zhiguo," 39.

88. Huang, *Inflation and Investment Controls*, provides a comprehensive study on cadre evaluation by the department of the organization focused on administrative monitoring.

89. "Zhongzubu renming Xu Xianping"; An, "Zhongzubu zaikaoli yiqi zongjingli."

90. Dickson, *Red Capitalists in China*, 43.

91. They are Xu Jianyi, Qin Huanming, Zhang Pijie, and An Tiecheng. See FAW-VW 2004 Annual Report, 3. Individual career profiles of members of the party committee are also found at http://www.southcn.com/news/china/hrcn/rsdifang/200412280416.htm (accessed November 1, 2015).

92. Xu, "Jialu WTO dui Changchun," 109.

93. Thun, *Changing Lanes in China*, 179–82.

94. Interviews no. A(C) 24, October 19, 2005; no. A(C) 25, October 20, 2005; no. A(C) 26, March 21, 2006. "Changchun to Forge Auto Parts Base," *People's Daily*, May 8, 2004.

95. Similar points are addressed in Geely's choice of Shanghai as the core venue of Geely-Volvo for sales and a research center. Refer to "Difang zhengfu daobijili"; Shanghai Auto Industry Corporation (SAIC), *Zhongguo qiche gongye fazhan yanjiu*, 53; Sit and Liu, "Restructuring and Spatial Change," 657.

96. SAIC, *Zhongguo qiche gongye fazhan yanjiu*, 53–55.

97. The SAIC recorded 843,000 sales units, RMB10 billion revenues, and RMB107 billion total assets in 2004 (SAIC Annual Report, 2004).

98. Interviews no. A(B) 14, February 17, 2006; no. A(B) 17, February 22, 2006.

99. Interview no. A(SH) 33, March 3, 2006.

100. Interviews no. A(SH) 36, March 7, 2006; no. A(SH) 38, March 9, 2006.

101. On Shanghai municipality's spending, see Schwarz, "Shanghai Aims to Be China's Detroit"; interview no. A(SH) 32, March 3, 2006.

102. Interview no. A(SH) 36, March 7, 2006.

103. Interview no. A(SH) 36, March 7, 2006.

104. SAIC is in the top twenty revenue earners among China's state-owned firms and therefore of substantial interest to the SASAC.

105. Interview no. A(B) 6, November 17, 2005.

106. In the cases of Beijing-Hyundai and SAIC-GM, Hyundai and GM were decided on by the top leaders at the center, not the Beijing or Shanghai government. Interview no. A(B) 5, November 10, 2005.

107. Wu, "Beijing Gives Local Government."

108. Interview no. A(SH) 31, March 1, 2006; no. A(SH) 43, April 26, 2006.

109. Interview no. A(SH) 31, March 1, 2006; no. A(SH) 43, April 26, 2006.

110. Interview no. A(SH) 38, March 9, 2006.

111. Communication with auto industry specialist Jian Sun, vice president of A.T. Kearney Greater China, Shanghai office (November 23, 2007).

112. Cheng Li uses the term *xunshizu* to refer to the inspection teams formed to review nominated candidates for provincial cadre positions, but I use this term to refer to a "floating supervisory body," focusing on its regulatory control over major SOEs in China. On the "official" function of *xunshizu*, see Li, "Reshuffling Four Tiers," 3.

113. *Jiemi xunshizu*, http://blog.ifeng.com/article/27752283.html (accessed November 1, 2015).

114. "Zhongzubu xunshizu zuzhang cheng."

115. The official ordinance on which the supervision of the *xunshizu* is based is "Dangzheng lingdao ganbu xuanba renyong gongzuo tiaoli" (Regulations on the Nomination and Appointment of the Party-state Leading Cadres), http://news.xinhuanet.com/ziliao/2003-01/18/content_695422.htm (accessed November 1, 2015). For additional information on the *xunshizu*, see "Zhongzubu guanyuan tan 'xunshi' zhidu" (The official of the Department of Organization discusses "*Xunshi*" system), http://news.eastday.com/eastday/news/news/node4938/node43662/userobject1ai731578.html (accessed November 1, 2015).

116. Yeo, "Complementing the Local Party Discipline."

117. Interview in DRC, Beijing (March 24, 2006).

118. *Xunshizu*'s supervision has been extended from cadre elites at the provincial level to the business management of key SOEs, and its monitoring of business management has come to be more formalized based on the party's guidelines. In 2004, the Central Committee of the CCP and the Department of Organization established *xunshizu* for the financial industry to strengthen regulation of the financial structure. See

"Zhongjiwei yu zhongzubu zujian guoqi xunshizu" (The Central Committee and the Department of Organization Establish *Xunshizu* for State-owned Firms), http://www .chinanews.com.cn/news/2006-04-13/8/716449.shtml (accessed March 8, 2007).

119. Moss, "China's Auto Market Slips."

120. Official website, http://global.geely.com/general/CompanyProfile.html (accessed June 23, 2013).

121. "Geely Automobile Holding Ltd," https://quotes.wsj.com/GELYF/financials /annual/balance-sheet (accessed April 30, 2018).

122. Geely official website, http://global.geely.com/general/CompanyProfile.html (accessed June 23, 2013).

123. Geely official website.

124. Zhang, "China's Private Sector."

125. Various sources point to the benefits of local auto companies for local governments, refer to Yun, "Dangzhengfu kaojin qiche jilide duice," 106–7; Yi, "Hude zhengfu yuanshou."

126. "Minqi zaoche de xinsuan lu."

127. "Minqi zaoche de xinsuan lu."

128. According to the EU Commission, Geely paid out US$2.7 billion for the acquisition of Volvo and management funds afterward, and half of the expense was from overseas investment. Among domestic sources, Daqing city's SASAC is one of the major stakeholders of Geely. Chen, "Oumeng pizhun jilishougou."

129. "Difang zhengfu daobijili."

130. Lu, "Woerwo zai huashoujia hezi."

131. Zhang, "Li Tiezheng."

132. State Council Secretariat, "Qiche chanye tiaozheng."

133. Liang, "Geely-Volvo Deal Approved."

134. Zhao and Liang, "Go-Abroad Geely on Verge," https://www.caixinglobal .com/2010-01-29/101018640.html.

135. Chen and Hu, "Geely Taps China Banks."

136. Zhao and Liang, "Go-Abroad Geely on Verge."

137. Similar logic is found in local government support for Geely. After Geely took over Volvo, it had to attract huge investments and capital to set up the manufacturing factories. In return for investments, Daqing came to hold the authority to review the progress of auto production and withdraw the funds if Geely failed to meet its agreements. Lu, "Woerwo zai huashoujia hezi."

138. Interview no. A(SH) 52, March 31, 2011.

139. Interview no. G9, July 20, 2012.

140. Wei and Young, "Geely Gets State Planner Approval for Volvo Buy," *Reuters*, July 30, 2010.

141. Zhao and Liang, "Go-Abroad Geely on Verge."

142. "Jili jituan shougou woerwo"; "Beiqi jinggou woerwo buleguan."

143. Campbell, "China's Carmakers."

144. Dunne, "Geely Just Bought Volvo."

## 4. The Telecommunications Service Industry

1. "Guoziwei mingque dianxin"; Luo, *Dianxin jingzheng guizhi*; Mou, *Qiyewu jingzheng xingshi*.

2. Unless otherwise noted, the telecoms industry in this study refers to "basic" service and does not include value-added or equipment services.

3. Li, "China's Telecom Industry on the Move," 3.

4. Pearson, "Governing the Chinese Economy."

5. Yuan, *Guanzhi zhili*, 131.

6. Wan, "Sector Reform," 161.

7. Zhang, "Universal Service Obligations," 3.

8. *Guanzhi zhili*, 131.

9. *Guanzhi zhili*, 6–7.

10. Because China was seriously deficient in investment capital for the telecom industry in the early stages of development, the Chinese government made up the deficit by charging high installation fees for telephone lines. During the seventh FYP (1986–90), installation fees and subcharges accounted for 30 percent of total investment capital in the telecom industry; over the eighth FYP (1991–95), it rose to 50 percent. Wan, "Sector Reform," 163.

11. Pei, *China's Trapped Transition*, 103.

12. Jordana, Levi-Faur, and Marin, "The Global Diffusion of Regulatory Agencies."

13. Pearson, "Governing the Chinese Economy."

14. See the official WTO website on the telecoms sector, http://www.wto.org/english/tratop_e/serv_e/telecom_e/telecom_e.htm.

15. WTO website. Upon entry, foreign firms may take up 50 percent ownership of value-added service firms within two years, and 49 percent ownership in mobile and fixed-line services within five to six years. DeWoskin, "The WTO and the Telecommunications Sector"; Yang, "Can the Chinese State Meet."

16. For more discussion on various barriers China Unicom has encountered, see Yan and Pitt, *Chinese Telecommunications Policy*, 82–83. For the prereform telecoms regime, see Lu, "The Management of China's Telecommunications Industry."

17. Interviews no. T2, December 7, 2005; no. T3, December 7, 2005; no. T6, December 15, 2005; no. T10, January 17, 2006.

18. Zhang and Peng, "Telecom Competition, Post-WTO Style." See also Mertha and Zeng, "Political Institutions, Resistance," 323.

19. Guan, *China's Telecommunications Reforms*, 21.

20. Kong, "China's Telecom Regulatory Regime," 165–66.

21. Guan, *China's Telecommunications Reforms*, 27.

22. Guan, *China's Telecommunications Reforms*, 27.

23. Dickie, "China Telecoms Move Raises Hopes"; "China Begins Revamp of Its Telecom Sector."

24. Dickie, "China Telecoms Move Raises Hopes"; "China Begins Revamp of Its Telecom Sector."

25. Meng et al., *Dianxin jingzheng guizhi*, 33.

26. Wang, "Zhongguo dianxianye de fazhan," 90.

27. Wang, "Zhongguo dianxianye de fazhan," 90.

28. Wang, "Zhongguo dianxianye de fazhan"; Yun, *Quanyewu jingzheng xingshi.*

29. Eaton, *Advance of the State,* 82–85.

30. Eaton, *Advance of the State,* 85.

31. Yun, *Quanyewu jingzheng xingshi,* 106.

32. Yun, *Quanyewu jingzheng xingshi,* 106.

33. Liu et al., *Zhongguo shige wunian,* 547, 566.

34. Freedom on the Net 2018, "China: Not Free," https://freedomhouse.org/report /freedom-net/2018/china (accessed March 5, 2019).

35. Wang, "Zhongguo dianxianye de fazhan," 90.

36. Huang, "Central-Local Relations," 663.

37. Huang, "Central-Local Relations," 663.

38. As figure 4.2 shows, they were named "offices" (Bangongshi) of Posts and Tele-communications at the municipal levels.

39. Mueller and Tan, *China in the Information Age,* 43.

40. Mueller and Tan, *China in the Information Age,* 43.

41. Liu and Feng, *Fazhan woguo zizhu zhishi,* 228.

42. Lieberthal *Governing China,* 187.

43. This leadership relationship is also found between the SASAC and telecoms giants, because the SASAC is the nominal ownership agency for central state-owned telecoms giants. Likewise, direct and formal regulation for telecoms firms cannot help but emerge.

44. Interviews no. T23, April 22, 2008; no. T25, April 29, 2008; no. T26, April 29, 2008.

45. Interviews no. T23, April 22, 2008; no. T25, April 29, 2008; no. T26, April 29, 2008. Other scholars have raised similar points. See Hu, "Dabuzhi gaige zhihou sheilai."

46. Wang, Xiao, and Tang, *Zhongguo longduan xing chanye,* 282–83.

47. Chen, "Zhongguo dianxinye," 132; Mou, *Qiyewu jingzheng xingshi,* 98; Yun, *Guan-zhi zhili,* 135; Wang, "Zhongguo dianxianye de fazhan," 90.

48. The SDPC was renamed the National Development and Reform Commission (NDRC) in the 2003 government restructuring.

49. Mou, *Qiyewu jingzheng xingshi,* 101.

50. Mou, *Qiyewu jingzheng xingshi,* 102.

51. Working Group on Research of the Problems of Government Control over Mono-poly Industry, "Dianxinye de zhengfu guanli," 5.

52. "Nation Cuts Telecoms Fees by 53 Percent in 5 Years," *Xinhua,* February 28, 2008.

53. "NDRC Will Fix Timetable for Mobile Phone One-Way Charging," *ChinaTech-News,* February 5, 2007.

54. Interview no. T3, December 7, 2005; Pearson, "Governing the Chinese Economy"; Pearson, "Variety Within and Without."

55. Pearson, "Regulation and Regulatory Politics."

56. See Yeo, "Between Owner and Regulator."

57. See Guan, *China's Telecommunications Reforms,* 24–30; Yu et al., "Market Perfor-mance of Chinese Telecommunications," 717–18.

58. According to the 2008 restructuring plan China Mobile would take over China Tietong and form New China Mobile; China Unicom would transfer its CDMA

network to China Telecom and merge with China Netcom; China Satcom would merge with China Telecom. Dickie, "China Telecoms Move Raises Hopes"; Jing, "Chinese Telecom Industry Consolidated."

59. Ming, "China Mobile Soars."

60. China Mobile is the largest player among operators, and as of 2007 controls about 70 percent of the domestic market in wireless services. Dickie, "China Telecoms Move Raises Hopes."

61. Ming, "Telecoms Undergo Restructuring-Again."

62. Interviews no. T27, May 8, 2008; no. T28, May 5, 2008; no. T29, May 14, 2008.

63. For more information on its origin and function, see Yang, *Remaking the Chinese Leviathan*; Pearson, "The Business of Governing Business."

64. Wang, *Ziran longduan chanye*, 137–38; Chen, "Zhongguo dianxinye," 132; Luo, "Cong zhengfu longduan," 59.

65. Yuan, *Guanzhi zhili*, 198; Su, *Dianxinye guanzhi moshi*, 46; Bai, "Woguo guoyou zichan jianguan," 61.

66. Author's correspondence interview with Chinese scholar, no. G13, July 15, 2008.

67. The operators independently compile the budget, but long-term, large-scale investment particularly needs the SASAC's oversight in the budgeting process. Author's correspondence interview, no. G13, July 15, 2008.

68. The other six industries are military, electricity, oil and chemistry, coal, civil aviation, and shipping. See "Guanyu tuijin guoyou ziben."

69. "Guanyu tuijin guoyou ziben."

70. For example, Eric Harwit analyzes the government's fiscal and regulatory industrial policies in China's telecoms equipment manufacturing industry. Harwit, "Building China's Telecommunications Network"; Clark, "Beijing Unveils Plans for Telecoms Super-Ministry."

71. It was restructured as the Central Network Security and Informatization LSG (Zhongyang Wanglu Anquan he Xinxihua Lingdao Xiaozu) in 2014, and its reinforced status can be seen in its head, Party General Secretary Xi Jinping, not the government head, Li Keqiang.

72. Wang, "Zhongyang wangleu anquan," 24; Dong, *Zhongxiao qiye xinxihua jianshe*, 36–39; Wang, *Zhongguo dianzi zhengfu*, 3–8.

73. Wang, "Zhongyang wangleu anquan," 25.

74. Zhou, *Zhongguo "xiaozu jizhi" yanjiu*, 71–80.

75. Interviews no. T27, May 8, 2008; no. T29, May 14, 2008. For details of the CCP formal organizational structure and functions, see Lieberthal, *Governing China*, 173–75, 178; Barton and Huang, "Governing China's Boards," 99–107.

76. See Article 13 of Interim Regulations on Supervision and Management of State-owned Assets of Enterprises (May 27, 2003), http://en.sasac.gov.cn/2003/11/24/c_118.htm.

77. Note that *bianzhi* (编制) refers to the authorized number of personnel in a party or government administrative organ, service organization (*shiye danwei*), or working unit (*qiye*), whereas the *nomenklatura* lists only the most important positions. Brødsgaard, "Institutional Reform and the *Bianzhi* System," 363–64. For more extensive studies on the *nomenklatura* system, see Burns, *The Chinese Communist Party's Nomenklatura*

*System*; Burns, "Strengthening CCP Control of Leadership Selection"; Brødsgaard and Zheng, *Bringing the Party Back In*; Brødsgaard and Zheng, *The Chinese Communist Party in Reform*; Chan, "Cadre Personnel Management."

78. Brødsgaard, "Institutional Reform and the *Bianzhi* System," 364.

79. Brødsgaard, "Institutional Reform and the *Bianzhi* System," 364.

80. Author's correspondence interview, no. G13, July 15, 2008.

81. Author's correspondence interview, no. G13, July 15, 2008.

82. Since Xi Jinping took office, private companies must establish a party committee inside the firms. Huang, "China's Communist Party Tightens Grip"; Heilmann, "How the CCP Embraces."

83. Wang, "Xiandai dianxin qiye dangwei." Wang served as deputy secretary of the party committee in Shanghai's telecom corporations in 2002.

84. Author's correspondence interview, no. G13, July 15, 2008.

85. According to the 2008 shake-up of the sector announced on May 23, 2008, China Netcom will be merged with China Unicom.

86. Chuan, "Why Is China's Telecommunications Market So Profitable?"

87. Yeo, "Contextualizing Corporate Governance."

88. For more information on the function and structure of the central inspection groups, refer to Yeo, "Complementing the Local Party Discipline."

89. Sheng and Wang, "Old Chums and a Troubled Telecom Chief."

90. Zhao and Yu, "Telecoms Carriers Put under Anti-Corruption Review."

91. "Zhongyang xunshixia de guoqi"; Qin, "Zhongguo liantong wanglufen."

92. Fligstein, *Architecture of Market*, 158.

93. Yuan, *Guanzhi zhili*, 134.

94. Harwit, *China's Telecommunications Revolution*, 50.

95. Wang, *Ziran longduan chanye*, 138.

96. Wu, *From Iron Fist to Invisible Hand*, table 5.1, 70–71.

97. Research unit for Longduanxing hangye de zhengfu guanzhi wenti yanjiu, *Jingji Yanjiu Cankao*, 5–7.

98. Luo, "Dianxin jingzheng guize," 83.

99. Li, "Chanye guizhi shijiao xiade," 42.

100. *Zhonghua renmin gongheguo fanlongduanfa.*

101. Bradsher, "China: Anti-Monopoly Law Approved."

102. Bradsher, "China: Anti-Monopoly Law Approved."

103. Lang, "Dianxin liantong falongduan'an"; Souhu Caijing, "Dianxin liantong cunzai longduanma?"

104. Chen, Liu, and Li, *Zhongguo weiji gongguan*, 179.

105. Livdahl, Sheng, and Li, "Potential Fines to Be Levied"; *Zhonghua renmin gongheguo fanlongduanfa.*

106. Chen, Liu, and Li, *Zhongguo weiji gongguan*, 179.

107. Chen, Liu, and Li, *Zhongguo weiji gongguan*, 179.

108. Chen, Liu, and Li, *Zhongguo weiji gongguan*, 181.

109. "Beijing Must Back NDRC in Probe."

110. Hille, "Beijing Probes Claims."

111. "NDRC Evaluating Rectification Results."

112. Wang, "Zhongguo dianxin, zhongguo liantong," 15; Jiao, "Dianxin, liantong longduan anzhong," 32.

113. Hille, "Beijing Probes Claims."

114. Zhang, "Fanlongduan fali 'jingji xianfa'," 45.

115. Gu and Zhou, "Dianxin liantong shexian longduan."

## 5. Beyond China

1. Yang, *Remaking the Chinese Leviathan*.

2. Martina, "Exclusive: In China."

3. Sun, "Ba jihua he tongji fangzai"; Sun, "Lun jiazhi"; Chen, "New Issues," 21–22.

4. Kennedy, *Business of Lobbying*; Naughton, "China's Distinctive System"; Pearson, "Variety Within and Without."

5. Heillmann, "Regulatory Innovation by Leninist Means."

6. He, "Regulation of the Financial Sector," 379.

7. He, "Regulation of the Financial Sector."

8. He, "Regulation of the Financial Sector."

9. He, "Regulation of the Financial Sector," 379.

10. Zhang, "Party, State, and Business."

11. Qi et al., "Fixing Wind Curtailment."

12. Email correspondence with Chinese scholar in Beijing (August 16, 2018).

13. Qi et al., "Fixing Wind Curtailment."

14. Email correspondence with Chinese scholar in Beijing (August 25, 2018).

15. Chung, "Political Economy of Industrial Restructuring," 68–69.

16. Eaton, "Political Economy of Advancing State."

17. Indeed, in spite of such regulatory difficulty, the CAAC tried to restructure the market by banning the establishment of a new airline. See Chung, "Political Economy of Industrial Restructuring"; Eaton, "Political Economy of Advancing State," 73.

18. Pearson, "The Business of Governing Business"; Eaton, "Political Economy of Advancing State."

19. Price et al., "How China Is Using State Power," 13.

20. National Development and Reform Commission, "Gangtie chanye fazhan zhengce."

21. In regression analysis, this can raise the issue of multicollinearity. But it would be hardly possible to consider only perfectly independent variables in a comparative case study that has an inherently limited number of observations. In addition, three explanatory variables in this book are derived from the theoretical framework of the market-institutional approach that attempts to disaggregate the market into institutions, aiming to highlight China's complex and diverse political economies. In this regard, the methodological concern of multicollinearity should not be taken seriously in this study.

22. Smith, "Life of the Party"; Chan, Kerevliet, and Unger, *Transforming Asian Socialism*.

23. Riedel and Comer, "Transition to a Market Economy," 193.

24. Kornai, *Highways and Byways*, xi.

25. Yeo and Painter, "Diffusion, Transmutation, and Regulatory Regime."

26. Doanh, "Market Economy with Socialistic Orientation," 163.

27. Doanh, "Market Economy with Socialistic Orientation."

28. Doanh, "Market Economy with Socialistic Orientation," 166.

29. Bartholomew et al., "Crossing the River by Feeling the Stones"; Yeo and Painter, "Diffusion, Transmutation, and Regulatory Regime."

30. Anh, Duc, and Chieu, "The Evolution of Vietnamese Industry," 241.

31. Riedel and Comer, "Transition to a Market Economy in Viet Nam," 193.

32. Thuy, "Economic *Doi Moi* in Vietnam," 102; Riedel and Comer, "Transition to a Market Economy in Viet Nam," 193.

33. Anh, Duc, and Chieu, "The Evolution of Vietnamese Industry," 18.

34. Anh, Duc, and Chieu, "The Evolution of Vietnamese Industry," 240–41.

35. Riedel and Comer, "Transition to a Market Economy in Viet Nam," 193.

36. Kikuchi, "Keeping Vietnam's Textile."

37. Hung, Thien, and Liem, "The Impact of Equitization on Firm Performance."

38. In Vietnam, a range of adaptive informal institutions—what Vietnamese scholars call "fence-breaking activities"—gradually dismantled socialist institutions, contributing to a more favorable political environment for economic experimentation. Malesky, "Leveled Mountains and Broken Fences"; Tsai, "Private Sector Development," 228–29.

39. Yeo, "Contextualizing Corporate Governance."

40. *Equitization* is a term used commonly in Vietnam to describe the transformation of an SOE into a joint stock company. See UNDP, "The State as Investor."

41. Yeo and Painter, "Diffusion, Transmutation, and Regulatory Regime"; CIEM, UNDP, and MPI, "Competitiveness and the Impact of Trade Liberalization," 14; Cheshier and Penrose, "Top 200 Industrial Strategies."

42. CIEM, UNDP, and MPI, "Competitiveness and the Impact of Trade Liberalization," 14.

43. Hung, Thien, and Liem, "The Impact of Equitization," 70.

44. North, *Understanding the Process.*

45. Refer to the following study comparing China and Vietnam: Kerkvliet, Chan, and Unger, "Comparing the Chinese and Vietnamese Reforms," 1, 7.

46. Boudarel, "Influences and Idiosyncrasies"; Womack, "Reform in Vietnam," 185.

47. Kerkvliet, Chan, and Unger, "Comparing the Chinese and Vietnamese Reforms," 7.

48. Abrami et al., "Vietnam through Chinese Eyes," 260.

49. Abrami et al., "Vietnam through Chinese Eyes," 259.

50. Abrami et al., "Vietnam through Chinese Eyes."

51. Abrami et al., "Vietnam through Chinese Eyes," 261.

52. Anh, Duc, and Chieu, "The Evolution of Vietnamese Industry," 248.

53. Anh, Duc, and Chieu, "The Evolution of Vietnamese Industry," 22.

54. Vogel, *Freer Markets, More Rules.*

55. Pearson, "Regulation and Regulatory Politics," 12.

56. Lindblom, *Politics and Markets.*

57. Chen, "New Issues since the Basic Competition," 21–22; Sun, "Ba jihua he tongji fangzai"; Sun, "Lun jiazhi."

58. Steinfeld, *Playing Our Game*, 24–39.

59. Steinfeld, *Playing Our Game*, 24–39.

60. Yeo, "Contextualizing Corporate Governance."

61. Holz, "Industrial Policies and the Changing Patterns," 23; Wildau, "US Tariffs Target"; see "President Donald J. Trump Is Confronting China's Unfair Trade Policies," https://www.whitehouse.gov/briefings-statements/president-donald-j-trump-confronting -chinas-unfair-trade-policies/ (accessed July 12, 2019).

62. Huang, *Capitalism with Chinese Characteristics*.

63. Huang, *Capitalism with Chinese Characteristics*, 41.

64. Thun, *Changing Lanes in China*; Huang, *Capitalism with Chinese Characteristics*, 42.

65. Huang, *Capitalism with Chinese Characteristics*, 41.

66. Huang, *Capitalism with Chinese Characteristics*, 43.

67. Brødsgaard, "Politics and Business Group Formation in China"; Eaton, *Advance of the State*; Yeo, "Contextualizing Corporate Governance."

68. The heart of the national economy includes armaments, electrical power and distribution, oil and chemicals, telecommunications, coal, aviation, and shipping; pillar sectors include machinery, automobile, IT, construction, steel, base materials, chemicals, land surveying, and R&D. Breslin, "Government-Industry Relations," 37.

69. Breslin, "Government-Industry Relations," 37; "2015 Zhongguo 500 qiang qiye gaofeng luntan," http://finance.sina.com.cn/focus/2015zgqy500q/ (accessed March 27, 2017).

70. Breslin, "Government-Industry Relations," 36.

71. Lardy, *Markets over Mao*, 75 and chapter 3.

72. Zhao and Su, "Xi Jinping guanyu quanmain," 45–46; Zhao and Ji, "Xi Jinping quanmin shenhua," 34.

73. Feng, "Xi Jinping Reminds China's State"; emphasis added.

74. In March 2018, it was transformed into the Central Comprehensive and Deepening Reform Commission (Zhongyang Quanmian Shenhua Gaige Weiyuanhui, 中央全面深化改革委员会).

75. Huang, "How Leading Small Groups Help Xi."

76. Xi, "Guanyu zhonggong zhongyang."

## Appendix 2

1. Pearson, "Variety Within and Without."

2. Gao and Yu, *Jichu sheshi chanye*, 2.

3. Gao and Yu, *Jichu sheshi chanye*, 30–31.

4. They include Zhang Xinzhu (Chinese Academy of Social Sciences), Gao Shiji (Development Research Center of State Council), and Ma Jun (Development Research Center of State Council); interview no. T16, February 9, 2006.

5. Gao and Qin, "Cong zhidu bianqian," 27–28.

6. Gao, "Cong fada guojia zhengfu."

7. They include Zhou Qiren (Beijing University), Yu Hui (Chinese Academy of Social Sciences), and Kan Kaili (Beijing University of Posts and Telecommunications).

8. Majone, *Regulating Europe*, 48; Vogel, *Freer Markets*; Jordana and Levi-Faur, *Politics of Regulation*.

9. Pearson, "The Business of Governing Business," 299.

10. Vogel, *Freer Markets*, 130.

11. Moran, *British Regulatory State*.

12. Levi-Faur and Gilad, "Rise of the British Regulatory State."

13. Vogel, *Freer Markets*.

14. Yang, *Remaking the Chinese Leviathan*; Pearson, "The Business of Governing Business"; Pearson, "Governing the Chinese Economy"; Pearson, "Variety Within and Without"; Yeo and Pearson, "Regulating Decentralized State Industries"; Yeo, "Between Owner and Regulator."

15. Clarke, "Corporatization, Not Privatization"; Pearson, "Governing the Chinese Economy."

16. Pearson, "The Business of Governing Business"; Pearson, "Variety Within and Without."

17. Yang, *Remaking the Chinese Leviathan*, 14.

18. Yang, *Remaking the Chinese Leviathan*, 18.

19. Yang, *Remaking the Chinese Leviathan*, 17–18.

20. Yang, *Remaking the Chinese Leviathan*, 18.

21. On the other hand, Andrew Mertha argues soft centralization in that "although bureaucracy is centralized from the township/county to the provincial level, it remains decentralized between the centre and the province." Mertha, "China's 'Soft' Centralization."

22. Gao, "Cong fada guojia zhengfu"; Gao and Yu, *Jichu sheshi chanye*; Pearson, "Variety Within and Without."

23. Pearson, "The Business of Governing Business," 298, 315, 332.

24. Yeo, "Between Owner and Regulator"; Hsueh, *China's Regulatory State*; Pearson, "Variety Within and Without"; Pearson, "State-Owned Business and Party-State Regulation."

25. Pei, *China's Trapped Transition*.

26. Shih, *Factions and Finance in China*.

27. The classic works include Johnson, *MITI and the Japanese Miracle*; Amsden, *Asia's Next Giant*.

28. Pearson, "The Business of Governing Business"; Nolan, *China and the Global Economy*.

29. Pearson, "The Business of Governing Business," 300.

30. Pearson, "The Business of Governing Business," 300.

31. Pearson, "The Business of Governing Business," 301.

32. See Kroeber, "Developmental Dreams."

33. Hsueh, *China's Regulatory State*.

34. Hsueh, *China's Regulatory State*, 3.

35. Tsai and Cook, "Developmental Dilemmas in China."

36. Chin, *China's Automotive Modernization*, 16.

37. Eaton, *The Advance of the State*, 22–24.

38. Hellmann, "Winners Take All"; Varese, " Transition to the Market and Corruption"; Solnick, "Breakdown of Hierarchies."

39. Pei, *China's Trapped Transition*, 40.

40. Pei, *China's Trapped Transition*, 34.
41. Edin, "State Capacity and Local Agent Control," 2.
42. Hood et al., *Regulation inside Government*, 194.
43. The terminology of "market socialism" was originally used by academic economists to highlight public ownership in the market economy, whereas "socialist market economy" is characteristic of the language of the official Chinese ideology. See Kornai, *From Socialism to Capitalism*, 47.
44. Pearson, "The Business of Governing Business"; Chin, *China's Automotive Modernization*; Hsueh, *China's Regulatory State*; Eaton, *Advance of the State*.
45. Pearson, "The Business of Governing Business"; Pearson, "Governing the Chinese Economy"; Pearson, "Variety Within and Without."
46. Heilmann, "Regulatory Innovation by Leninist Means," 4.
47. Heilmann, "Regulatory Innovation by Leninist Means," 2. On the other hand, Victor Shih emphasizes factional rivalry as a key variable in accounting for centralization of the financial industry in China. See Shih, "Authoritarian Power Imperatives."

# Glossary

Beijing Qiche Gongye Gongsi Ban-
gongsi 北京汽车工业办公司 Beijing
Auto Industry Corporation General
Office

*chongzu* 重组 market restructuring

*dabuzhi gaige* 大部制改革 super-ministry
reform
*dang* 党 party
*dangnei jiandu* 党内监督 internal party
supervision
*daxing qiye* 大型企业 large enterprises
Dianxin Guanliju 电信管理局 Telecommunications Administration Bureau
Dongshihui 董事会 board of directors
Dongshizhang 董事长 chairman of
the board

*fanlongduan fa* 反垄断法 Anti-monopoly
Law
Fanlongduan Weiyuanhui 反垄断委员会
Anti-monopoly Commission
*fanlongduan zhixingjiegou* 反垄断执行
结构 Anti-monopoly enforcement
structure
*gaige kaifang* 改革开放 reform and
opening

Guangzhou Qiche Gongye Bangongsi
广州汽车工业办公司 Guangzhou Auto
Industry Office
*gufenzhi* 股份制 shareholding system
*gugan qiye* 骨干企业 key enterprises
*guihua* 规划 program
Guojia Jingji Xinxi Guanli Lingdao
Xiaozu 国家经济管理领导小组
National Economy and Information
Management Leading Small
Group
Guojia Wanglu Yu Xinxi Anquan Xietiao
Xiaozu 国家网路与安全协调小组
National Network and Information
Security Coordination Small Group
*guojin mintui* 国进民退 "state advance,
private retreat"
*guoying qiye* 国营企业 state-run
enterprises
*guoyou zhongxin jingji* 国有中心经济 state
ownership-centered economy
Guoziwei Dangwei 国资委党委 SASAC
Party Committee
Guoziwei Xunshizu 国资委巡视组
SASAC Inspection Group

*huan jishu he shichang* 换技术和市场
exchange technology with market

Jiage Jianchaju 价格检查局 Pricing Supervision Bureau

*jiandu* 监督 oversight

*jianguan* 监管 regulation

Jianshihui 监事会 Supervisory Commission

*jianyi* 建议 suggestion

*jiefang* 解放 liberation

*jihua* 计划 planning

*jingji mingmai* 经济命脉 economy lifeline

Jingying Guanli Weiyuanhui 经营管理委员会 Business Management Commission

*jingyingzhe chengren zhidu* 经营者承认制度 system of manager approval

*juedui kongzhili* 绝对控制力 absolute control

*laobaixing* 老百姓 ordinary people

*lingdao guanxi* 领导关系 leadership relationship

*lingdao xiaozu* 领导小组 leading small groups

*longtou* 龙头 driving force

*pizhun* 批准 approval

Qiche Gongye Guanli Ju 汽车工业管理局 Auto Industry Managing Bureau

*sanda, sanxiao* 三大三小 "three large, three small"

*shenghua gaige* 深化改革 deepening reform

*shidian* 试点 experiment

*shuangzhong lingdao* 双中领导 dual leadership

*tiaotao* 条条 vertically

Tongxin Guanliju 通信管理局 Communication Administration Bureau

Wujiaju 物价局 Pricing Bureau

*xietiao* 协调 coordination

Xinxihua Lingdao Xiaozu 信息化领导小组 Informatization Leading Small Group

Xunshizu Lingdao Xiaozu 巡视组领导小组 Inspection Work Leading Small Group

*yangqi* 央企 central state-owned enterprises

*yewu guanxi* 业务关系 professional relationship

*yindao* 引导 guide

Youxian Gongsi 有限公司 limited liability companies

*zhanlue zhongyao bufen* 张略重要部分 strategically important sectors

*zheng* 政 government

*zhengqi fenkai* 政企分开 separating government from enterprise

*zhidao xing jihua* 指导计划 guidance planning

*zhiling* 指令 command

*zhilingxing jihua* 指令性计划 mandatory planning

*zhizhu chanye* 支柱 pillar sectors

Zhongguo Dianxin Zongju 中国电信总局 General Bureau of China Telecom

Zhongguo Qiche Gongye Gongsi 中国汽车工业公司 Chinese National Auto Industry Corporation

Zhongguo Qiche Gongye Lianhehui 中国汽车工业联合会 Chinese Auto Industry Association

Zhongguo Qiche Gongye Zonggongsi 中国汽车工业总公司 Chinese National Auto Industry General Corporation

Zhongyang Caijing Lingdao Xiaozu 中央财经领导小组 Central Finance and Economy Leading Small Group

*Zhongyang Caijing Lingdao Xiaozu Bangongsi* 中央财经领导小组办公司 Central Finance and Economy Leading Small Group (CFELSG) Office

Zhongyang Jingji Gongzuo Huiyi 中央经济工作会议 Central Economy Work Conference

Zhongyang Xunshizu 中央巡视组 central inspection groups

*zhongyao zhizhu chanye* 重要支柱产业 important pillar sectors

*zhuada fangxiao* 抓大放小 "grasping large, letting go small"

*zhuti* 主体 main system

*zifei* 资费 service pricing

*zizhu chuangxin* 自主创新 indigenous innovation

*zizhu pinpai* 自主品牌 indigenous brands

*zonghe hangye* 综合行业 comprehensive industry

Zongjingli 总经理 president

*zouchuqu* 走出去 going out

# References

Abrami, Regina, Edmund Malesky, and Yu Zheng. "Vietnam through Chinese Eyes: Divergent Accountability in Single-Party Regimes." In M. Dimitrov (ed.), *Why Communism Did Not Collapse: Understanding Authoritarian Regime Resilience in Asia and Europe*, 237–75. New York: Cambridge University Press, 2013.

Amsden, Alice. *Asia's Next Giant: South Korea and Late Industrialization*. New York: Oxford University Press, 1989.

An, Limei. "Zhongzubu zaikaoli yiqi zongjingli Xu Xianping neimu" (The Organization Department of CPC tested FAW again, the secret story of competition of a general manager). *Qicheren*, 24 May 2012. http://auto.cntv.cn/20120524/101169_1.shtml (accessed 26 February 2015).

Andrews-Speed, Philip, Stephen Dow, and Zhiguo Gao. "The Ongoing Reforms to China's Government and State Sector: The Case of the Energy Industry." *Journal of Contemporary China* 9, no. 23 (2000): 5–20.

Anh, Nguyen Thi Tue, Luu Minh Duc, and Trinh Duc Chieu. "The Evolution of Vietnamese Industry." WIDER Working Paper no. 19, April 2014.

———. "The Evolution of Vietnamese Industry." In C. Newman, J. Page, J. Rand, A. Shimeles, M. Söderbom, and F. Tarp (eds.), *Manufacturing Transformation: Comparative Studies of Industrial Development in Africa and Emerging Asia*. Oxford Scholarship Online, August 2016.

Arrighi, Giovanni. *Adam Smith in Beijing: Lineages of the Twenty-First Century*. New York: Verso, 2007.

Bai, Jinyai. "Woguo guoyou zichan jianguan tizhi de liche yanjin yu fazhan yanjiu" (A research on the historical evolution and development of China's state-owned assets supervision system). *Xinzheng yu Fa*, no. 7 (2016): 57–73.

Barma, Naazneen H., and Steven K. Vogel. "Economic Sociology." In N. H. Barma and S. K. Vogel (eds.), *The Political Economy Reader: Markets as Institutions*, 117–20. New York: Routledge, 2008.

Bartholomew, Ann, Stephen Lister, Edward Mountfield, and Nguyen Van Minh. "Crossing the River by Feeling the Stones: Vietnam's Experiment with Block Grant Budgeting." *International Journal of Public Administration* 28, no. 3 (2005): 337–54.

Barton, Dominic, and Richard He Huang. "Governing China's Boards: An Interview with John Thornton." *McKinsey Quarterly* 1 (2007): 99–107.

"Beijing Must Back NDRC in Probe of Telecoms Giants Monopoly of State-owned Firms over Key Sectors Submitting a Block to Nation's Economic Growth." *South China Morning Post*, 14 November 2011.

Beijing shifan daxue jingji yu ziyuan guanli yanjiusuo (Institute of Economics and Resource Management, Beijing Normal University). *2003 nian zhongguo shichang jingji fazhanbaogao* (Report on the Development of China's Market Economy in 2003). Beijing: Zhongguo duiwai jingji maoyi chubanshe, 2003.

"Beiqi jinggou woerwo buleguan yiqi kanzhong fadongli" (It is not optimistic BAIC bidding for Volvo, FAW prefers engine). *Chexunwang*, 20 August 2009. http://www.chexun.com/news/20090820/26771.html (accessed 18 February 2015).

Bian, Morris L. *The Making of the State Enterprise System in Modern China: The Dynamics of Institutional Change*. Cambridge, MA: Harvard University Press, 2005.

———. "Explaining the Dynamics of Change: Transformation and Evolution of China's Public Economy through War, Revolution, and the Peace, 1928–2008." In B. Naughton and K. L. Tsai (eds.), *State Capitalism, Institutional Adaptation, and the Chinese Miracle*. New York: Cambridge University Press, 2015.

Boudarel, Georges. "Influences and Idiosyncrasies in the Line and Practice of the Vietnam Communist Party." In W. S. Turley (ed.), *Vietnamese Communism in Comparative Perspective*, 158–66. Boulder, CO: Westview Press, 1980.

Bradsher, Keith. "China: Anti-Monopoly Law Approved." *New York Times*, 31 August 2007.

———. "China's Embrace of Foreign Cars." *New York Times*, 8 April 2014.

Brandt, Loren, and Eric Thun. "The Fight for the Middle: Upgrading, Competition, and Industrial Development in China." *World Development* 38, no. 11 (November 2010): 1555–74.

Breslin, Shaun. "Capitalism with Chinese Characteristics: The Public, the Private, and the International." Asia Research Center Working Paper no. 104, 2004.

———. "Government-Industry Relations in China: A Review of the Art of the State." In A. Walter and X. Zhang (eds.), *East Asian Capitalism: Diversity, Continuity, and Change*. Oxford: Oxford University Press, 2012.

Brødsgaard, Kjeld Erik. "Institutional Reform and the *Bianzhi* System in China." *China Quarterly*, no. 170 (June 2002): 361–86.

———. "Politics and Business Group Formation in China." *China Quarterly*, no. 211 (September 2012): 624–48.

Brødsgaard, Kjeld Erik, and Yongnian Zheng, eds. *Bringing the Party Back In: How China Is Governed*. Singapore: Times Academic Press, 2004.

———. *The Chinese Communist Party in Reform*. London: Routledge, 2006.

Burns, John P. *The Chinese Communist Party's Nomenklatura System*. Armonk, NY: M. E. Sharpe, 1989.

————. "Strengthening CCP Control of Leadership Selection: The 1990 *Nomenklatura.*" *China Quarterly*, no. 138 (1994): 458–91.

Cai, Ruipengai. "Zhongyang caijing lingdao xiaozu" (Leading Group for Finance and Economic Affairs). *Jinrong Shijie*, 16 June 2016.

Campbell, Peter. "China's Carmakers: Too Many Are Too Small to Be Viable." *Financial Times*, 23 October 2017.

Cao, Yingwang. "1958 nian yu 1962 nian zhongyang caijing xiaozu" (The central finance and economy leading small groups in 1958 and 1962). *Dangshi Bolan*, no. 11 (2013): 4–8.

Cao, Yu, Zengyou Pan, and Xiaoqiang Wu. "Woguo qiche chanye butong zibenjian binggou chongzu tedian fenxi" (Analysis on the characteristics among different capital merging and acquisition in China's auto industry). *Shangye Qiche*, no. 5 (2013): 126–29.

Carrigan, Christopher, and Cary Coglianese. "The Politics of Regulation: From New Institutionalism to New Governance." *Annual Review of Political Science* 14 (2011): 107–29.

Chai, Joseph C. *China: Transition to a Market Economy*. Oxford: Oxford University Press, 1997.

Chan, Anita, Benedict J. Tria Kerevliet, and Jonathan Unger, eds. *Transforming Asian Socialism: China and Vietnam Compared*. St. Leonards, NSW: Allen & Unwin, 1999.

Chan, Hon S. "Cadre Personnel Management in China: The Nomenklatura System, 1990–1998." *China Quarterly*, no. 179 (September 2004): 703–34.

Chen, Xianhong, Xiaocheng Liu, and Huajun Li. *Zhongguo weiji gongguan anli yanjiu baogao 2011 juan* (A Case Study of China Crisis Public Relations). Huazhong: Huazhong Keji Daxue Chubanshe, 2012.

Chen, Xiaohong. "Zhongguo dianxinye: zhengce, chanye zuzhi de bianhua ji ruogan jianyi" (China's telecoms industry: changes of policy and industrial organizations, and some suggestions). *Guanli Shijie*, no. 1 (1999): 126–38.

Chen, Yunhen. "New Issues since the Basic Competition of the Socialist Transformation." In N. Lardy and K. Lieberthal (eds.), *Chen Yun's Strategy for China Development: A Non-Maoist Alternative*, 7–22. Armonk, NY: M. E. Sharpe, 1982.

Chen, Zhijue. "Oumeng pizhun jilishougou woerwo touzizhe daqing guoziwei fuchu shuimian" (The EU approved Geely will purchase Volvo, the situation of investors congratulating SASAC will rise to the surface). *Nanfang ribao*, 8 July 2010. http://finance.sina.com.cn/roll/20100708/08118255165.shtml (accessed 24 February 2015).

Cheng, Lingen. "Zhongguo gaoceng lingdao xiaozu de yunzuo jizhi jiqi yanhua" (The operational mechanism and evolution of China's top-level leadership small group). In Y. Keping (ed.), *Zhonggong de zhili yu shiying: bijiao de shiye* (Governance and Adaptation of Chinese Communist Party: A Comparative Perspective), 20–47. Beijing: Zhongyang Bianyi Chubanshe, 2015.

Cheshier, Scott, and Jago Penrose. "Top 200 Industrial Strategies of Viet Nam's Largest Firms." UNDP, 2007. http://www.un.org.vn/en/publications/un-wide-publications/doc_details/27-the-top-200-industrial-strategies-of-viet-nams-largest-firms.html.

Chin, Gregory. *China's Automotive Modernization: The Party-State and Multinational Corporations*. London: Palgrave Macmillan, 2010.

China Association of Automobile Manufacturers and China Automotive Technology and Research Center. *China Automobile Industry Yearbook 1988–2013*. Beijing: Jixie gongye chubanshe, 1989–2015.

"China Begins Revamp of Its Telecom Sector." Reuters, 23 May 2008.

"China Defines Key National Economic Sectors." *China Daily*, 18 December 2006. http://english.people.com.cn/200612/18/print20061218_333734.html.

"Chinese Automaker Hoping for Revival." *Xinhua News*, 28 April 2013. http://english .people.com.cn/90778/8226355.html (accessed 11 March 2014).

Chuan, Tong. "Why Is China's Telecommunications Market So Profitable?" *Epoch Times*, 11 October 2006.

Chung, Jae Ho. "Reappraising Central-Local Relations in Deng's China: Decentralization, Dilemmas of Control, and Diluted Effects of Reform." In C. Chao and B. J. Dickson (eds.), *Remaking the Chinese State: Strategies, Society, and Security*, 46–75. London: Routledge, 2001.

———. "The Political Economy of Industrial Restructuring in China: The Case of Civil Aviation." *China Journal* 50 (July 2003): 61–82.

———. *Centrifugal Empire: Central-Local Relations in China*. New York: Columbia University Press, 2016.

CIEM, UNDP, and MPI. "Competitiveness and the Impact of Trade Liberalization in Vietnam: The Case of Telecommunications." Hanoi, May 2006.

Clark, Robert. "Beijing Unveils Plans for Telecom Super-Ministry." *Bloomberg*, 13 March 2008.

Clarke, Donald. "Corporate Governance in China: An Overview." *China Economic Review* 14, no. 4 (2003): 494–507.

———. "Corporatization, Not Privatization." *China Economic Quarterly* 7, no. 3 (2003): 27–30.

Cui, Xiaosu. "Zhongyang caijing lingdao xiaozu de bianchen" (The evolution of the Central Finance and Economy Leading Small Group). *Shidai Qingnian*, July 2014.

DeWoskin, Kenneth J. "The WTO and the Telecommunications Sector in China." *China Quarterly* 167 (2001): 630–54.

Dickie, Mure. "China Telecoms Move Raises Hopes of Overhaul." *Financial Times*, 23 May 2008.

Dickson, Bruce J. *Red Capitalists in China: The Party, Private Entrepreneurs, and Prospects for Political Change*. New York: Cambridge University Press, 2003.

———. *Wealth into Power: The Communist Party's Embrace of China's Private Sector*. New York: Cambridge University Press, 2008.

"Difang zhengfu daobijili: woerwo xiangmuluo dingjiading" (Local government forced Geely: Volvo's projects settled in Jiading). *Diyi caijing ribao*, 24 August 2010. http:// auto.163.com/10/0824/08/6ERCVKKV00084IJH.html (accessed 24 February 2015).

Ding, Changqing. "Jixie gongye shixing sanzhong jihua guanli xiangshi de jinglian yu wenti" (The experience and problems of implementing the three forms of planning and management in the machinery industry). *Jingji Guanli*, no. 4 (1984): 8–10.

Doanh, Le Dang. "Market Economy with Socialistic Orientation: The Evolution in Vietnam." In J. Kornai and Y. Qian (eds.), *Market and Socialism: In the Light of the Experiences of China and Vietnam*, 162–81. New York: Palgrave Macmillan, 2009.

Dong, Yan. *Zhongxiao qiye xinxihua jianshe yu zhili* (Information building and management of small and medium-sized enterprises). Zhishi chanquan chubanshe, 2012.

Dunne, Michael. "Geely Just Bought Volvo. Now What?" *Wall Street Journal*, 7 April 2010.

Eaton, Sarah. "Political Economy of Advancing State: The Case of China's Airlines Reform." *China Journal* 90 (2013): 64–86.

———. *The Advance of the State in Contemporary China: State-Market Relations in the Reform Era*. Cambridge: Cambridge University Press, 2016.

Edin, Maria. "State Capacity and Local Agent Control in China: CCP Cadre Management from a Township Perspective." *China Quarterly* 173 (2003): 35–52.

Eisner, Marc Allen. *Regulatory Politics in Transition*. Baltimore, MD: Johns Hopkins University Press, 2000.

Ernst, Dieter, and Barry Naughton. "China's Emerging Industrial Economy." In C. A. McNally (ed.), *China's Emergent Political Economy: Capitalism in the Dragon's Lair*, 39–59. New York: Routledge, 2008.

Estrin, Saul, and Peter Holmes. *French Planning in Theory and Practice*. London: Allen & Unwin, 1983.

Evans, Peter. *Embedded Autonomy: States and Industrial Transformation*. Princeton, NJ: Princeton University Press, 1995.

Fan, Maoyouan, and Gufu Zhang. "Shehuizhuyi jingji zhong guihua yu shichang guanxi wenti" (Problems on the relationship between planning and market in the socialist economy). *Jingji Yanjiu*, no. 3 (1979): 61–65.

Feigenbaum, Evan A. "A Chinese Puzzle: Why Economic 'Reform' in Xi's China Has More Meanings than Market Liberalization." *Macro Polo: Decoding China's Economic Arrival*, 26 February 2018. https://macropolo.org/analysis/chinese-puzzle-economic-reform-xis-china-meanings-market-liberalization/.

Feng, Emily. "Xi Jinping Reminds China's State Companies of Who's the Boss." *New York Times*, 13 October 2016.

———. "Chinese Tech Groups Display Closer Ties with Communist Party." *Financial Times*, 11 October 2017.

Fligstein, Neil. *The Architecture of Market*. Princeton, NJ: Princeton University Press, 2001.

Gao, Shiji. "Cong fada guojia zhengfu jianguan zhineng de kuozhang licheng kan shichang jingji zhong zhengfu zhineng yanjin" (Looking at the state in the market economy from the historical process of the function of state regulation in an advanced country). Forum: Zhongguo zhengfu tizhi gaige (Chinese Government System Reform), Zhejiang, China, 9–10 June 2007. http://www.chinareform.org.cn/cirdbbs/dispbbs.asp?boardID=12&ID=131038 (accessed 12 August 2007).

Gao, Shiji, and Hai Qin. "Cong zhidu bianqian de jiaodu kan jianguan tixi yanjin he jianguanguojia xingqi: guoji jinglian de yi zhong quanshi he zhongguo de gaige shijian fenxi" (From the view of institutional transition looking at the improvement of the regulatory system and the rise of the regulatory state: explanation from international experience and analysis of China's reform and practice). Paper prepared for OECD *Governance in China*, 2004.

Gao, Shiji, and Yanshan Yu. *Jichu sheshi chanye de zhengfu jianguan: zhidu sheji he nengli jianshe* (Government Regulation of Infrastructure: Institutional Design and Capacity Building). Beijing: Shehui kexue wenxian chubanshe, 2010.

Gilardi, Fabrizio. "Institutional Change in Regulatory Policies: Regulation through Independent Agencies and the Three New Institutionalisms." In J. Jordana and D. Levi-Faur (eds.), *The Politics of Regulation: Institutions and Regulatory Reforms for the Age of Governance*, 67–89. Cheltenham, UK: Edward Elgar, 2004.

Gu, Xiaoyu, and Zhou Yu. "Dianxin liantong shexian longduan huochi dafadan" (Alleged monopolistic conduct by China Telecom and China Unicom or eat a menu of infringement). *Xinlang Caijing*, 10 November 2011. http://finance.sina.com.cn/chanjing/gsnews/20111110/072510787933.shtml.

Guan, Scott Yunxiang. *China's Telecommunications Reforms: From Monopoly towards Competition*. New York: Nova Science Publishers, 2003.

"Guanyu tuijin guoyou ziben tiaozheng he guoyou qiye zhongzu de zhidao yijian" (Leading opinion on enhancing state capital coordinating and state firm restructuring). *SINA*, 18 December 2006. http://finance.sina.com.cn/g/20061218/11133173443.shtml.

*Guanzhi zhili: zhongguo dianxin chanye gaige shizheng yanjiu* (Regulatory Governance: Chinese Telecoms Industry Reform Empirical Study). Beijing: Renmin youdian chubanshe, 2009.

Gui, Tiantian. "Xunshizu zhiqi xiaoshou fubai duofa shiyu gaoguanbei 'dianmin'" (Inspection group pointed out corruption in sales several times, ten executives or more were called the roll). *Beijing qingnian bao*, 30 October 2014. http://business.sohu.com/20141030/n405596184.shtml (accessed 26 February 2015).

"Guowuyuan yuanze tongguo qiche, gangtie chanye jinxing guihua" (The State Council's principle is passed that the automobile and iron/steel industry is going to implement revitalization plan). *Shanghai zhengquanbao*, 15 January 2009.

"Guoziwei mingque dianxin hangye wei guoyou jingji yankong yangye" (SASAC strictly controls the telecom industry for the state-owned economy). *Beijing yuele xinbao*, 12 December 2006.

Guven, Ali Burak. "Reforming Sticky Institutions: Persistence and Change in Turkish Agriculture." *Studies in Comparative and International Development* 44 (2009): 162–87.

Han, Maoqianan. "Jiji zuohao xunshi gongzuo cujin qiye youhao youkuai fazhan" (In order to complete inspection work and rapidly and well improve development of enterprises). *Guoyou zichan guanli* (December 2010): 44–46.

Harwit, Eric. *China's Automobile Industry: Policy, Problems, and Prospects*. Armonk, NY: M. E. Sharpe (1995).

———. "Building China's Telecommunications Network: Industrial Policy and the Role of Chinese State-owned, Foreign and Private Domestic Enterprises." *China Quarterly* 190 (June 2007): 311–42.

———. *China's Telecommunications Revolution*. New York: Oxford University Press, 2008.

He, Jianzhange, Jiye Wang, and Kaitai Wu. "Guanyu jihua tiaojie he shichang tiaojie xiangjiehe wenti" (On the problems of combining planning and markets). *Jingji Yanjiu*, no. 5 (1980): 21–25.

He, Weiping. "The Regulation of the Financial Sector in China: A Tale of Two Governments." *Journal of Corporate Law Studies* 18, no. 2 (2018): 339–80.

Heilmann, Sebastian. "Regulatory Innovation by Leninist Means: Communist Party Supervision in China's Financial Industry." *China Quarterly* 181 (March 2005): 1–21.

———. "Policy-Making and Political Supervision in Shanghai's Financial Industry." *Journal of Contemporary China* 14, no. 45 (November 2005): 643–48.

———. "How the CCP Embraces and Co-opts China's Private Sector." MERICS, 21 November 2017. https://www.merics.org/en/blog/how-ccp-embraces-and-co-opts -chinas-private-sector (accessed 23 September 2018).

Heilmann, Sebastian, and Oliver Melton. "The Reinvention of Development Planning in China, 1993–2012." *Modern China* 39, no. 6 (2013): 580–628.

Hellmann, Joel S. "Winners Take All: The Politics of Partial Reform in Post-Communist Transition." *World Politics* 50, no. 2 (1998): 203–34.

Hille, Kathrin. "Beijing Probes Claims of Telecoms Monopolies." *Financial Times*, 9 November 2011.

Holz, Carsten A. "Industrial Policies and the Changing Patterns of Investment in the Chinese Economy." *China Journal*, no. 81 (January 2019): 23–57.

Hood, Christoper, Colin Scott, Oliver James, and Tony Travers. *Regulation inside Government: Waste-Watchers, Quality Police and Sleaze-Busters*. Oxford: Oxford University Press, 1998.

Hsu, Robert C. "The Political Economy of Guidance Planning in Post-Mao China." *Weltwirtschaftliches Archiv*, Bd. 122, H. 2 (1986): 382–94.

Hsueh, Roselyn. *China's Regulatory State: A New Strategy for Globalization*. Ithaca, NY: Cornell University Press, 2012.

Hu, Yaobang. *Quanmian kaichuang shehuizhuyi xiandaihua jianshe de xin jumian* (Pioneering a New Era of Socialist Modernization). Beijing: Renmin Chubanshe, 1982.

Hu, Yaqing. "Dabuzhi gaige zhihou sheilai jianguan dianxinye" (Who will regulate the telecoms industry after super-ministry reform?). *Zhongguo Jingying Bao*, 17 March 2008.

Huang, Carry. "How Leading Small Groups Help Xi Jinping and Other Party Leaders Exert Power." *South China Morning Post*, 20 January 2014.

———. "China's Communist Party Tightens Grip on Private Firms, Joint Ventures." *South China Morning Post*, 18 June 2015.

Huang, Yasheng. "Central-Local Relations in China during the Reform Era: The Economic and Institutional Dimensions." *World Development* 24, no. 4 (1996): 655–72.

———. *Inflation and Investment Controls in China: The Political Economy of Central-Local Relations during the Reform Era*. New York: Cambridge University Press, 1996.

———. "Between Two Coordination Failures: Automotive Industrial Policy in China with a Comparison to Korea." *Review of International Political Economy* 9, no. 3 (2002): 538–73.

————. *Capitalism with Chinese Characteristics: Entrepreneurship and the State.* New York: Cambridge University Press, 2008.

Huang, Zhiling. "Guojiajiwei zai xin shiqi hongguan tiaokong zhong de diwei he zuoyong" (The State Planning Commission's status and roles for a new era of macro-control). *Shoudu Jingji,* no. 1 (1994): 43–45.

Hung, Duong Nhu, Nguyen Dinh Thien, and Nguyen Thanh Liem. "The Impact of Equitization on Firm Performance: The Case of Vietnam." *International Research Journal of Finance and Economics* 164 (November 2017): 68–74.

Jiang, Mengweiiang. "Guoziwei xunshizu jinzhu liujia yangqi xunshi" (SASAC Inspection Group scrutinizes six enterprises). *Beijing Shangbao,* 9 September 2014.

Jiao, Haitaoao. "Dianxin, liantong longduan anzhong chengnuode xiaoji xiaoying" (The negative effects of accepting the monopoly probing against China Telecom and China Unicom). *Faxue,* no. 3 (2012): 31–37.

"Jili jituan shougou woerwo qiche woerwo xiaoshoude manchang lichen" (Geely purchased Volvo, the long history of the acquisition of Volvo by Geely Group). *Changchengwang,* 28 December 2019. http://www.hebei.com.cn/ggzxzx/qypd/qyfl/qcjd/200912 /t20091229_948834.html.

Jing, Li. "Chinese Telecom Industry Consolidated into Three Giants." *Economic Observer Online,* 28 May 2008. https://www.eeo.com.cn/ens/Industry/2008/05/28/101652 .html

Johnson, Chalmers. *MITI and the Japanese Miracle: The Growth of Industrial Policy, 1925– 1975.* Stanford, CA: Stanford University Press, 1982.

Jordana, Jacint, and David Levi-Faur, eds. *The Politics of Regulation: Institutions and Regulatory Reforms for the Age of Governance.* Cheltenham, UK: Edward Elgar, 2004.

————. "The Politics of Regulation." In J. Jordana and D. Levi-Faur (eds.), *The Politics of Regulation: Institutions and Regulatory Reforms for the Age of Governance.* Cheltenham, UK: Edward Elgar, 2004.

Jordana, Jacint, David Levi-Faur, and Xavier Fernandez Marin. "The Global Diffusion of Regulatory Agencies: Channels of Transfer and Stages of Diffusion." *Comparative Political Studies* 44, no. 10 (2011): 1343–69.

Kennedy, Scott. *The Business of Lobbying in China.* Cambridge, MA: Harvard University Press, 2005.

————. "Comparing Formal and Informal Lobbying Practices in China: The Capital's Ambivalent Embrace of Capitalists." *China Information* 23, no. 2 (June 2009): 195–222.

Kerkvliet, Ben, Anita Chan, and Jonathan Unger. "Comparing the Chinese and Vietnamese Reforms: An Introduction." *China Journal,* no. 40 (July 1998): 1–7.

Kikuchi, Tomo. "Keeping Vietnam's Textile and Garment Industry Competitive." *East Asia Forum,* 30 July 2016.

Kim, Taeho. "Leading Small Groups: Managing All under Heaven." In D. M. Finkelstein and M. Kivlehan (eds.), *China's Leadership in the 21st Century: The Rise of the Fourth Generation.* Armonk, NY: M. E. Sharpe, 2003.

Kirby, William C. "Continuity and Change in Modern China: Chinese Economic Planning on the Mainland and on Taiwan, 1943–1958." *Australian Journal of Chinese Affairs*, no. 24 (July 1990): 121–41.

Kohli, Atul. *State-Directed Development: Political Power and Industrialization in the Global Periphery*. New York: Cambridge University Press, 2004.

Kong, Qingjiang. "China's Telecom Regulatory Regime on the Eve of WTO Accession." *Issues & Studies* 37, no. 4 (July/August 2001).

Kornai, Janos. *The Socialist System: The Political Economy of Communism*. Princeton, NJ: Princeton University Press, 1992.

———. *Highways and Byways: Studies on Reform and Post-Communist Transition*. Cambridge, MA: MIT Press, 1995.

———. *From Socialism to Capitalism*. Budapest: Central European University Press, 2008.

Kroeber, Arthur R. "Developmental Dreams: Policy and Reality in China's Economic Reforms." In S. Kennedy (ed.), *Beyond the Middle Kingdom: Comparative Perspectives on China's Capitalist Transformation*. Stanford, CA: Stanford University Press, 2011.

Laing, Dongmei Liang. "Geely-Volvo Deal Approved by Chinese Regulator." *Caixin*, 30 July 2010. http://english.caixin.com/2010-07-30/100165511.html (accessed 20 June 2013).

Lang, Lang. "Dianxin liantong falongduan'an xuannian guangdian huyu checha" (China Telecom and China Unicom's anti-trust case is full of suspense). *21 Shiji Jingji Baodao*, 22 November 2011.

Lardy, Nicholas. *Markets over Mao: The Rise of Private Business in China*. Washington, DC: Peterson Institute for International Economics, 2014.

Lardy Nicholas, and Kenneth Lieberthal, eds. *Remaking the Chinese State: Strategies, Society, and Security*. New York: Routledge, 2001.

Lau, Lawrence, Yingyi Qian, and Gerard Ronald. "Reform without Losers: An Interpretation of China's Dual-Track Approach to Transition." *Journal of Political Economy* 108, no. 1 (2000): 120–43.

Lee, Ching Kwan. *The Specter of Global China: Politics, Labor, and Foreign Investment in Africa*. Chicago: University of Chicago Press, 2018.

Lee, Peter N. S. *Industrial Management and Economic Reform in China, 1949–1984*. Hong Kong: Oxford University Press, 1987.

Levi-Faur, David, and Sharon Gilad. "The Rise of the British Regulatory State: Transcending the Privatization Debate." *Comparative Politics* 37, no. 1 (October 2004): 105–24.

Li, Cheng. "Reshuffling Four Tiers of Local Leaders: Goals and Implications." *China Leadership Monitoring*, no. 18 (Spring 2006).

———. "China's Telecom Industry on the Move: Domestic Competition, Global Ambition, and Leadership Transition." *China Leadership Monitors*, no. 19 (Fall 2006).

Li, Cheng, and Ryan McElveen. "Pessimism about China's Third Plenum Is Unwarranted." *China & US Focus*, 4 November 2013. https://www.chinausfocus.com/society-culture/pessimism-about-chinas-third-plenum-is-unwarranted (accessed 1 March 2020).

Li, Junfengi. "Chanye guizhi shijiao xiade zhongguo fanlongduan zhifa jiagou" (The framework of China's antimonopoly law enforcement from the view of industrial regulation). *Fashang Yanjiu*, no. 2 (2010): 32–43.

"Li Rongrong chuxi guoziwei xunshi gongzuo zuotanhui bing jianghua" (Li Rongrong attended the meeting of the SASAC inspection and gave a speech). *Guoziwei xunshiban* (SASAC Inspection Office), 29 October 2000. http://www.sasac.gov.cn/n85463 /n327265/n327817/n327825/c370986/content.html.

Li, Weiao. "Jiemi zhongyang caijing lingdao xiaozu" (Unveiling the central finance and economy leading small group). *Ganbu Wenzhai*, September 2014.

———. "Juemi zhongyang caijing lingdao xiaozu" (Deciphering the central financial economy leading small group). *Dangzheng Luntan*, no. 18 (2014): 26–27.

———. "Zhongyang caijing lingdao xiaozu xiankai" (Central finance and economy leading a small group to reveal itself). *Nanfang Zhoumo*, 19 June 2014.

Li, Yuqian. "Plenum Insight: Conclave Didn't Change Status of SOEs." *Caixin*, 13 November 2013. http://english.caixin.com/2013-11-13/100604443.html (accessed 26 February 2015).

Liang Xueping. *Zhongguo gonggong wupin de gonggei yanjiu* (Research on the provision of the public good in China). Tianjin: Nankai daxue chubanshe, 2014.

Lieberthal, Kenneth. *Governing China: From Revolution through Reform.* New York: Norton, 2002.

Lieberthal, Kenneth, and Michael Oksenberg. *Policy Making in China: Leaders, Structures, and Processes.* Princeton, NJ: Princeton University Press, 1988.

Lin, Xuchen, Ting-jie Lu, and Xia Chen. "Reform and Development of Basic Telecommunication Service Industry in China and Its Evaluation: A Perspective Technological Progress." *Information Science and Management Engineering* (2016): 58–62.

Lindblom, Charles E. *Politics and Markets: The World's Political-Economic Systems.* New York: Basic Books, 1977.

Liu, Chenglui, Naiwu Hu, and Guanghua Yu. "Jihua he shichang xiangjiehe shi woguo jingji guanli gaige de jiben tuijing" (Combining planning and markets is the basic approach to reforming national economic management). *Jingji Yanjiu*, no. 7 (1979): 37–46.

Liu, Feng, and Kaidong Feng. *Fazhan woguo zizhu zhishi chanquan qiche gongye de zhengce xuanze* (Developing Policy Selection for the National Indigenous Intellectual Property in the Automobile Industry). Beijing: Beijing daxue chubanshe, 2005.

Liu, Guoguang. "Luelun jihua tiaojie yu shichang tiaojie de jige wenti" (Brief discussion on issues of planned readjustment and market regulation). *Jingji Yanjiu*, no. 10 (1980): 3–11.

———. *Zhongguo shi ge wu nian jihua yanjiu baogao* (Research Report on Ten Chinese Five-Year Plans). Beijing: Renmin Chubanshe, 2006.

Liu, Guoguang, and Renwei Zhao. "Lun shehuizhiyi jingji zhong jihua yu shichang de guanxi" (Discussion on the relationship between planning and markets in the socialist economy). *Jingji Yanjiu*, no. 5 (1979): 46–55.

Liu, Guoguang, et al. *Zhongguo shige wunian jihua yanjou baogao* (Research Report on China's 10 Five-Year Plans). Beijing: Renmin chubanshe, 2006.

Liu, Weidong, and Henry Wai-chung Yeung. "China's Dynamic Industrial Sector: The Automobile Industry." *Eurasian Geography and Economics* 49, no. 5 (2008): 523–48.

Liu Zhiming. "Zhongguo jingji zhuanxing zhong gonggong wupin tigong tizhi de yanbian yu gaige" (The evolution and reform of the provision of public goods mechanism in China's economic transition). *Huanan shiban daxue xuebao*, no. 2 (April 2003): 31–40.

Livdahl, David, Jenny Sheng, and Huiyan Li. "Potential Fines to Be Levied on SOEs May Total Billions of Yuan." *South China Morning Post*, 28 December 2011.

Lu, Ding. "The Management of China's Telecommunications Industry." *Telecommunications Policy* 18, no. 3 (1994): 630–33.

Lu, Nanu. "Woerwo zai huashoujia hezi gongshi chengli." *Qiche shangbao*, 7 June 2013. http://www.autobusinessnews.com.cn/showMarket.aspx?id=1573 (accessed 23 February 2015).

Luo, Gengmo. "Guanyu jihua jingji shichang jingji he qita" (On planned economies, market economies, and others). In Zhongguo Shehui Kexueyuan Jingji Yanjiusuo (Chinese Academy of Social Sciences Economy Research Institute) (ed.), *Shehuizhuyi jingji zhong jihua yu shichang de guanxi* (Planning and Markets in a Socialist Economy). Beijing: Zhongguo Shehui Kexue Chubanshe, 1980.

Luo, Haipinguo. "Cong zhengfu longduan dao zhengfu guizhi—lun woguo dianxinye fazhan zhong de zhengfu xingwei bianqian" (From administration monopoly to government regulation: the changing government behavior in the telecoms industry). *Ningbo Zhiye Jishu Xueyuan Xuebao* 15, no. 3 (2011): 56–60.

Luo, Mingweiuo. *Dianxin jingzheng guize yu shichang jianguan* (Telecom Competition Rules and Market Regulation). Beijing: Renmin youdian chubanshe, 2014.

Ma, Honga. "Guanyu jingji guanli tizhi gaige de jige wenti" (Several problems concerning the reform of the economic managerial system). *Jingji yanjiu*, no. 7 (1981): 11–24.

———. *Xiandai Zhongguo jingji shidan* (The Contemporary Chinese Economy: A Compendium). Beijing: Zhongguo Sehui Kexue Chubanshe, 1982.

Ma, Kai, and Yushu Cao. *Jihua jingji tizhi gaige xiang shehui zhuyi shichang jingji tizhi de zhuangui* (The Changing Trajectory of the Planned Economic System toward the Socialist Market Economic System). Beijing: Renmin Chubanshe, 2002.

Majone, Giandomenico. "The Rise of the Regulatory State in Europe." *West European Politics* 17 (1994): 77–101.

———. *Regulating Europe*. London: Routledge, 1994.

Malesky, Edward. "Leveled Mountains and Broken Fences: Measuring and Analyzing De Facto Decentralization in Vietnam." *European Journal of Southeast Asian Studies* 3, no. 2 (2004): 307–37.

Mao, Zedong. "On the Ten Major Relationships (*Lun shi da guanxi*)." In *Selected Works of Mao Zedong* (*Mao Zedong xuanji*), vol. 5, 272–76. Beijing: People's Publishing House, 1977.

———. "Eighteen Issues Discussed at the Lushan Meeting" (Lushan huiyi taolun de shiba ge wenti). In *Collected Works of Mao Zedong* (*Mao Zedong wenti*), vol. 8, 75–82. Beijing: People's Publishing House, 1999.

Martina, Michael. "Exclusive: In China, the Party's Push for Influence inside Foreign Firms Stirs Fears." Reuters, 24 August 2017. https://www.reuters.com/article/us-china -congress-companies/exclusive-in-china-the-partys-push-for-influence-inside -foreign-firms-stirs-fears-idUSKCN1B40JU (accessed 8 March 2019).

Marukawa, Tomoo. "Why Are There So Many Automobile Manufacturers in China?" *China: An International Journal* 11, no. 2 (August 2013): 170–85.

McGowan, Francis, and Helen Wallace. "Towards a European Regulatory State." *Journal of European Public Policy* 4 (1996): 560–76.

Meng, Mingweing, ed. *Dianxin jingzheng guizhi yu shichang jianguan* (Telecom Competition Control and Market Regulation). Beijing: Renmin youdian chubanshe, 2014.

Mertha, Andrew. "China's 'Soft' Centralization: Shifting Tiao/Kuai Authority Relations." *China Quarterly* 184 (December 2005): 791–810.

Mertha, Andrew C., and Ka Zeng. "Political Institutions, Resistance and China's Harmonization with International Law." *China Quarterly* 182 (June 2005): 319–37.

Meyer, John W., and Brian Rowan. "Institutionalized Organizations: Formal Structure as Myth and Ceremony." *American Journal of Sociology* 83, no. 2 (1977): 340–63.

Milhaupt, Curtis J., and Wentong Zheng. "Beyond Ownership: State Capitalism and the Chinese Firm." *Georgetown Law Journal* 103, no. 665 (2015): 655–22.

Ming, Shuliang. "China Mobile Soars on Sector's New Shakeup." *Caijing*, 23 April 2008.

———. "Telecoms Undergo Restructuring-Again." *Caijing*, 13 June 2008.

"Minqi zaoche de xinsuan lu, Geely qiche fazhanshi huigu" (The rough road walked by a private auto firm: a retrospect of Geely's history). *Qiche zhijia*, 6 December 2013.

Mo, Xiurong. "Sun Yefang chanye jiegou sixiang yu xinxing gongyehua" (Sun Yefang's thought on industrial structure and new industrialization). *Xiandai Guanli Kexue*, no. 10 (2009): 73–75.

Moore, Thomas. *China in the World Market: Chinese Industry and International Sources of Reform in the Post-Mao Era*. Cambridge: Cambridge University Press, 2002.

Moran, Michael. "Review Article: Understanding the Regulatory State." *British Journal of Political Science* 32, no. 2 (2002): 391–413.

———. *The British Regulatory State: High Modernism and Hyper-Innovation*. Oxford: Oxford University Press, 2003.

Moss, Trefor. "China's Auto Market Slips into Slow Lane—Except for EVs." *Wall Street Journal*, 11 January 2018.

Mou, Qingou. *Qiyewu jingzheng xingshi xia zhongguo dianxinye guizhi yanjiu* (Research on the Rules of the Chinese Telecom Sector under Corporate Service Competition). Shanghai: Shanghai caizheng daxue chubanshe, 2011.

Mueller, Milton, and Zixiang Tan. *China in the Information Age: Telecommunications and the Dilemma of Reform*. Washington, DC: Center for Strategic Studies, 1997.

National Bureau of Statistics of China. *Zhongguo tongji nianjian* (China Statistical Yearbook). Beijing: Zhongguo tongji chubanshe, various years.

National Development and Reform Commission. "Gangtie chanye fazhan zhengce" (Steel industry development policy). 8 July 2005. http://www.mofcom.gov.cn/article /b/g/200508/20050800238200.shtml (accessed 14 July 2019).

Naughton, Barry. "China's Experience of Guidance Planning." *Journal of Comparative Economics* 14, no. 4 (1990): 743–67.

———. "The Pattern and Legacy of Economic Growth in the Mao Era." In K. Lieberthal (ed.), *Perspectives on Modern China: Four Anniversaries.* Armonk, NY: M. E. Sharpe, 1991.

———. *Growing Out of the Plan: Chinese Economic Reform, 1978–1993.* New York: Cambridge University Press, 1995.

———. "SASAC Rising." *China Leadership Monitor,* no. 14 (Spring 2005).

———. *The Chinese Economy: Transition and Growth.* Cambridge, MA: MIT Press, 2007.

———. "A Political Economy of China's Economic Transition." In L. Brandt and T. G. Rawski (eds.), *China's Great Economic Transformation,* 91–135. New York: Cambridge University Press, 2008.

———. "Market Economy, Hierarchy, and Single-Party Rule." In J. Kornai and Y. Qian (eds.), *Market and Socialism: In the Light of the Experiences of China and Vietnam,* 13–161. Hampshire: Palgrave Macmillan, 2009.

———. "Understanding Chinese Stimulus Package." *China Leadership Monitor,* no. 28 (Spring 2009).

———. "China's Distinctive System: Can It Be a Model for Others?" *Journal of Contemporary China* 19, no. 65 (June 2010): 437–60.

———. *Wu Jinglian: Voice of Reform in China.* Cambridge, MA: MIT Press, 2013.

Naughton, Barry, and Kellee S. Tsai. *State Capitalism, Institutional Adaptation, and the Chinese Miracle.* New York: Cambridge University Press, 2015.

"NDRC Evaluating Rectification Results of Monopoly-Accused Telecom Giants." *Xinhua News Agency,* 24 February 2014.

Nolan, Peter. *China and the Global Economy: National Champions, Industrial Policy and the Big Business Revolution.* London: Palgrave Macmillan, 2001.

North, Douglas. *Understanding the Process of Economic Change.* Princeton, NJ: Princeton University Press, 2005.

Oertel, Jenka. "Why the German Debate on 5G and Huawei Is Critical." *Transatlantic Take,* 15 February 2019.

Page, Scott E. *Diversity and Complexity.* Princeton, NJ: Princeton University Press, 2010.

Pearson, Margaret M. "The Business of Governing Business in China: Institutions and Norms of the Emerging Regulatory State." *World Politics* 57 (January 2005): 296–322.

———. "Regulation and Regulatory Politics in China's Tiered Economy." Paper presented at the conference "Capitalism with Chinese Characteristics: China's Political Economy in Comparative and Theoretical Perspectives," Indiana University, 19–20 May 2006.

———. "Governing the Chinese Economy: Regulatory Reform in the Service of the State." *Public Administration Review* 67, no. 4 (July/August 2007): 718–30.

———. "Variety Within and Without: The Political Economy of Chinese Regulation." In S. Kennedy (ed.), *Beyond the Middle Kingdom: Comparative Perspectives on China's Capitalist Transformation,* 25–43. Stanford, CA: Stanford University Press, 2011.

———. "State-Owned Business and Party-State Regulation in China's Modern Political Economy." In B. Naughton and K. Tsai (eds.), *State Capitalism, Institutional Adaptation, and the Chinese Model.* New York: Cambridge University Press, 2015.

Pei, Minxin. "China's Governance Crisis." *Foreign Affairs* 81, no. 5 (September/October 2002): 96–109.

———. *China's Trapped Transition: The Limits of Developmental Autocracy.* Cambridge, MA: Harvard University Press, 2006.

———. "The Dark Side of China's Rise." *Foreign Policy*, no. 153 (March/April 2006).

Polanyi, Karl. *The Great Transformation: The Political and Economic Origins of Our Time.* Boston: Beacon Press, 1944.

Price, Alan H., Timothy C. Brightbill, Christopher B. Weld, and Tessa V. Capeloto. "The Reform Myth: How China Is Using State Power to Create the World's Dominant Steel Industry." American Iron and Steel Institute, October 2010.

Qi, Ye, Wenjuan Dong, Changgui Dong, and Caiwei Huang. "Fixing Wind Curtailment with Electric Power System Reform in China." China's Energy in Transition series, Brookings-Tsinghua Center for Public Policy, July 2018.

Qian, Yingyi. "How Reform Worked in China." William Davidson Institute Working Paper 473, June 2002.

Qin, Meiin. "Zhongguo liantong wanglufen gongsi fuzongjingli zhang zhijiang beidiaocha" (Zhang Zhijiang as a vice president of China Unicom Network branch was investigated). *Caixin*, 15 December 2014.

Qu, Wanwen. "Chaogan gongshi jiandu xiade zhongguo chanye zhengce yangshi: yi qiche chanye weilie" (China's industrial policy model beyond the supervision of a commonsense: taking the automobile industry as an example). *Jingjixue* 8, no. 2, (January 2009): 501–32.

Research unit for Longduanxing hangye de zhengfu guanzhi wenti yanjiu (Studying the problems of the government's control over the monopoly sector). "Dianxinye de zhengfu guanzhi wenti yanjiu" (Studying the problems of government control over telecoms Industry). *Jingji Yanjiu Cankao* 25 (2003).

Riedel, James, and Bruce Comer. "Transition to a Market Economy in Vietnam." In W. T. Woo, S. Parket, and J. D. Sachs (eds.), *Economies in Transition: Comparing Asia and Europe*, 189–216. Cambridge, MA: MIT Press, 1997.

Rutland, Peter. *The Myth of the Plan.* London: Huchison, 1985.

Schwarz, Brian. "Shanghai Aims to Be China's Detroit." *Asian Times*, 12 October 2006.

Segal, Adam, and Eric Thun."Thinking Globally, Acting Locally: Local Governments, Industrial Sectors, and Development in China." *Politics & Society* 29, no. 4 (December 2001): 557–88.

Shan, Liuhan. "Fengyong er shanag zizhu pinpai kuangken zhengfu butie" (Rush on like a swarm of hornets, the independent brand of automobile enterprises is crazily eating government subsidies). *Zhongguowang*, 16 April 2012. http://auto.china.com.cn /industry/view/20120416/37901.shtml (accessed 18 February 2015).

Shanghai Auto Industry Corporation (SAIC). *Zhongguo qiche gongye fazhan yanjiu* (China Auto Industry Development Research). Shanghai: Shanghai Technology Press, 2005.

Sheng, Huhen, and Heyan Wang. "Old Chums and a Troubled Telecom Chief." *Caixin*, 3 February 2010. http://english.caixin.com/print/print_en.jsp.

Shi, Qingqi, Xiaobing Yang, and Tianhua Huang. "Changing Pattern of Development Planning in China." In S. Tambunlertchai (ed.), *Development Planning in Asia*, 91–114. Kuala Lumpur: Asia and Pacific Development Centre, 1993.

Shi, Yaodong, and Bi Zhi. "Woguo qiche chanye zhengfu guanli tizhi de xianzhuang,wenti, yu chengyin" (Condition, problem, and factors of the governmental management system in China's auto industry). *Neibu zhiliao*, Development Research Center of the State Council, 2004.

Shih, Victor. "Authoritarian Power Imperatives and the Chinese Banks." Presented at the American Political Science Associations' annual conference, San Francisco, August/September 2001.

———. *Factions and Finance in China: Elite Conflict and Inflation*. New York: Cambridge University Press, 2008.

Sit, Victor F. S., and Weidong Liu. "Restructuring and Spatial Change of China's Auto Industry under Institutional Reform and Globalization." *Annals of Association of American Geographers* 90, no. 4 (December 2000): 653–73.

Smith, Benjamin. "Life of the Party: The Origins of Regime Breakdown and Persistence under Single-Party Rule." *World Politics* 57, no. 3 (April 2005): 421–51.

Solinger, Dorothy J. *China's Transition from Socialism: Statist Legacies and Market Reforms 1980–1990*. New York: Routledge, 1993.

Solnick, Steve. "The Breakdown of Hierarchies in the Soviet Union and China: A Neoinstitutional Perspective." *World Politics* 48, no. 2 (January 1996): 209–38.

State Council of the PRC. "Guanyu gaijin jihua guanli tizhi de guiding" (Provisions on the Planning Administration System). September 1958.

———. "Made in China 2015 Strategy for the Auto Sector." http://english.gov.cn/policies/infographics/2015/06/02/content_281475119391820.htm (accessed 19 April 2018).

State Council Secretariat. "Qiche chanye tiaozheng he jinxing guihua" (Auto industry adjusting and rejuvenating plan). 20 March 2009. http://www.gov.cn/zwgk/2009-03/20/content_1264324.htm (accessed 27 February 2015).

State Planning Commission (SPC). "Guanyu gaijin jihua tizhi de ruogan zanxing guiding" (Temporary regulation on state planning). 4 October 1984.

———. "Zhonghua Renmin Gongheguo guomin jingji he shehui fazhan di-qige wunian jihua" (Seventh five-year plan for the national economic and social development of the People's Republic of China). 23 September 1985. http://www.china.com.cn/ch-80years/lici/12/12-0/8.htm.

Steinfeld, Edward S. *Forging Reform in China: The Fate of State-Owned Enterprises*. Cambridge: Cambridge University Press, 1998.

———. *Playing Our Game: Why China's Economic Rise Doesn't Threaten the West*. New York: Oxford University Press, 2010.

Su, Jinshengu. *Dianxinye guanzhi moshi yu fazhan janjiu* (A Research on Mode of Regulation and Development in Telecoms). Beijing: Remin youdian daxue chubanshe, 2007.

Sun Yafeng. "Ba jihua he tongji fangzai jiazhi guilu de jichushang" (Place planning and statistics on the basis of the law of value). *Jingji Yanjiu* 6 (1956): 30–38.

———. "Lun jiazhi" (On value). *Jingji Yanjiu* 9 (1959): 42–69.

———. *Selected Works of Sun Yefang* (Sun Yefang xuanji). Taiyuan: People's Publishing House, 1984.

Sun, Zongfu. "Woguo shangye jihua guanli tizhi de yange" (History of Chinese business economy's planning and management system). *Shangye Jingji Yanjiu*, no. 2 (1985): 55–59.

Teiwes, Frederick. "The Chinese State during the Maoist Era." In *The Modern Chinese State*, 105–60. New York: Cambridge University Press, 2000.

Tenev, Stoyan, and Chunlin Zhang. *Corporate Governance and Enterprise Reform in China: Building the Institutions of Modern Markets*. Washington, DC: World Bank, 2002.

Thun, Eric. "Industrial Policy, Chinese-Style: FDI, Regulation, Dreams of National Champions in the Auto Sector." *Journal of East Asian Studies*, 4 (2004): 453–89.

———. *Changing Lanes in China: Foreign Direct Investment, Local Governments, and Auto Sector Development*. Cambridge: Cambridge University Press, 2006.

Thuy, Le Duc. "Economic Doi Moi in Vietnam: Content, Achievements, and Prospects." In W. S. Turley and M. Selden (eds.), *Reinventing Vietnamese Socialism: Doi Moi in Comparative Perspective*, 97–106. Boulder, CO: Westview Press, 1993.

Tsai, Kellee S. "Adaptive Informal Institutions and Endogenous Institutional Change in China." *World Politics* 59, no. 1 (October 2006): 116–41.

———. "Cause or Consequence? Private Sector Development and Communist Resilience in China." In M. K. Dimitrov (ed.), *Why Communism Did Not Collapse: Understanding Authoritarian Regime Resilience in Asia and Europe*, 205–36. New York: Cambridge University Press, 2013.

Tsai, Kellee S., and Sarah Cook. "Developmental Dilemmas in China: Socialist Transition and Late Liberalization." In S. M. Pekkanen and K. S. Tsai (eds.), *Japan and China in the World Political Economy*, 11–28. New York: Routledge, 2005.

Tsai, Lily L. "Solidarity Groups, Informal Accountability, and Local Public Goods Provision in Rural China." *American Political Science Review* 101, no. 2 (May 2007): 355–72.

UNDP. "The State as Investor: Equitisation, Privatisation and the Transformation of SOEs in Vietnam." UNDP Vietnam Policy Dialogue Paper 2006/3, October 2006.

Varese, Federico. "The Transition to the Market and Corruption in Post-socialist Russia." *Political Studies* 45, no. 3 (1997): 579–96.

Vogel, Steven K. *Freer Markets, More Rules: Regulatory Reforms in Advanced Industrial Countries*. Ithaca, NY: Cornell University Press, 1996.

———. "Why Freer Markets Need More Rules." In M. K. Landy, M. A. Levin, and M. Shapiro (eds.), *Creating Competitive Markets: The Politics of Regulatory Reform*, 25–42. Washington, DC: Brookings Institution Press, 2007.

———. "Why Freer Markets Need More Rules." In Naazneen H. Barma and Steven K. Vogel (eds.), *The Political Economy Reader: Markets as Institutions*, 341–54. New York: Routledge, 2008.

Wan, Yan. "Sector Reform." In J. Lin et al. (eds.), *Telecommunications in China: Development and Prospects*, 159–80. New York: Nova Science Publishing, 2001.

Wang, Junhaoang. *Ziran longduan chanye zhengfu guanzhi lilun* (Government Control Theory of the Natural Monopoly Industry). Hangzhou: Zhejiang daxue chubanshe, 2000.

Wang, Junhaoang, Xingzhi Xiao, and Yaojia Tang. *Zhongguo longduan xing chanye guanzhi jigou de sheli yu yunxing jizhi* (Establishment and Operation Mechanism of Chinese Monopoly Industry Regulation Institution). Beijing: Shangwu yinshuguan, 2008.

Wang, Ouang. "Zhongguo dianxianye de fazhan yu chanye zhengce de yanbian" (China's telecom industry development and the changes in industrial policy). *Zhongguo Jingji Yanjiu*, no. 4 (2000): 87–101.

Wang, Qingang. "Woguo gonggongpin gongji yanbian ji queshi yuanyin fenxi" (Analysis of the evolution of public goods supply and its deficiency in China). *Tianjin Xingzheng Xueyuan Xuebao* 15, no. 5 (September 2013): 76–82.

Wang, Sanwen, "Xiandai dianxin qiye dangwei shishi zhengzhi lingdao de sikao" (The current party committees in telecoms enterprises reflect the political leaders' thought). *Youdian Qiye Guanli*, no. 17 (2001): 7–9.

Wang, Xiaoye. "Zhongguo dianxin, zhongguo liantong shexian longduan de zaisikao" (Rethinking the case of China Telecom and China Unicom antimonopoly). *Jiaoda Faxue*, no. 2 (2013): 5–15.

Wang, Yukai. *Zhongguo dianzi zhengfu moshi yu xuanze* (Chinese Electronic Government Model and Choice). Guojia xingzheng xueyuan chubanshe, 2010.

———. "Zhongyang wanglu anquan he xinxihua lingdao xiaozu de youlai jiqi yingxiang: (The origin and influence of the Central Network Security and Informatization Leading Small Group). *Zhongguo Xinxi Anquan* 3 (2014): 24–28.

Wang, Zhuhao. *Ziran longduan chanye de zhengfu guanzhi lilun* (Theory on the Government Rules of the Natural Monopoly Industry). Hangzhou: Zhejiang daxue chubanshe, 2000.

Wedeman, Andrew. "Crossing the River by Feeling for Stones or Carried Across by the Current?" In S. Kennedy (ed.), *Beyond the Middle Kingdom: Comparative Perspectives on China's Capitalist Transformation*, 70–82. Stanford, CA: Stanford University Press, 2011.

Wei, Liqunei, et al. *Shehuizhuyi shichang jingji yu jihua moshi gaige* (Socialist Market Economy and Reform of the Planned Model). Beijing: Zhongguo jihua chubanshe, 1994.

White, Gordon. *Riding the Tiger: The Politics of Economic Reform in Post-Mao China*. Stanford, CA: Stanford University Press, 1993.

Wildau, Gabriel. "US Tariffs Target China Industrial Policy, not Trade Deficit." *Financial Times*, 23 March 2013.

Womack, Brantly. "Reform in Vietnam: Backwards towards the Future." *Government and Opposition*, no. 27 (April 1992): 177–89.

Working Group on Research of the Problems of Government Control over Monopoly Industry. "Dianxinye de zhengfu guanli wenti yanjiu" (Research on government management of the telecommunications industry). *Jingji Yanjiu Cankao* 25, no. 1698 (2003).

Wu, Irene S. *From Iron Fist to Invisible Hand.* Stanford, CA: Stanford University Press, 2009.

Wu, Jichian. *Zhongguo tongxin fazhan zhilu* (The Road of Development of Communication in China). Beijing: Xinhua chubanshe, 1997.

Wu, Jinglian. *Understanding and Interpreting Chinese Economic Reform.* Mason, OH: Thomson South-Western, 2005.

Wu, Junyang. "Zhidao xing jihua tantao" (On guidance planning). *Jingji Yanjiu* 3 (1985): 3–8.

Wu, Wanlin. "Xiaozu zhengzhi yanjiu: neihan, gongneng yu yanjiu zhangwang" (Studying "small group politics": implications, functions, and prospects for research). *Ai Sixiang,* 7 July 2009. http://www.aisixiang.com/data/28773-2.html.

Xi, Jinping. "Guanyu zhonggong zhongyang guanyu quanmian gaige ruogan zhongda wenti de jueding" (The Central Committee of the Communist Party of China's Decision on Deepening Reforms). *Renmin Ribao,* 16 November 2013.

Xia, Ming. "The Communist Party of China and the 'Party-State.'" *New York Times,* n.d. https://archive.nytimes.com/www.nytimes.com/ref/college/coll-china-politics -002.html.

Xiang, Anboand Wenkui Zhang."Zhongguo chanye zhengce de tedian, pinggu yu zhengce tiaozheng jianyi" (Features, assessment, and policy adjustment and suggestions on Chinese industrial policies). *Zhongguo Fazhan Guancha,* no. 12 (2013): 19–21.

Xinkuaibao. "Dijiuhui: Shang-Nan hezuo zhengfu lalangpei jingshi chongzu cheqi baochengtuan" (The ninth: The government forced into SAIC and NAC cooperation, it was surprised to restructure automobile companies). *Jingyangwang,* 7 January 2009. http://auto.163.com/09/0107/10/4V23LSIN000834TJ.html (accessed 1 November 2015).

Xu, Yajun. "Jialu WTO dui Changchun qiche gongye de yingxiang" (The effect of WTO entry on the Changchun auto industry). *Shehui Kexue Zhanxian,* May 2001.

Xue, Muqiaoue. *Zhongguo shehuizhuyi jingji wenti de yanjiu* (A Study of Problems in China's Socialist Economy). Beijing: Renmin Chubanshe, 1979.

———. "Shehuizhuyi jingji de jihua guanli" (Management by planning in the socialist economy). In Zhongguo Shehui Kexueyan Jingji Yanjiusuo (Chinese Academy of Social Sciences, Institute for Economic Research) et al. (eds.), *Shehuizhuyi jingji zhong jihua yu shichang de guanxi* (Planning and Markets in a Socialist Economy), vol. 1. Beijing: Zhongguo Shehui Kexue Chubanshe, 1980.

Yan, Xu, and Douglas C. Pitt. *Chinese Telecommunications Policy.* Boston: Artech House, 2002.

Yang, Dali L. "Governing China's Transition to the Market: Institutional Incentives, Politicians' Choices, and Unintended Outcomes." *World Politics* 48, no. 3 (April 1996): 424–52.

———. "Can the Chinese State Meet Its WTO Obligations? Government Reforms, Regulatory Capacity, and WTO Membership." *American Asian Review* 20, no. 2 (Summer 2002): 191–222.

———. *Remaking the Chinese Leviathan: Market Transition and the Politics of Governance in China*. Stanford, CA: Stanford University Press, 2004.

Yeo, Yukyung. "Between Owner and Regulator: Governing the Business of China's Telecommunications Service Industry." *China Quarterly* 200 (December 2009): 1013–22.

———. "Contextualizing Corporate Governance: The Case of China's Central State Enterprise Groups." *Journal of Contemporary China* 22, no. 81 (January 2013): 460–75.

———. "Complementing the Local Party Discipline Commissions of the CCP: Empowerment of the Central Inspection Groups." *Journal of Contemporary China*, 25 (January 2016): 59–74.

Yeo, Yukyung, and Martin Painter. "Diffusion, Transmutation, and Regulatory Regime in Socialist Market Economies: Telecoms Reform in China and Vietnam." *Pacific Review* 24, no. 4 (September 2011): 375–95.

Yeo, Yukyung, and Margaret M. Pearson. "Regulating Decentralized State Industries: China's Auto Industry." *China Review* 8, no. 2 (Fall 2008): 231–59.

Yi, Zhao. "Hude zhengfu yuanshou" (Sudden government help). *Soufunwang*, 9 September 2010. http://www.fang.com/news/2010-09-09/3770686_3.htm (accessed 24 February 2015).

"Yiqi-dazhong liuren weifan zhongyang baxiang jingshen guiding beichuli" (Six people in FAW-VW violated the provisions of the central eight spirit). *Zhonggongwang*, 29 December 2014. http://auto.china.com.cn/news/corp/20141229/643841.shtml (accessed 26 February 2015).

Yu, Liangchun, Sanford Berg, and Qing Guo. "Market Performance of Chinese Telecommunications: New Regulatory Policies." *Telecommunications Policy* 28, nos. 9–10 (2004): 715–32.

Yu, Linglinu. "Shanghai qiche nanqi hezuo quanjiemi congdanxiang he zuodao quanmian hezuo" (SAIC and NAC have secret cooperation, from single project cooperation to full cooperation). *21 Shiji jingji baodao*, 9 January 2008.

Yuan, Chunhui. *Guanzhi zhili: zhongguo dianxin chanye gaige shizheng yanjiu* (Regulatory Governance: An Empirical Study of China's Telecoms Industry Reform). Beijing: Renmin youdian chubanshe, 2009.

Yun, Qingun. *Quanyewu jingzheng xingshi xia zhongguo dianxinye guizhi yanjiu* (Study of China Telecoms Industry Control under the Service Competition Situation). Shanghai: Shanghai caizheng daxue chubanshe, 2011.

Yun, Xiao. "Dangzhengfu kaojin qiche jilide duice" (The time that the government is close to Geely's counterstrategy). *Zhongguo Touzi*, February 2003. http://www.fang.com/news/2010-09-09/3770686_3.htm (accessed 24 February 2015).

Zhang, Bing, and Mike W. Peng. "Telecom Competition, Post-WTO Style." *China Business Review* (May–June 2000).

Zhang, Bo. "Dangnei lingdao xiaozu changyu zhong de zuzhi zhiduhua: yi zhongyang caijing xiaozu weili" (Institutionalizing the structure of the leading small group scope within the party: From the case of the central finance and economy leading small group). *Lilun yu Gaige*, April 2015.

Zhang, Jie. "Shida chanye zhenxing jihua chuqi: erjidu dailai de chongjing" (Ten sectoral rejuvenation plans all appear: looking forward to the second quarter). *21 Shiji Jingji Baodao*, 28 February 2009.

Zhang, Jin. "Party, State, and Business: the Case of the Chinese Oil Industry." In X. Zhang and T. Zhu (eds.), *Business, Government and Economic Institutions in China*, 281–312. Cham: Springer International Publishing/Palgrave Macmillan, 2018.

Zhang, Jincaihang. "Chen Yun yu zhongyang caijing gongzuo lingdao jigou de bianqian" (Chen Yun and the evolution of the central finance working leading structure). *Beijing Dangshi*, no. 1 (2013): 24–28.

Zhang, Moninghang. "Fanlongduan fali 'jingji xianfa' youduoyuan-zhuanfang guowuyuan fanlongduan weiyuanhui zhuanjia zixunzu fuzuzhang huangyong" (How far away is the "anti-monopoly law" from the "economic constitution"—an interview with Huang Yong, deputy head of the expert advisory group of the State Council's Anti-monopoly Committee). *Nanfengchuang*, no. 23 (2013): 45–47.

Zhang, Xinzhu. "Universal Service Obligations in China's Telecom Sector: Situations, Reforms, and Implementation." Research Center for Regulation and Competition, Chinese Academy of Social Sciences, May 2002.

Zhang, Yihang. "Shanghai nanqi hebing neimu pilu buwei rensuozhi de xiaoxi" (The inside story of SAIC and NAC merge, exposing information that people can't be known). *Qiche zazhi*, 13 January 2008.

Zhang, Yu. "Li Tiezheng: zhongyang zhengfu liting jili shougou woerwo" (Li Tiezheng: the central government supports Geely's acquisition of Volvo). *Tengxun qiche*, 28 March 2010. http://auto.qq.com/a/20100328/000094.htm (accessed 24 February 2015).

Zhang, Zoe. "China's Private Sector in Shadow of the State." *Financial Times*, 4 October 2008.

Zhao, Fukehao, and Zhengju Ji. "Xi Jinping quanmin shenhua gaige sixiang lungang" (A study on Xi Jinping's idea of deepening reform). *Zhonggong Zhongyang Dangxiao Xuebao* 18, no. 6 (2014): 29–34.

Zhao, Hejuanhao, and Dongmei Liang. "Go-Abroad Geely on Verge of Volvo Deal." *Caixin*, 29 January 2010.

Zhao, Hejuanhao, and Ning Yu. "Telecoms Carriers Put under Anti-Corruption Review." *Caixin*, 27 May 2011. http://english.caixin.com/2011-05-27/100263581.html.

Zhao, Linglinghao, and Tengfei Ren. "Guozi jianguan ruhe zaiyifa zhiguo beijingxia youxu tuijin" (How do state-owned assets supervision and administration improve orderly in the rule of law background?). *Xianfengdui*, December 2014.

Zhao, Lingyunhao, and Na Su Si. "Xi Jinping guanyu quanmain shenhua gaige de shida zhongyao lundian" (Xi Jinping's ten important points regarding the comprehensive and deepening reform). *Lilun Daobao*, no. 1 (2015): 44–46.

Zhong, Wuhong. "Beijing Gives Local Government More Say." *Asian Times*, 18 October 2006.

*Zhongguo Gongchandang Zhongyang Weiyuanhui guanyu jianguo yilai dang de rushi lishi wenti de jueyi* (The Central Committee of the Chinese Communist Party on the

Party's Resolution of Historical Issues since its Establishment). Beijing: Renmin chubanshe, 1981.

Zhongguo qiche gongye xiehui (China Auto Industry Association). *Zhongguo qiche gongye gaige kaifang 30 zhounian huigu yu fazhan*. Beijing: Zhongguo wuzi chubanshe, 2009.

Zhongguo qiche gongye xiehui (China Auto Industry Association) and Zhongguo qiche gongye zixun weiyuanhui (China Auto Advising Industry Commission). *Zhongguo qiche chanye chengzhang zhanlue*. Beijing: Qinghua daxue chubanshe, 2014.

*Zhonghua renmin gongheguo fanlongduanfa* (People's Republic of China Anti-monopoly Law). 30 August 2007. http://www.gov.cn/flfg/2007-08/30/content_732591.htm (accessed 5 June 2014).

"Zhongyang Qiye Gongwei yu Xin Guoziwei de Weimiao Shike" (Central enterprise work group and a new state asset commission's subtle time). *21 Shiji Jingji Baodao*, 29 January 2003.

"Zhongyang xunshixia de guoqi bufai kaosha chisha chengtongbing" (State-owned enterprises' corruption under the central inspection, it is going to get any kinds of sick depends on what to eat). *Caixin*, 16 March 2015. http://datanews.caixin.com/2015-03 -16/100791599.html.

"Zhongzubu renming Xu Xianping wei yiqijituan zongjingli Xu Jianyi churen dongshizhang" (The Organization Department of CPC appointed Xu Xianping as a general manager of FAW Group and Xu Jianyi as a chairman). 24 October 2011. http:// forum.home.news.cn/thread/89917174/1.html (accessed 26 February 2015).

"Zhongzubu xunshizu zuzhang cheng wuniannei dui shengji gaoguan xunshi yibian" (The director of the Central discipline inspection commission: supervision of high-profile cadres at the provincial level within five years). *Beijing Qingnian Bao*, 12 March 2004. http://www.chinanews.com/n/2004-03-12/26/412489.html (accessed 25 February 2015).

Zhou, Taihehou. *Dangdai Zhongguo de jingji tizhi gaige* (Contemporary China: The Structural Economic Reforms). Beijing: Zhongguo Dangdai Chubanshe, 2009.

Zhou, Wang. *Zhongguo "xiaozu jizhi" yanjiu* (Research on Chinese "Small Group Mechanism"). Tianjin: Tianjin renmin chubanshe, 2010.

Zou, Ximing. *Zhongguo zhongyang jigou yanse shilu* (A Chronicle of the Evaluation of CCP Central Organs). Beijing: Zhongguo Dang'an Chubanshe, 1998.

# Index

Page numbers for figures and tables are in italics.

## Harvard East Asian Monographs
(most recent titles)

# Harvard East Asian Monographs